RICE AS SELF

RICE AS SELF

JAPANESE IDENTITIES
THROUGH TIME

Emiko Ohnuki-Tierney

PRINCETON UNIVERSITY PRESS   PRINCETON, NEW JERSEY

Published by Princeton University Press, 41 William Street,
Princeton, New Jersey 08540
In the United Kingdom: Princeton University Press,
Chichester, West Sussex

Library of Congress Cataloging-in-Publication Data

Ohnuki-Tierney, Emiko
Rice as self : Japanese identities through
time / Emiko Ohnuki-Tierney
p. cm.
Includes bibliographical references and indexes.
1. National characteristics, Japanese.   2. Japan—
Civilization.   3. Rice—Social aspects—Japan.
I. Title.
DS830.033   1993
952—dc20   92-43711   CIP
ISBN 0-691-09477-2

This book has been composed in Adobe Sabon

Princeton University Press books are printed
on acid-free paper and meet the guidelines for
permanence and durability of the Committee
on Production Guidelines for Book Longevity
of the Council on Library Resources

Printed in the United States of America

10   9   8   7   6   5   4   3

To the late Fujita Sensei
and Kōnan Elementary School

Contents

Acknowledgments

I BEGAN this work at the Center for Advanced Study in the Behavioral Sciences during my fellowship year there in 1989–1990. It was indeed an idyllic year for full-time research. I am most grateful to the center and the National Science Foundation (grant no. BNS87-00864), and the graduate school of the University of Wisconsin, Madison, for their support. This study could not have been completed without the generous support of the Vilas Research Professorship from the William F. Vilas Trust. Words cannot express my appreciation for the Trust, the graduate school of the University of Wisconsin, Madison, and the university.

Miyata Noboru has not only supplied me with information but has also patiently listened to some of my arguments and has offered invaluable suggestions and critiques. Jan Vansina read an earlier version of the manuscript, offering me almost page by page comments and suggestions. He demands meticulous historical and ethnographic data for his own work but has been most encouraging about my interpretations. Donald Keen wrote an extensive critique of my article on the emperor, and his suggestions and criticisms were extremely helpful when I revised the section on the imperial system. Chester S. Chard introduced me to Japanese archaeology, enormously easing my dealings with prehistory. Many others generously contributed to this work, only some of them are mentioned here: Joseph Nagy, Mathew Kramer, Kishima Takako, the late Robert M. Bock, Stephen Gudeman, Lawrence Sullivan, and Kenji Tierney.

As I developed this book, I was fortunate to be invited to lecture on material from various sections of it. Space does not allow me to thank each host for the marvelous feedback I received: the Department of Anthropology, University of Minnesota (1992); the Center for World Religions, Harvard University (1991); the East-West Center, Hawaii (1991); the Department of Social Anthropology, London School of Economics (1990); the Center for Japanese Studies, University of California at Berkeley (1989); and the East Asian Program, Stanford University (East Asian Program) (1989).

I must include a special acknowledgement to my colleagues in Paris. The feedback for the seminars I was invited to give at the École des Hautes Études en Sciences Sociales during April 1992 turned out to be so valuable that I revised the entire manuscript after my return from France. I warmly thank Marc Augé for his invitation and his lively discussion with me. It was through his insistence on *l'espace* that I came to realize the enormous symbolic significance of rice paddies. Discussions with Françoise Héritier-Augé on the food and the body, with Jean Bazin on the divine kingship, with Maurice Godelier on rice as money, with Francis Zimmermann on sacrifice, and with Claude Meillasoux on food and stratification were all much appreciated.

A long and most engrossing discussion with Pierre Bourdieu recast the relation of food to power inequality both within and without Japan into sharper relief, thereby pushing my arguments in chapters 8 and 9 much further.

I thank two anonymous reviewers for the Princeton University Press, especially the one who so enthusiastically endorsed the version he read. Although in hindsight I found the manuscript quite underdeveloped, he offered brilliant suggestions and his generosity resulted in my determination to improve it.

My special and warm thanks are due Mary Murrell, whose professional expertise, coupled with warm encouragement, has made the publication process exceptionally pleasant. I hope whatever improvement I made on the manuscript will in a small way return her generosity and patience in allowing me to revise yet again after I returned from France. I also acknowledge my gratitude to Walter Lippincott, who has extended his unfailing support of my work over a decade and four books. Since the publication of my previous Princeton book, Janet Stern has extended her friendship and professional guidance, which have been crucial to my sustained relationship with Princeton University Press. I thank her warmly.

I feel extremely fortunate to have such generous colleagues and am grateful for their warm and stimulating collegiality. The book's shortcomings, however, are my own responsibility.

I dedicate this book to the late Mr. Fujita Akira, or Fujita Sensei (*sensei* 'teacher' in Japanese). Toward the end of the war, schoolchildren were forced to relocate in the countryside. My school, the Kōnan Elementary School, took its students to a Zen temple in a remote mountain area. As time went on, our meals took a turn for the worse from rice gruel, so diluted that we could count the rice grains, with red beans added for volume, to two or three small potatoes with salt. After a formal recitation of a Zen sutra in the morning, back in our large communal room we re-chanted the sutra, changing the words to "We are hungry! We are hungry!" to the tune of the sutra. After a while I could no longer down potatoes and opted for hunger. Fujita Sensei went home to his farm and brought rice from his family's private supply to feed me. When the war ended, we returned to Kōbe only to find out that our school had been completely destroyed. But, school must continue if it had to continue even under the worst bombing. One day he took us all to a movie. It was the life story of Marie Curie. Her image, always clothed in black, and her singular dedication to her science impressed me so vividly that I could scarcely contain myself. I slept very little that night. The next morning I went to Fujita Sensei and declared that I wanted to be a Madame Curie and laid out my plan for a scientific experiment. Fujita Sensei, whose specialty was science, became excited and the two of us started an ill-fated experiment every day after school. Although I did not realize it at the time, in hindsight, I am astonished. In 1946 very few Japanese, especially men, took professional aspiration in a girl seriously. For the rice he fed me, and even more for his encouragement of my studies, I dedicate this book to his memory. I express my indebtedness to the Kōnan Elementary School, which, under the charismatic leadership of Principal Tsutsumi Tsuneya, provided the free, open, and stimulating environment in which I first learned the deep satisfaction and joy of learning.

July 9, 1992
Madison

A Note to the Reader _____

FOLLOWING the Japanese practice, I have rendered Japanese personal names with the surname first. A Japanese word is italicized only the first time it appears in the text, except in those instances when it reappears in quotations or in book titles or when the meaning of the word itself is under discussion.

RICE AS SELF

One

Food as a Metaphor of Self:
An Exercise in Historical Anthropology

INTENSIVE INTERACTION among peoples through trade, warfare, religion, and so forth, is a familiar historical picture in any part of the world. As anthropologists have become increasingly aware, few peoples have lived in isolated pockets insulated from historical flows of people and goods. An encounter with another culture, directly or indirectly through an exchange of cultural artifacts and institutions, often prompts people to think about who they are in relation to other peoples.

Food plays a dynamic role in the way people think of themselves and others. Parry (1985:613) notes of Hindu culture: "A man *is* what he eats. Not only is his bodily substance created out of food, but so is his moral disposition," and Braudel (1973:66) tells of similar sayings in Europe. "Tell me what you eat, and I will tell you who you are" is similar to the German proverb, "*Der Mensch ist was er isst*" (Man is what he eats). Food tells not only how people live but also how they think of themselves in relation to others. A people's cuisine, or a particular food, often marks the boundary between the collective self and the other, for example, as a basis of discrimination against other peoples. Thus, although the Japanese are quite attached to raw food, the Ainu take pride in long, thorough cooking methods and distinguish their "civilized" way from the "barbaric" ways of the Japanese and Gilyaks—their neighbors—who eat food raw. Many Japanese, in turn, used to or continue to distinguish themselves from the neighboring Koreans and Chinese by pointing out their use of garlic, which is not used in *washoku* (Japanese cuisine). People have a strong attachment to their own cuisine and, conversely, an aversion to the foodways of others, including their table manners (Ohnuki-Tierney 1990a).

In many urban areas of the world today, ethnic foods are popular, and food has become truly internationalized. In the United Kingdom, daily cuisine now includes foods introduced by people from the former colonies—Africa, the East and West Indies, Pakistan, China (Hong Kong)—as well as "Italian" pizza and American hamburgers and "American steak." I saw with amazement and amusement in south London that "fish and chips" is now sometimes advertised as "traditional." In Japan, even before the recent introduction of fast foods from McDonald's,

A & W, and Kentucky Fried Chicken, a large number of foreign foods had been adopted, and some had become part of Japanese cuisine, for example, a Chinese noodle dish (*rāmen*) and Indian curry.

As cuisines internationalize in many parts of the world, ethnic festivals and foodways "revive." These "ethnic revivals" often are "invention[s] of the tradition" (Hobsbawm and Ranger 1986).[1] Retrospectively constructed practices, including cuisine, are presented as "genuine, authentic traditions" when they are simply latter-day inventions like the kilt or the "Highland tradition of Scotland" known today (Trevor-Roper 1983). In contemporary Japan traditional washoku has made a tremendous comeback precisely because Japan is undergoing an unprecedented transformation under the impact of global geopolitics. Similarly, "Scottish Highland culture" was created during the Union with England. In both cases, these "inventions" relate to the urgent need of peoples to redefine their own identities. The worldwide phenomenon of "ethnic" or "cultural" revivals, then, must be seen as a presentation and representation of the self, using foods as "metaphors of self."

For this process of dialectic differentiation and representations of self and other, people select not just any food but important foods and cuisine as metaphors. So-called staple foods often play powerful roles among, for example, the wheat-eating people in north India versus the rice-eating south Indians; the dark bread of European peasants versus the white bread of the upper class in past centuries; and rice-eating Asians versus bread-eating Europeans.

To explore how a people use the metaphor of a principal food to think about themselves in relation to other peoples, I chose, as an example, rice for the Japanese. As a people, the Japanese have repeatedly reconceptualized themselves as they encountered different others—Chinese and Westerners—by using rice as a metaphor for themselves. In addition to rice grains as food, rice paddies have played an enormously important role in the self-identity or identities of the Japanese. Thus, the symbolism of rice is bifurcated: on the one hand, "rice as *our* food" and, on the other hand, "rice paddies as *our* land," each reinforcing the other.

As my research on this project began, it became clear that the notion that rice had been "the staple food"—quantitatively the most important food—of the Japanese since its introduction to Japan must be questioned in light of postwar research. Although this notion was held to be an unquestionable historical fact before the war, postwar scholarship began uncovering evidence that rice has not always been quantitatively important to many Japanese (chap. 3). Most of these scholars, nonetheless, contend that it has always been of crucial symbolic significance for them. Of all the meanings assigned to rice, rice as a dominant metaphor of self has been the most important. In other words, rice has been a dominant metaphor of the Japanese but *not* because rice was *the* food to fill the stomach.

Metaphors used in day-to-day discourse, or "metaphors we live by," as Lakoff and Johnson (1980) say, may not always be articulated in the mind of the people. For example, as I explain later, the metaphor "bread" has layers of meaning, for example, as a metaphor for food in general and for the body of Christ. But people usually are not articulate about its meanings and the interrelationships among them.

Here I differ from the late V. Turner, a major figure in symbolic anthropology, whose concepts of "exegetical meaning" (1967:50) and "dominant symbols" (1967:20, 30–33) emphasize the articulation by the people who use symbols and who interpret meanings. My own experience with both the Ainu and the Japanese is that they follow their customs rather than being conscious about the meanings of their behavior or of symbols they use. The presence of metaphors in verbal and nonverbal discourse and their meanings are often abstracted by those who interpret them, such as anthropologists. Fernandez (1990) tells how profound meanings embodied in a key to a house in Asturian mountain villages in Spain gradually surface in the individuals' consciousness through a certain incident and how the meanings are deeply embedded in broader sociocultural contexts as well as long-term historical processes. The use of day-to-day metaphors by the folk contrasts with metaphors used by literary figures and other cultural elites whose ingenuity is measured by the original creation of a metaphor to call attention to a hitherto unexpected similarity between the metaphor and its referent (for details, see Ohnuki-Tierney 1990c).

By *dominant*, I mean *significant* in two senses. First, it occurs frequently, or its presence, both itself and its iconic representations, is quite conspicuous. Second, it serves as a "window," revealing something important about the culture. There are always a number of dominant symbols in a culture. For example, the mountains, the sea, bamboo, oxen, and countless others are dominant symbols in Japanese culture, each informative about something significant about the culture and society.

The purpose of this book is to show *how* the Japanese notion of the self has taken on a different contour as a different historical other has emerged and rice and rice paddies have served as the vehicle for deliberation, although not always conscious, in these processes.

Although it is easy to understand how people conceptualize themselves as a single collective self in their encounters with another people, it is far more taxing to understand how a particular mode of representation has gained such prominence because a number of contesting modes of representations and multiple voices exist in any social group. In fact, now that anthropologists have become acutely aware of the multiplicity within any social group, the term *contested* or *contesting* appears in book and article titles with extreme frequency. Japanese culture and society, too, have always been heterogeneous, as I delineated in my earlier work (Ohnuki-Tierney 1987). A study of rice as a metaphor of the Japanese self, then, involves the question of *how* rice has become a dominant metaphor of the Japanese despite the fact that a large segment of the population has always been engaged in occupations other than rice agriculture and, as mentioned, rice has not been a quantitatively important source of food for a large segment of the Japanese population.

In a broader framework it is a question of the development of a powerful representation of the self by the people themselves, on the one hand, and of how to reconcile a dominant representation with apparent multiplicity within a culture, on the other hand (chap. 6). How does a certain representation become strategic, and how does it acquire the power to naturalize its significance? My use of the term *naturalize* is similar to that of Barthes, Bourdieu, and Foucault. I use *naturalization* to refer to a historical process whereby culturally determined values and norms acquire a state that makes them seem "natural," not arbitrary, to the people (cf. Bourdieu 1977:164). For example, in many cultures of the world, even today, menstrual blood is thought to be "naturally" polluting and dirty—a concept often used to justify barring women from various religious practices.

It is too easy to conclude that powerful individuals institute a certain structure of meaning that the rest of the population blindly adopts. A superficial application of such conceptual tools as "false consciousness," "mystification," "hegemony," or even "naturalization" too often encourages the researcher to evade confronting the questions and to ignore culture-specific meanings and particular historical processes.

The particular problem I have chosen for this book cannot be answered by examining Japanese culture and society synchronically. I have, therefore, chosen to examine historical processes in which cultural practices and institutions involving rice and rice paddies have played prominent roles. When historicizing anthropology,[2] one can select various time scales: long-term, middle-range (for example, one century), or very short. Braudel ([1958] 1980) of the Annales school originally proposed the tripartite scheme—*longue durée*, conjuncture, and event—in which he gave pride of place to ecological and geographical factors.[3] Each has its own advantages and disadvantages. Most common approaches within historicized anthropology are studies of either a middle-range or short period. They enable the examination of vivid cultural dynamics in which actions and roles of individual agents can be identified. One can examine the role of agents whose interests conflict with those of others, use of the past for the present or for the future, and various "dynamics" between agents and cultural forces. (For a review of some of the issues in historicized anthropology see Moore 1986; Ohnuki-Tierney 1990b).

Although the extension of the Braudelian longue durée to a study of *mentalités* has not been altogether successful (cf. Chartier 1982; Hunt 1986; see also Bailey 1985; Santamaria and Bailey 1981), and I do not give primacy to ecology, I have opted to examine Japanese culture and society through a long period because of its extraordinary advantages. Ricoeur (1980:11) has stated that "history characterized by short, rapid, nervous oscillations" is "richest in humanity" although "the most dangerous" (see also Furet 1972, especially 54–55; Le Goff 1972). Although I would not categorically regard short-term oscillations as dangerous unless they are prejudged as permanent changes, it is well to note Ricoeur's distinction between long-term enduring changes compared to short-term oscillations whose impact on culture may be superficial and temporary. Most importantly, a long-term study enables the examination of a life-course, as it were, of a particular society, rather than snapshots taken at different times of development, thereby enabling one to confront the problem of *plus ça change, plus c'est la même chose*. The problem of change and continuity, or structure and its transformations, has been convincingly argued by a number of scholars who examined a culture over a long time, for example, Chang (1977) on the Chinese foodways, Tambiah (1976) on the galactic polity in Thailand, and Watson and Rawski (1977) on the Chinese death ritual.

As I take a long-term view in this book, my aim is not to cover historical and ethnographic details exhaustively. Nor is it on individual actions per se. My concern here is primarily social groups within Japan or the Japanese as a whole in relation to other peoples. My findings are based on the distinct advantages of taking a broad and long-term view.

In anthropology recent emphasis on the individual[4] has often cast references to a larger social group in a negative light. If the purpose of a study is the *intra*group dynamics, individuals, either as subjects or agents, receive focal importance. But it should not lead to a total ban on generalizations because individuals cannot be divorced from sociocultural context. Those who eschew generalizations at times suggest that it is a sin of "totalizing" to use terms such as "the Japanese." But generalizations cannot be avoided altogether. Even if one qualifies "the Japanese" in every occurrence with "many," "most," "some," "a few," or, even "73.2 percent," these adjectives add only an illusion of quantitative specificity. I trust that the reader will exercise common sense and understand that "the Japanese" does not necessarily mean "every Japanese." I also use the terms "Japan" and "Japanese" loosely throughout, realizing that neither Japan as a nation nor the Japanese as a well-bounded social group have existed throughout history—as B. Anderson (1991) points out, the birth of a nation is often difficult to pinpoint.[5]

Following the practice of the "natives," I also use the terms *West* and *Western*, not only because there are no better terms but also because the Japanese use most frequently the term *gaijin* (foreigners) to refer primarily to Westerners, especially Americans and West Europeans, including the French, the Germans, and the British, although they occasionally use *seiyōjin* (Westerners) as well.[6]

Historians and anthropologists no longer treat society or culture as well delineated and separate from the rest of the world. Most, if not all, historical changes are dialectic processes between internal developments and forces outside the boundaries of a political unit called society. Culture, in contrast to society, is never bounded (Leach 1965:282; 1982:41–43). Whether the agent of change is the development of capitalism, the growth of worldwide trade, or the spread of religion, most historical changes have been stories of conjunctures, as well articulated in Braudel's original work on sixteenth-century Europe (see n. 3) and publications by Sahlins on Hawaii (1985; 1988). During these conjunctures people are often forced to redefine their concepts of self as a result of an encounter with the other. This is so because the self, in any culture, is always defined in relation to the other either dialogically with other individuals in a given social context or dialectically with other peoples (chap. 7).

Contrary to the stereotype of Japan as an island country tucked away in the northeast corner of the world, the people on these archipelagoes have always interacted with other peoples. As a metaphor for the self of the Japanese, rice is necessarily involved when the Japanese situate themselves in their interaction with the rest of the world. Although ironic in one sense, the Japanese chose rice and rice paddies as metaphors for themselves when wet-rice agriculture was originally introduced from the Asian continent. This fact speaks eloquently to how *the Japanese self was born through discourse with the other.* Since then, rice and rice paddies have intimately and persistently appeared in the discourse of selves and others. The stories of conjunctures with the Chinese and with Westerners have been told as stories of Japanese short-grain rice versus Chinese long-grain rice, Japanese rice versus the meat of Westerners, and in contemporary Japan, domestic short-grain rice versus foreign short-grain rice (chap. 7). This book, then, is about "rices as selves."

In the following chapters I show that throughout history, the symbolic importance of rice has been deeply embedded in the Japanese cosmology both of the elite and the common folk: rice as soul, rice as deity, and ultimately, rice as self. In ancient Japan, human reproduction and agricultural production were conterminous; the same term was used for sexual intercourse and growth under the sun. In addition, ritual and polity were synonymous. Harvest rituals both among the folk and at the imperial court have been a major cultural institution, an important agent in constituting and reconstituting the importance of rice. These agrarian rituals enact a cosmic cycle of gift exchange during which a new crop of rice is offered in return for the original seeds given by the deities. Because rice embodies a soul, harvest rituals celebrate cosmic rejuvenation through an exchange of their souls, that is, selves, as objectified in rice and, possibly, semen (chaps. 4, 8).

These rituals also embody the single most important social role of rice—its use as food for commensality at both a cosmic level between deities and humans (chap. 4) and among the folk (chap. 6). In fact, the symbolic power of rice derives to a large degree from the day-to-day sharing of rice among the members of a social group and its uses in the discourse. Commensality is an important cultural institution everywhere, whether at a family table or at a college in Oxford or Cambridge and is a crucial cultural institution whereby people who eat together become "we," as opposed to "they," and the food shared becomes a metaphor for the social group.

The centrality of rice in Japanese cosmology is related to the use of rice as "pure money" and its place in aesthetics (chap. 5). A by-product of this research is a critique of a number of assumptions of *la pensée bourgeoise*, which has long portrayed food for survival, money as the fetish of capitalism, wealth as a result of hard work, and so forth. I demonstrate in this book that rice can be a pure or even sacred medium of exchange. Contrary to the image of the workaholic behind the Japanese economic miracle, a view exists in Japanese culture that wealth is a gift from a deity rather than a result of sweat. The rational choice of the "economic person" is an inappropriate model for understanding the importance of rice as wealth to the Japanese.

Only when the symbolic-cultural significance of rice for the Japanese is recognized can the contemporary phenomenon be understood: in the post-industrial era the Japanese have strenuously resisted the importation of California rice. Economically, the importation of California rice, which is very similar to the domestic rice, makes good sense because it is cheaper than the domestic rice. Furthermore, the total amount of money spent for rice by the Japanese today is too small to be of concern. Yet even many urbanites, who otherwise resent their taxes being used for rice farm subsidies, are opposed to rice importation.

As important as rice grains are as food, rice paddies are equally if not more important as "rice as self." Rice paddies have been a common theme portrayed in woodblock prints, paintings, and contemporary posters in travel agents' offices to attract urbanites to "the countryside." They are imbued with aesthetics. They have been intimately portrayed in representations of agriculture, the countryside, the seasons, and the past. As a metaphor of self, rice paddies are *our* ancestral land, *our* village, *our* region, and ultimately, *our* land, Japan. They also represent *our* pristine past before modernity and foreign influences contaminated it. Rice paddies then embody Japanese space and time, that is, Japanese land and history (chap. 6).

But the self represented by rice and rice paddies has undergone significant changes at historical conjunctures when the self was forced to redefine itself in relation to a particular other it encountered (chap. 7). The double-sided development of rice as self and rice paddies as our land offers two fascinating findings about the historical transformations of the Japanese concepts of self and other. First, the self turned into selves through successive historical conjunctures because each "other" required redefinition of the self. Second, and even more important, the process whereby the self became selves also involved a process whereby the other became others, not only successively through history but through a creation of *marginalized others*, both within Japanese society and without. Within Japanese society, some of the self became the *marginalized internal other*, that is, minorities who were originally nonsettled people (*hiteijūmin*), people without rice paddies. Outside of Japanese society, *marginalized external other* was created. They are peoples, like the Chinese and Koreans, who have lost the privileged status as the culturally superior other. They are then represented as eating wrong rice. One sees, then, a paradoxical phenomenon whereby rice represents the collective self of the Japanese as a whole while it has also played an important role in the stratification within the society and in the power inequality with different others.

In an anthropological study one must wrestle with cross-cultural comparisons in a way that neither denies the specificity of a particular culture under the rubric of cultural universals nor examines culture in isolation to herald its uniqueness as has often been done with Japanese culture. Assigning meanings and uses to rice and rice paddies in Japanese culture is far from unique. I introduce some cross-cultural comparisons throughout the book (more systematically in chap. 8) to show some parallels between Japanese culture and that of others. In most cultures, the landscape (city and country), historicity (past and present), and economic activities (hunting-gathering, agriculture, industry) are representations embedded in the conceptualization of the self in relation to the other at a particular vantage point (chap. 8). Agricultural protectionism in many of the postindustrial societies relies in part on this conceptual association between agriculture and *our* nature cum *our* land, and ultimately, *us* (chap. 8).

This is not a book about rice or rice agriculture per se. Therefore, chapter 2 on rice agriculture and chapter 3 on "rice as staple food" constitute only brief background information. My symbolic argument begins with chapter 4. I have not included a systematic discussion of rice wine (*sake*), except in passing, which would offer additional ethnographic and historical information on many of the issues. Because this study of rice includes research on highly complex subjects, such as the Japanese imperial system in a historical perspective, I was forced to confine the scope of my investigation. For references I emphasize publications in Japanese to introduce Japanese scholarship and sources in Japanese to an English-speaking audience.

Two

Rice and Rice Agriculture Today

Rice in Today's World

Rice, along with wheat and corn, is one of the three most important grains in the world today. In 1984 wheat occupied 31.8 percent, rice 20.2 percent, and corn 17.8 percent of the cultivated acreage in the world while wheat constituted 29 percent, rice 26.1 percent, and corn 24.9 percent of all agricultural production (Soda 1989:11). More than one-third of the world's population (34.9 percent; 1,166,474,000 people) eat rice as the only staple food. If one includes those who rely on both rice and other staples, such as corn and potatoes, the figure increases to 38 percent, and 17.5 percent depend on a combination of wheat, rice, and other grains. These figures compare with 10.5 percent of the world population who use wheat as the only staple and 3.0 percent who use both wheat and other foods, such as corn and potatoes (Watanabe 1987:19).

Debates over the origin of the rice plant continue. Scholars recently refuted a theory that it originated in tropical Asia near the equator in India and propose a source in the mountainous areas of subtropical Asia between Yunnan in the east and Assam in the west (Watanabe 1989:084; Bray 1986:8–9). Ethnologists and geneticists have proposed an alternative origin as a result of a symposium on the origin of rice, held at the National Museum of Ethnology (Kokuritsu Minzokugaku Hakubutsu-kan) in 1992 (S. Yoshida 1992). They question the Yunnan-Assam region as the origin, pointing to the definite presence of tropical *japonica* before the Heian period (794–1185). Yoshida concurs with Satō Yōichirō, a geneticist and a participant in the symposium, who suggests delaying a conclusive statement on the origin until the origins of tropical *japonica* and *indica* are identified. Whatever the origin, rice is decisively an Asian crop: 90 percent of world yields are grown in monsoon Asia, and 64 percent of this figure is produced in East and Southeast Asia alone (Swaminathan 1984 cited in Bray 1986:8; for detailed technical information on the rice plant and rice agriculture, see Barker and Herdt 1985).

The major rice-producing countries in 1986 were the People's Republic of China (36 percent); India (20 percent); Indonesia (8 percent); Bangladesh (5 percent); Thailand (4 percent); Japan (3.1 percent); Burma

(2.7 percent) and Korea (1.6 percent). The major non-Asian rice-producing countries were Brazil (2.1 percent), which has many Japanese and other Asian residents, and the United States (1.3 percent), but non-Asian production is insignificant compared to that of Asian countries (Statistics Appendix of Nōrinshō White Papers for 1987, cited in Soda 1989:13).

The Asian domesticated rices, *Oryza sativa*, have two major subspecies.[1] The *indica* type, commonly referred to as long-grain rice, has longer, more slender grains that remain separate when cooked, whereas the *japonica*, or short-grain type, has shorter, rounder, more translucent grains that become sticky when cooked. Both subspecies have glutinous and nonglutinous varieties. In Japan the *indica* subspecies was cultivated early on but only briefly (Shirota 1989:076; see also Shirota 1987) and *japonica* rice became the exclusive type cultivated and consumed by the Japanese.

Rice cultivation is far more labor intensive than either wheat or corn cultivation, but under favorable conditions rice produces a good yield and is easy to thresh (Sasaki 1985:52). Seedlings are grown in separate beds and then transplanted individually in flooded paddies (for details, see Bray 1986). Bray (1986) argues that apparently inefficient rice agriculture cannot be understood in terms of the "rational" or the "Economic Person (Man)" model of economic activities developed in the Western social sciences.

Rice in all countries has undergone many changes as a result of deliberate efforts to improve the species. The most dramatic genetic engineering produced new rice varieties at the International Rice Research Institute in the Philippines, which have short stems, do not lodge easily, even in strong wind and rain, and can benefit more from fertilizers than other varieties. The new varieties were disseminated through the Green Revolution, as the new technology has been called, and have been widely accepted in many Asian countries, especially India. Japan did not participate in the Green Revolution as I explain in chapter 3.

Rice differs from other staple foods in that it is cooked and consumed without any processing other than threshing and milling, unlike wheat and corn, which are first ground and then made into bread and tortillas. In part for this reason, almost every rice-consuming population insists on "quality" in their rice, a composite of appearance, fragrance, and, most important, taste. Preferences differ from one population to the next. The taste of any food is a complex perception, involving even tactile senses, and is always acquired. Nonsticky long-grain rice does not taste good to the Japanese, whereas it is the preferred rice in many other Asian countries. The Thai people emphasize the "jasmine fragrance" of their rice. The cooking method influences which kind of rice is considered good. The Japanese use plain cooked rice or mix it with vinegar and cool it for sushi. They, therefore, prefer a rice that tastes good when used either way. When the Japanese cook rice with other ingredients to make *kate-gohan* (mixed rice), they do not use oil. The culinary repertoire of non-Japanese Asians, however, more frequently includes rice cooked with other ingredients or fried after boiling. Short-grain rice becomes too soggy or crumbles too easily when cooked in these ways.

The rice plant provides other useful material. In Japan, rice straw and chaff are used as fertilizer. In *Bizen* style pottery, rice straw is wrapped around the clay items during firing to protect them and to imprint aesthetic designs. In the past, the Japanese used ash from rice husks or straw to remove oil from animal fur before making it into writing brushes. Rice straw is used in many other ways to make straw hats, sandals, rain gear (*mino*), *tatami* mats, and so forth. As I explain in chapter 5, these objects, which were vital in the daily life of the Japanese, acquired an aesthetic value in Japanese culture and contributed greatly to the way the Japanese feel about rice and rice agriculture, a cultural valuation that is far greater than pure economic value.

Types of Rice in Japan

Whatever the original variety of rice introduced to Japan was, it was suited to the warm, humid climate. Some claim that red rice (*akamai*, or *akagome*) was the rice introduced originally from the Asian continent although opinions differ about what constitutes "red rice" (Watanabe 1987:28). Red rice has special ritual value; some shrines, located primarily in remote areas of southern Japan, still cultivate red rice for ritual use (Shirota 1989; Watanabe 1987). The Japanese custom of using *se-kihan* (red meal) for auspicious occasions may derive from the early use of red rice (Yanagita 1981a:208), although now *sekihan* is made by combining red beans (*azuki*) with rice to produce the desired color.

At present, there are many varieties of rice in Japan. The rice plants had to be adapted to regional climates within Japan that range from subtropical to subarctic. The tradition whereby each rice-growing family keeps its own rice for the next year's planting maintained genetic variety. Self-seeding (planting homegrown seed), a practice endorsed and protected by the Japanese government, also eliminated the need for large rice seed companies. Urban consumers' rice has been supplied by farmers in nearby regions. This situation contrasts with other nations, such as the United States, where the presence of seed companies results in the reduction of varieties of agricultural products.

The situation has changed drastically, however. With affluence and a reduction in rice consumption, most Japanese have developed a preference for varieties grown in the cold climate of Niigata and northeastern (*Tōhoku*) Japan, which includes six prefectures: Fukushima, Miyagi, Iwate, Aomori, Yamagata, and Akita. Among them, two varieties— koshihikari, grown in Niigata, and sasanishiki, grown in Miyagi and Yamagata—are the favorites, with Akita komachi, grown in Akita a close third. These two varieties were developed during the Meiji period and their quality has been improved since then (*Asahi Shinbun*, November 16, 1988). Their nationwide distribution is a recent phenomenon, promoted, according to some, by the government (Hasegawa 1987).

An important implication is that the rice preferred by the Japanese today is very different not only from the rice originally introduced to Japan from monsoon Asia but also from the rice the Japanese in each region have consumed until recently. The rice that the Japanese today identify as *the* Japanese rice comes from northeastern Japan where rice agriculture arrived last.

Not only has rice undergone changes over time, so have the methods of processing. For most Japanese today, rice means white rice (*haku-mai*)—rice that is thoroughly polished. The consumption of white rice, however, is a relatively recent phenomenon. Most scholars agree that it was some time during the Genroku and Kyōho periods, the end of the seventeenth century through the beginning of the eighteenth century, that the Japanese began using polished rice. Until then, they consumed unpolished brown rice (*genmai*).[2] After the health food movement became popular some individuals used genmai. One sees a similar scene in the United States and elsewhere where some prefer the dark bread that used to be the food of peasants. Nutritionists agree that the switch to white rice was unfortunate because the polishing process removes many important nutrients, including vitamin B[3] although some Japanese argue that white rice is equally, if not more, nutritious.

Japanese Government Intervention in
   ## Rice Agriculture

To understand contemporary rice agriculture in Japan, which involves many contradictions, it is essential to briefly review the intervention of the Japanese government in agriculture, especially rice agriculture (for details, see Donnelly 1978). The government's intervention is, from a world perspective, unparalleled in its degree. During the Medieval (1185–1392) and the Early Modern (*Kinseki*) (1603–1868) periods, rice was a tax taken by the regional and central governments. Thus, rice was never directly in a free-market economy during premodern times in Japan.

Essentially the same system has continued to the present. During the Modern period (1868–present), the national government took over the role of the Shōgunate government and assumed the control of agricultural products, especially rice, in an effort to increase the export of manufactured goods during the early phases of industrialization. The government envisioned that providing inexpensive rice to industrial workers would keep living costs down, which, in turn, would justify low wages for workers and high profit margins for industrialists through larger exports of manufactured goods. Thus, early in the twentieth century, the government began to consider the purchase, sale, and even the storage of all the rice harvested in Japan. The government initiated a rice control policy in 1920 thereby taking legal control of rice distribution in 1939. In 1942 it instituted the famous, or infamous, *shokuryō kanrihō* (Food Control Act), which gave the government legal authority over almost all food items. In the post–World War II period, the government gradually lifted many of these controls but not those on rice, wheat, and barley. Contrary to the original intent of the policy to protect consumers, the government doubly subsidized rice farmers by subsidizing both farmland and rice production (for details see Calder 1988:241–244). Several times in the 1960s, it increased the price of rice to boost farmers' incomes to the level of urban workers, whose incomes had increased as a result of the development of high technology. In other words, government policy changed from protecting consumers in times of crises to protecting farmers in times of economic growth (Reich, Endō, and Timmer 1986:168).

The protection of farmers took an ironic turn as a result of the steadily decreasing demand for rice as Japan became affluent. The Japanese diet shifted toward side dishes (*fukushoku*) rather than rice although rice continues to be called the main dish (*shushoku*). An influx of foreign dishes, including pizza and hamburgers, further contributed to the reduction in rice consumption. In 1990 the expected consumption was only ten million tons, whereas fourteen million tons of rice could potentially be produced if all rice land was effectively used for rice cultivation (*Asahi Shinbun*, May 31, 1990). Thus, Japan has experienced overproduction of rice in recent years, especially in 1968–1971 and 1976–1979 when bumper crops were harvested, and the government had to purchase and store huge quantities of surplus rice (*Nihon Keizai Shinbun*, February 12, 1989; Ōshima 1984).[4]

Although this is the general picture portrayed in mass media and held by the people, Hasegawa (1987:16–20) points out that, during a rice shortage in 1984, the government "sneaked in" 150,000 tons of rice from Korea and Thailand, a move strenuously opposed by the farm unions. Likewise, Calder (1988:231–232) notes that Japan imported Korean rice worth $70 million in 1984, an act by the Japanese government, according to many observers, designed to establish leverage over the farm unions (Calder 1989).

In addition to the double subsidies for farmers, the government took two additional steps to alleviate the impact of the deteriorating rice economy. First, it instituted a policy to encourage farmers to reduce production capacity. The government *pays* rice farmers *not* to use their land for rice, a practice known as the reduction of cultivated land (*gentan*) (*Asahi Shinbun*, May 31, 1990). In 1988 the government forced farmers to reduce land used for rice cultivation by 30 percent (*Asahi Shinbun*, January 27, 1988). Today of the 3 million hectares of rice paddies in Japan 770,000 hectares lie fallow (Kano 1987:40).

Second, the government encouraged an increase in rice consumption. Farmers were exempted from reducing rice production if they could implement ways to increase rice consumption, for example, by using it in school lunch programs or by increasing the consumption of sake (*Asahi Shinbun*, January 27, 1988). The government even devised a ploy using one of the most culturally central customs, gift exchange. The government lifted its ban that restricted farmers to delivering rice only to neighboring districts and allowed nationwide delivery. In 1988 a new gift item appeared in the Mitsukoshi Department Store in Nihonbashi, Tokyo—gift-wrapped koshihikari rice (*Nihon Keizai Shinbun*, November 20, 1988) from Niigata, considered the best rice in Japan today.

In 1986 the government spent ¥ 1 trillion on farm subsidies, as they had in previous years, but in 1987 the amount declined to ¥ 560 billion (*The Economist*, December 1987:32).[5] In the face of mounting financial difficulties, the government loosened its control of the rice market and no longer controls all harvested rice. In 1990 one finds three types of rice: *seifumai*, government rice that is purchased and sold to consumers by the government; *jishu ryūtsūmai*, rice sold for profit although it is sold through the local governments; and *jiyūmai*, rice sold on the market.

Rice and Rice Agriculture in Contemporary Japan

At the beginning of the Meiji period (1868–1912), the population of Japan was 34,800,000, of which 80 percent were engaged in farming. In 1985 Japan's population was 120 million of which only 4.3 million (3.5 percent) were in the farming and lumber industries (Sahara 1990:4).[6] Today only a small number of farmers are full-time, and fully 85 percent of the rice crop is grown by part-time farmers (*New York Times*, April 19, 1987). In rural Japan today, the older generation farms part-time while the younger generation works primarily in cities. Moon

(1989) details an agricultural community that revitalized itself by turning homes into boarding houses, much like the "bed and breakfast" places in the United Kingdom and the United States, to accommodate skiers who flock to a nearby ski slope. The future of the tradition of family farming on ancestral land is tenuous.

The power held by farmers and the continuation of farm policies were usually attributed to the Liberal Democratic party (LDP), the ruling party of postwar Japan, which has traditionally relied on rural votes. Kelly (1989) argues that since the late 1960s rural electoral support for the LDP has come not from the few full-time farmers but from the far more numerous part-time farmers who have benefited from the LDP's government price subsidies to part-time rice farmers and from the services and public works provided in their regions.

In 1985 the average income of all farmers, the majority of whom also drew income from nonagricultural sources, was ¥ 7.3 million, more than ¥ 1 million more than the average income of urban salaried workers (Yayama 1987:67). Despite higher incomes than urbanites, farmers are not well-off financially because of the high cost of farm operation. Thus, investments in farm equipment and other expenditures caused 16 percent of farmers to default on their mortgages; only 60 percent paid their debts regularly. Many farmers in Hokkaidō, where 10 percent of the rice in Japan is grown, and even some farmers in the rice country, are in extreme financial difficulty. For example, in 1990, the Itōs, father-son full-time farmers in Hokkaidō, were ¥ 62 million in debt—¥ 45 million from the purchase of an additional 6.5 hectares of farmland in 1988 and the remainder operating costs not subsidized by the government. In 1989 their income was ¥ 20 million of which ¥ 15 million came from the sale of rice. The cost of operating the farm was ¥ 10 million and the cost of living for the family was ¥ 6 million. The remainder was used to pay off the debt (*Asahi Shinbun*, May 31, 1990).

Although urbanites feel that farmers are overprotected by the government, farmers do not feel privileged or adequately protected financially and are ambivalent about their occupation. In a "Voice of the People" column in the *Asahi* newspaper (June 12, 1990), Tokunaga Atsuyoshi, a fifty-eight year-old farmer, chronicled the family tradition of farming and the importance of their ancestral land since the Russo-Japanese War. He was disappointed when his daughter, whom he had hoped would continue farming, married a white-collar worker (*sararīman*) in the city and left the farm. Now that he sees little future in farming, he feels he should congratulate his daughter who had the foresight to leave. He reluctantly anticipates the day when he, too, will cease to be a farmer. He was prompted to write the article by the pressure from the United States to open Japan's rice market. The title of his article, "Kome yunyū yōnin, jidai no nagareka" (Rice importation—A sign of the time?) portrays the ambivalent attitude of contemporary Japanese—an unequivocal surface opposition to the importation of foreign rice and a perception that it may be inevitable.

Another rice farmer, Gotō Masayoshi, is quoted, "As a father, I have second thoughts about telling my son to succeed to [sic] my farm." A forty-one-year-old farmer, Kuroda Yūichi, converted his entire 1.1-hectare (2.7-acre) rice farm into an organic farm where he grows tomatoes, flowers, spinach, and other vegetables in plastic greenhouses (Thorson 1989).

Farmers I interviewed in 1989 also seemed quite ambivalent. They recognized the potential of becoming rich by selling their subsidized farmland at stupendous prices if land prices went up. They felt, however, that farm work was hard; often wives tended the farm while husbands worked in a nearby city to earn additional income. Their ambivalence is clearly expressed in the fact that many farmers, according to them, often preferred that their daughters not marry farmers while wishing that their sons would stay on the ancestral farm. These farmers pointed to several reasons for not wanting their daughters to marry farmers. First, farming involves too much work, and the future seems precarious. Second, as they themselves have experienced, rural life has retained too many expensive traditional rituals. A wedding alone, they say, costs ¥ 10 million, and many other ceremonies are far more elaborate than those in the cities. Rural life, according to them, is very expensive,[7] especially for those with daughters because the financial burdens of traditional rituals performed before and after the wedding fall on the bride's family. If a daughter marries in a city, a wedding can be less costly because not only are a wedding ceremony and its accompanying rituals far less complicated and less expensive but the bride's parents are not obliged to invite innumerable relatives and neighbors (sometimes everyone in a settlement).

The preference both by parents and their daughters to leave farming has created a situation whereby young farmers have a hard time finding women willing to marry them, so much so that mass media inside and outside Japan report that women from the Philippines, Thailand, and elsewhere in Asia have been recruited.

Today, a new term, rinō (leaving farming) appears frequently in the mass media. In Hokkaidō, in one city (Fukagawa) alone 136 farm families left farming during a three-year period (1986–1988) primarily because of huge debts incurred by purchasing land and machinery to expand their farms (Asahi Shinbun, November 20, 1988). Nationwide statistics indicate that one-third of farm families are headed by people more than sixty years of age, of whom 40 percent have no successors (Asahi Shinbun, November 20, 1988).

The following is a list of those prefectures, starting from the north, that produced more than three hundred thousand kilos of rice (wet rice) in 1988 (Nōrin Suisanshō Keizaikyoku Tōkei Jōhōbu 1990:66):

Prefectures	Kilos of Wet Rice
Japan total	9,888,000
Hokkaidō	763,100
Aomori	327,900
Iwate	324,500
Miyagi	379,100
Akita	573,900
Yamagata	454,500
Fukushima	344,600
Ibaragi	377,900
Tochigi	319,700
Chiba	323,100
Niigata	736,000

Note that Hokkaidō is not divided into prefectures, thus its total production is far larger than that of any prefecture.

With the decline of rice agriculture, three strategies have been adopted by rice farmers: farmers in Kyūshū, where the rice is not good enough to bring commercial profits, have decided to confine rice production to their own consumption; farmers in Hokkaidō are striving to cut costs; and only those in the northeastern prefectures where "the best rice" is grown continue rice agriculture as before (*Asahi Shinbun*, June 14).

The plight of rice farmers indicates that, even for them, rice agriculture is not a matter of rational choice by the economic person, just as urbanites' attitudes toward rice are not solely based on economic rationality.

Consumers' Attitudes toward Rice and Rice Agriculture

The Price of Rice

Obviously, the government subsidies have removed rice from the supply and demand of a market economy; the price of rice in Japan today is several times higher than in the United States. The prices of several varieties of rice at a food cooperative (*kōpu*) in the Kobe area in the spring of 1990 were similar to prices at department stores I checked in Tokyo (see table 2.1). Although the high price of rice has been cited, especially by non-Japanese media, to confirm the fallacy of the Food Control Act, the

TABLE 2.1
Price for Ten Kilograms of Rice

Rice Vareity	November 1989	May 1990	October 1992ᵃ
Koshihikari			
from Niigata Prefecture	¥ 5,800	¥ 5,980	¥ 6,600
Sasanishiki			
from Miyagi Prefecture	¥ 5,460	¥ 5,400	¥ 5,800
Hyōjun Kakakumai			
(Standard rice)	¥ 3,750	¥ 3,610	¥ 3,616

ᵃ The figures are based on 5-kg bags, sold for half the price listed here, at a supermarket in Tokyo. Koshihikari from Niigata Prefecture was sold under the name of "Shirayukimai" (white-snow rice), although they also had another type of Koshihikari from Niigata Prefecture at ¥ 3,250 for 5 kg and the price at a department store in Tokyo for it was ¥ 3,050 for 5 kg.

first two types of rice in table 2.1, whose prices are not controlled by the government, command much higher prices than other varieties and yet are eagerly sought by consumers. Therefore, unless one takes the view that Japanese consumers have been completely co-opted by the government, government policy is not the sole villain behind the high price of rice.

Rice consumption varies considerably from household to household, depending not only on the number of people but also on their ages and the family's life-style. For example, soon after World War II, in many urban households people began eating toast, eggs, and salad (usually finely sliced cabbage) for breakfast while those in rural households (and former rural residents who moved to cities) continued to eat rice for breakfast. The recent decline in rice consumption, however, is reported to be more acute in rural areas than in cities (*Asahi Shinbun*, January 11, 1989).

In 1987 rice consumption per individual was 72 kilos per year (*Asahi Shinbun*, January 11, 1989), a figure that contrasts sharply with the average of 150 kilos per individual per year before World War II (Ōshima 1984:121). As a rough estimate, 10 kilos of rice lasted about ten days to two weeks for a family of four. A Japanese family of three to four persons in 1988 thus spent on the average about ¥ 1,200 for rice each month. The amount of money spent on rice is usually far less than the Japanese now spend on side dishes (fukushoku). For example, a couple in their forties with a monthly income of only ¥ 138,000, spent ¥ 47,183 on side dishes but ¥ 5,800 on rice (*Asahi Shinbun*, November 13, 1988). The proportion of money spent on rice by middle- to high-income families is far less than money spent on other foods. A nation-

2.1. Kentucky Fried Chicken in Kōbe, Japan, 1991. Foreign foods have almost saturated the market. Photo by the author.

wide survey in 1989 revealed that a family's average expenditure on rice was 2 percent of its total expenditures. Again, this contrasts sharply with consumer habits in prewar periods. For example, during the Taishō period (1912–1926) an average 27 percent of the budget of laborers was spent on rice (Ōshima 1984:121).

Considering the high prices prevalent in Japan in the 1990s, ¥ 1,200 for rice per month is not an enormous amount of money. When I asked people in June 1990 if they considered rice expensive, a surprising number replied that rice was inexpensive because they no longer ate much rice. From their point of view the amount of rice they eat is so small that it seems inexpensive, even though the price per kilogram is about eight times higher than that in the United States. It is a very noneconomic argument that "makes sense" to the Japanese. Therefore, consumers are willing to buy the two most expensive varieties—koshihikari and sasanishiki. These species are difficult to grow and are always in short supply. To verify whether the willingness to buy expensive rice was confined to the well-to-do, I interviewed a number of Japanese in street cars and public places, purposely targeting those who looked less affluent. They, too, held the same opinion. Because what is sold as koshihikari or sasanishiki rice on the market is often mixed with cheaper rice, urban Japanese usu-

2.2. A Department Store Promoting the Sale of Rice in Kōbe, Japan, 1990. Photo by the author.

ally rely on a local store that can be trusted to deliver the nonmixed rice of their choice. Cheaper types of rice are used in less exclusive restaurants, cafeterias, and other establishments and for less expensive rice products such as inexpensive sake and rice crackers. I tried sushi, rice balls (*onigiri*), and other samples of cooked rice in inexpensive stores in the fashionable Roppongi district in Tokyo and found that many of them lacked "quality."

Although urbanites are willing to pay a high price for "tasty" rice, they also harbor considerable resentment against farmers. Ōmae Kenichi, an MIT graduate, and a business strategist cum managing director for McKinsey & Company's Tokyo office, is most articulate as he presents the feeling of urbanites in his 1986 book, *Shin-Kokufuron* (A new theory on the wealth of nations). In the book, entitled after Adam Smith's *An Inquiry Into the Nature and Causes of the Wealth of Nations*, he outlines strategies for Japan's further prosperity; it was a bestseller in Japan. He decries Japan's farm policy, which was laid down forty years ago when 40 percent of the Japanese population were farmers. He points out that farmers, who constitute only 6 percent of the population, now hold 18 percent of the votes. He calls urbanites "the silent majority" and shows that their taxes underwrite government subsidies for farmland and rice.

Japan is a small, mountainous country; 70 percent of its land is too mountainous for agricultural use. Of the remaining 30 percent, only 2.9 percent is in urban areas where 120 million people are cramped in small houses while the rest of the flat land is taken by rice-growing farmers. Ōmae points out that, because of the government's protectionist policies, urbanites are held hostage in tiny apartments ("rabbit huts") while farmers are held hostage on their land because of their dependence on government subsidies. He reminds the reader that in 1986 of one hundred billionaires (*okuman chōja*) in Japan, sixty to seventy were farmers who had sold their farmlands. He blames the astronomical price of urban land on the high price of rice, which discourages conversion of rural land to urban uses. Rural areas in Japan are often near cities; thus, this land could easily house urbanites.

Ōmae's is not a lone voice. A man in his forties who sat next to me on a plane from San Francisco to Narita in November 1989 proudly announced that he and his officemates ate spaghetti and other noodle dishes (*menrui*) for lunch, eating rice only at dinner time. He emphatically claimed that children today prefer bread to rice. As our conversation continued, he added, "When they start participating in sports, they start eating rice because rice supplies the energy they need." As our plane descended to the Narita airport, he pointed to the rice paddies below and said in disgust that the farmers were waiting for land prices to go up so they could sell their land and go off on world tours. He is openly hostile to farmers who are doubly subsidized by the government at the expense of urbanites. Despite this man's hostility toward farmers and his modern food preferences, he still considers rice to be *the* source of energy—an important point that I return to in chapter 4.

In discussions about agriculture, urbanites are pitched against rural farmers. One must remember, however, that a significant segment of the Japanese population has been neither farmers nor urban industrial and commercial workers but fishermen, miners, craft specialists, entertainers, and so forth (see chap. 6). Of these other occupations, fishermen often reside in rural areas but do not benefit from government subsidies. While interviewing people in 1989 in Kanazawa in Ishikawa prefecture, I talked with a taxi driver who used to be a fisherman by occupation. He advocated opening up the rice market and pointed out that only rice farmers, not fishermen, had benefited from the government's protectionist policy.

The Rice Importation Issue

Discussions about the price of rice would probably not have surfaced in Japan, at least not as acutely, had there not been pressure from the United States and some European countries to open Japan's rice market, an issue widely reported in mass media inside and outside Japan. The United States Rice Millers Association (RMA) asked for a quota of up to 2.5 percent of the Japanese market in the first year after the agreement is made, increasing to 10 percent in the fourth year (Darlin 1988; Take-uchi 1988). Although the United States Trade Representative (USTR) turned down this request in October 1986, it agreed to put it on the agenda for the Uruguay Round of multilateral trade negotiations in 1987. Through the 103-nation General Agreement on Tariffs and Trade Japan continues in 1992 to wrestle with agricultural issues in general and this one in particular.

As expected, RMA's demand met immediate and violent opposition in Japan, spearheaded by Zenchū, the powerful Central Union of Agricultural Cooperatives.[8] The Japanese government, too, initially resisted the pressure quite stubbornly.

Most surprising is that rice importation is opposed by Japanese consumers. The results of opinion polls taken at various times are shown in table 2.2.

Women tended to oppose rice importation more than did men. This is curious because in most families, women hold the decision-making power over the household budget. If women are *not* opposed to rice im-

TABLE 2.2
Opinion Polls on the Rice Importation Issue
(percentage of respondents)

Opinion	For (sansei)			Against (hantai)
	A	B	C	A
Allow free trade (*jiyūka*) of rice	23	24	21	52
Allow importation within certain limits (*wakunai*)	41	60	44	33
Allow no importation of rice		16	30	

Sources: A figures from the opinion polls conducted by the National Broadcasting Company (NHK) on October 22 and 23, 1988, covering eighteen thousand individuals over age twenty; B figures from a survey by a leading newpaper, the *Nihon Keizai Shinbun*, in 1988 (*Nihon Keizai Shinbun*, November 26, 1988); and C figures from a survey by another leading newspaper, the *Asahi*, on May 20 and 21 (*Asahi Shinbun*, June 4, 1990).

portation, then, Japan's opposition is not based on consumers' concerns about price. The younger generation supports importation with restrictions, whereas people over sixty are most opposed to importation. In terms of occupation, those most opposed to importation are people in farming, lumbering, and fishing (58 percent) and laborers (36 percent), whereas the percentage of those supporting importation is fairly uniform among most occupational groups, including managers (27 percent), industrial laborers (22 percent), laborers in business sectors (24 percent), self-employed industrialists and business people (24 percent), and self-employed people (24 percent). Among farming, lumbering, and fishing occupations, however, only 12 percent favor importation (*Asahi Shinbun*, June 4, 1990). As noted earlier, attitudes toward importation differ considerably between farmers and those engaged in lumbering and fishing; differences are not shown in these statistics because these three occupations are traditionally lumped together.

That the rice problem primarily is not an economic issue for the Japanese is again evident in the following survey by the *Nihon Keizai Shinbun* (November 26, 1988). Within the context of the rice importation issue respondents were asked what they look for in future rice policies.

Increase organic cultivation and variety selection	46%
Reduce the price of rice	23%
Offer tasty rice even at a higher price	19%
Others and no response	12%

Thus, a reduction in price was the major concern of 23 percent, whereas 65 percent listed noneconomic preferences. A similar result emerged in a survey of consumers' opinions on the price of rice by the National Broadcasting Company (NHK) aired on November 3, 1988.

Price high/relatively high	33%
Price inexpensive/relatively inexpensive	30%

One recalls the noneconomic argument of the consumers that "the price of rice is not high if one consumes only a small amount." Therefore, many Japanese feel that even if the Japanese lose economically on this issue, the importation of rice will not profit Americans. Japanese consumers will continue to buy domestic rice because "it tastes far better than foreign rice and does not cost much," and imported rice will be purchased only by low-class restaurateurs. Some individuals who tried to import California rice to sell in Japan not only met government sanctions but could not sell it (Nagaoka 1987; Tracey 1988).

In 1992 when rice importation was no longer a "hot" topic in mass media or among the Japanese in general, an importation of frozen sushi from the United States, using California rice, won government approval after a brief struggle. Matsumoto Fujio is president of a chain, called Sushi Boy, which serves inexpensive sushi on a conveyer belt; sushi are placed on plates of different colors, depending upon the price. Customers take whatever they wish as sushi passes in front of them and bring their empty plates to the register to pay. Mr. Matsumoto built a factory in the United States that produces one hundred thousand sushi a day, all made by robots. He is already very successful in the United States where he can scarcely keep up with orders (*Asahi Shinbun*, October 3, 1992). His attempt to import his sushi into Japan, however, met opposition by the Shokuryōchō (Food Agency of the Japanese government). The government, in the end, was forced to approve its importation because it met the regulation that food containing rice must include 20 percent by weight of other food. In 1991 Japan imported thirteen hundred tons of shrimp pilaf, squid rice, and others (*Asahi Shinbun*, September 30 and October 3, 1992).

In other words, foreign rice has been imported into Japan and has been for a long time. The incident, therefore, discloses that Japanese opposition to the importation of California rice is more in principle than in fact. Whether the Sushi Boy victory is a sign of things to come, a prediction that Japanese opposition to California rice is weakening, is difficult to say.

Japan's stubborn opposition, at least so far, to rice importation contrasts starkly with its eagerness to import foreign goods that are prestige items among the Japanese. Revlon lipsticks are sold at prices several times higher than domestic lipsticks, just as Ivory soap is a fancy and expensive gift item, not to mention French wines and cognac, Polo clothing, Gucci handbags; all are fads purchased enthusiastically at astronomical prices (Ohnuki-Tierney 1990a).

Not only luxury goods but a surprising amount of day-to-day foods are also imported. In 1988 the percentage of foods imported into Japan were fish and shellfish 35.9 percent, grains 14.6 percent, meat 14.8 percent, and fruits and vegetables 12.7 percent; so-called Japanese dishes are increasingly made from imported ingredients (Tsūshō Sangyōshō 1989: 149–150; JETRO 1989:138–140). Thus, Japanese consumers scarcely resisted the importation of other agricultural products. In 1987 American farmers exported to Japan corn and sorghum feed grains worth more than $1 billion, roughly 70 percent of Japan's total feed grain imports (Ashbrook 1988). Reich, Endō, and Timmer (1986:159) show that agricultural trade between Japan and the United States increased rapidly from 1960 to 1980, representing a highly successful trade relationship (see also I. Yamaguchi 1987:40). In 1980 the United States provided about 40 percent of Japan's overall agricultural imports; 15 percent of the United States's total agricultural exports went to Japan, more than to any other country. According to these scholars, "the United States is the largest food supplier for Japan, and Japan is the largest export market for U.S. agricultural products. In fact, more land in the United States is devoted to growing food and fiber for Japan than is cultivated in Japan itself" (Reich, Endō and Timmer 1986:159). They conclude that rice prices are "not so much a consumer issue as they are a tax and budget issue," and the problem of a large budget deficit makes "rice price policy an important political and economic issue" (Reich, Endō, and Timmer 1986:190).[9]

Undoubtedly, the rice importation issue has a political dimension: the support of the rural electorate remains critical for Japanese political parties. In 1990, under increasing pressure from the United States and other countries, the LDP government strained to find ways to accommodate rice importation while the Japan Socialist party (JSP) adamantly opposed it and instead favored a policy of self-sufficiency in rice, thereby gaining support from people in both rural and urban areas. The third largest party, Kōmeitō, once expressed a desire "to meet the wishes of the consumers" and advocated rice importation, only to reverse their stance after meeting strenuous opposition from members representing rural Japan (*Asahi Shinbun*, June 7, 1990). The strength of the rural vote owes, to a considerable extent, to the fact that farmers and their families can mobilize voters through farmers' unions, whereas urban voters are isolated from each other and cannot form an effective voting block. The important point is that some urbanites voted with farmers to oppose rice importation, and, more important, they did not oppose the farmers' support of a closed market.

Symbolic Importance of Rice Today

Rice and rice agriculture in Japan constitute a complex phenomenon. Although rice farmers are protected by government policy, they are, nonetheless, ambivalent about their occupation. It is no longer economically profitable, yet it is difficult to discontinue it altogether. Urbanites resent farmers whose subsidies are paid for by urban taxes. Farmers are doubly subsidized: both farmland and rice are subsidized. Urbanites are enraged to see farmers on the annual billionaires' list. These farmers, according to urbanites, waited until land values went up and then sold their land at stupendously high prices, whereas urbanites cannot afford to own even one shovelful of "gold sand," that is, land in Japan. Yet these same urbanites are willing to pay high prices for the types of rice that are *not* controlled by the government. Even more surprisingly, they oppose rice importation, thus working against their own economic interests.

To capitalize the cultural aspect of Japanese feeling about rice, I focus on the noneconomic argument. Many Japanese are open to rice importation. The business/industry sector would rather see rice importation permitted and the friction reduced between the United States and Japan on the trade imbalance issue. For more than one generation, Keidanren, representing big business interests, has been vocal about their opposition to farm subsidies (Calder 1988:231).

Yet from a cultural perspective the argument about rice in contemporary Japan demonstrates beyond doubt that, for the Japanese, rice is not simply food to fill the stomach. Japanese attitudes and behaviors toward rice are not governed by economic rationale. The rice importation issue, which has a political dimension, is based on broader cultural issues involving the meaning of rice. An understanding of rice in Japan requires an understanding of the broader cultural and historical landscape in which the meanings of rice and rice agriculture are embedded.

Three

Rice as a Staple Food?

"STAPLE FOOD" is a household term with a seemingly commonsense meaning. People identify certain foods as staple foods—bread, rice, tortillas, and so forth. What makes a food a staple? Is it the food eaten the most, quantitatively? The food used by most or all of the people in a society? The food that defines the meal, regardless of quantity? The Japanese term *meshi* (*gohan* in the polite form) means either cooked rice or the meal in general. "Have you eaten *gohan*" means "Have you eaten a meal?" Equating rice with food in general may have diffused to Japan from China where *chih fan* (to eat rice) means "to eat," and *fan* (rice) means "food" in general (E. Anderson 1988:139). There is no question that rice has been crucially important to most Japanese throughout history. In this chapter I examine in a historical perspective, *how* rice became the staple food of the Japanese.

Around 350 B.C. wet-rice agriculture was introduced to Japan from somewhere in Asia via the Korean Peninsula to Kyūshū, the southernmost major island of the Japanese archipelago. From there, it spread northeastward in three successive waves, reaching the northeastern Tōhoku region by the beginning of the Christian era (Kokuritsu Rekishi Minzoku Hakubutsukan 1987:14). Arguably, from its sociopolitical ramifications, no other historical event was as significant for the development of what is now known as the Japanese nation. In the areas it penetrated, wet-rice agriculture replaced a long tradition of hunting-gathering during the period known as Jōmon (table 3.1). The scenario of subsequent developments is similar to that in other parts of the world where hunting-gathering economies were replaced by agriculture. Plant domestication enabled permanent settlement, which, in turn, made possible large populations and property accumulation and eventually led to the formation of nation-states.[1] In Japan, too, wet-rice agriculture heralded the beginning of the agricultural Yayoi period (350 B.C.–A.D. 250), which provided the basis for the subsequent Tomb period (A.D. 250–A.D. 646) during which regional lords, all located in central and western regions, controlled large territories. One of these regional lords was ancestral to those who established the Yamato state, whose leaders, in turn, founded the imperial family.

TABLE 3.1
Japanese Prehistory

Period	Subperiods	Dates
Kyūsekki	Early	About 50,000–30,000 B.P.
(Palaeolithic)	Late	30,000 B.C.–11,000 B.C.
Jōmon	Incipient	11,000 B.C.–7500 B.C.
	Earlier	7500 B.C.–5300 B.C.
	Early	5300 B.C.–3600 B.C.
	Middle	3600 B.C.–2500 B.C.
	Late	2500 B.C.–1000 B.C.
	Latest	1000 B.C.–300 B.C.
Yayoi	Early	300 B.C.–100 B.C.
	Middle	100 B.C.–A.D. 100
	Late	A.D. 100–A.D. 250
Kofun	Early	A.D. 250–A.D. 400
	Middle	A.D. 400–A.D. 500
	Late	A.D. 500–A.D. 646

This seeming natural development from hunting-gathering to agriculture to nation building, however, does not necessarily translate into a continuity in population and/or culture (for details, see Ohnuki-Tierney 1974:2–7; 1981:204–212). A dominant interpretation of the populations on the Japanese archipelago has been that a continuity existed between the hunting-gathering Jōmon population and the Yayoi agricultural population and that possibly some Jōmon population in the north, where agriculture did not reach, eventually became the Ainu who occupied northern parts of the main island, Hokkaidō, Kuriles, and Sakhalin and engaged in a hunting-gathering economy until recently. Others have argued that the Ainu are of a different population stock but have seen a continuity, biological and cultural, between the Jōmon and the Yayoi periods. Although these interpretations see continuity between the Jōmon and Yayoi populations, in a 1990 symposium both C. Turner (1976; 1991) and Hanihara (1991), on the basis of dentition, propose that the Japanese originated primarily in Yayoi when a substantial number of migrants from the mainland rapidly replaced the aboriginal Jōmonese, who constitute a common ancestry for the Ainu and the Ryūkyū (Okinawans).

At any rate, there is no question that Yayoi agriculture laid the foundation for what became the nation-state, Japan, and for the rice cultivation that became the symbolic emblem of the nation. One point has not

TABLE 3.2
Japanese History

Period	Dates
Ancient (Kodai)	
(Yayoi)	(300 B.C.–A.D. 250)
Kofun (Tomb period)	A.D. 250–646
Nara	A.D. 646–794
Heian	A.D. 794–1185
Medieval (Chūsei)	
Kamakura	A.D. 1185–1392
(Nanbokuchō)	(A.D. 1336–1392)
Muromachi	A.D. 1392–1603
Early Modern (Kinsei)	
Edo (Tokugawa)	A.D. 1603–1868
Modern period (Kin-Gendai)	
Meiji	A.D. 1868–1912
Taishō	A.D. 1912–1926
Shōwa	A.D. 1926–1989
Heisei	A.D. 1989–present

Note: I follow the periodization conventions prevalent in the historiography of Japan (e.g., K. Inoue 1967:viii–ix). Among the historical periods in table 2, the Early Modern is often referred to in English publications as the Tokugawa period. Japanese scholars, however, usually refer to this period as the *Kinsei* (Early Modern period) or as the *Edo Jidai* (the Edo period). Needless to say, historical periods are artificial constructs—one historical period is not transformed overnight into another. The beginning and ending dates for each period are debatable. I generally follow Sansom (1943) except when I use 1603 as the beginning date for the Early Modern period instead of his 1615 because 1603 is used most often in Japan. Within the Kamakura period, the turbulent period between 1336 and 1392 when there were two emperors is referred to as the *Nanbokuchō* period.

received adequate attention. Although wet-rice cultivation has been practiced for more than two thousand years since its introduction around 350 B.C., all of the population of the islands did *not* adopt wet-rice cultivation nor has rice been the staple food for all the people.

Before World War II, most scholars assumed the importance of rice for all Japanese and held the opinion that rice had been the staple food for all Japanese throughout history. Since the war, scholars have been widely divided on two related issues: the relative importance of rice agriculture versus other types of agriculture and the importance of rice as the *staple food*, that is, its quantitative or caloric value among various segments of Japanese society.

These controversies, which are often phrased in terms of "rice cultivation culture" (*inasaku bunka*)" versus "nonrice cultivation culture" (*hiinasaku bunka*); the latter is also called the "miscellaneous grain culture" (*zakkoku bunka*) because of its emphasis on various nonrice grains as staple foods for the Japanese. I shorten these labels, using "rice culture theory" and "miscellaneous grains theory." I also discuss the extent to which peasants were rice producers as well as consumers, the role of rice as the staple food for the Japanese generally, and the effect of affluence on rice consumption in contemporary Japan.

The Rice Culture (*Inasaku Bunka*) School

Kitō (1983a; 1983b) and a group of scholars from the National Museum of Ethnology—Ishige (1983; 1986), Koyama (1983), and Matsuyama (1990)—emphasize the importance of rice for the Japanese throughout history and challenge the "miscellaneous grains theory," which they argue was based on skewed samples and often constitutes subjective opinions (Ishige 1986). Kitō (1983a; 1983b) envisions four stages in each of which the Japanese relied on a different staple food:

Period	Staple Food
4000 B.C.–2000 B.C.	Nuts
2000 B.C.–A.D. 1000	Rice
A.D. 1000–A.D. 2000	Rice and miscellaneous grains
After A.D. 2000	Rice, miscellaneous grains, sweet potatoes, and others

In his scheme the staple food during the second period was exclusively rice, which was replaced by a mixed diet of rice and miscellaneous grains in the third period. Kitō contends that this change was a result of a rice tax that forced farmers to rely on miscellaneous grains. Even with the rice tax, Kitō believes that farmers during the Early Modern period consumed large amounts of rice but also consumed other foods as well (Kitō 1983a; 1983b).

The aforementioned scholars at the National Museum of Ethnology carried out a quantitative analysis of the energy values and caloric values of foods recorded in the *Hita no Gofudoki*, a survey of demographic characteristics and economic activities in the Hida region (Gifu Prefecture) during the Early Modern period (1603–1868) compiled by an official during the early Meiji period. They point out that, in the nineteenth-century Hida region, 53 percent of food energy came from rice (Ishige 1986:18; Koyama 1983:35). Koyama states, "At the time of *Hita no Go-fudoki*, millet (*hie*) was quickly being replaced by rice in the lowland area"(Koyama et al. 1981:505). They project this conclusion to the entire Japanese population, reasoning that if rice was so important in the Hida region where conditions were not favorable for growing rice, then it must have been important for the rest of Japan.[2]

Their data suggest marked regional differences within the Hida district. In fact, Matsuyama (1990:69–70) finds a clear difference between the thirteen villages along the upper streams that engaged in slash and burn agriculture and relied on millet (*hie*) and the fourteen villages along the lower streams that cultivated wet rice. Regional variation is also acknowledged by Koyama (1983:36) who writes, "Millet (*hie*) in a certain sense was more basic as staple food."

The Nonrice Culture (Hi-Inasaku Bunka) School

Scholars of "the miscellaneous grains" theory hold that miscellaneous grains have always been a major food source for many Japanese and that rice as a staple food was confined to a small segment of the population, primarily the elite.

Wet-rice Agriculture versus Slash and Burn Agriculture

Championed by such scholars as Amino (1980; 1984), Miyamoto (1981), Sasaki (1983, 1986), and Tsuboi (1984) a number of researchers have challenged the thesis that rice agriculture represents Japanese culture (Amino 1984:63–75; Sugiyama 1988; Tsuboi 1984:85–86). An influential interpretation at present is that other grains and tubers[3] were more important as staple foods than rice to many Japanese. These grains included wheat (*mugi*), buckwheat (*soba*), Italian millet (*awa*), true millet (*kibi*), Deccan grass (barnyard millet, hie), and sesame (*goma*). These grains grow on poor soil and require far less attention than rice. It is important to note, however, that these nonrice grains were called "miscellaneous grains" (zakkoku),[4] that is, they were labeled as a residual category.

Miscellaneous grains were cultivated by the Japanese before the introduction of wet-rice cultivation techniques. The question is the extent to which they were replaced, on the one hand, by rice agriculture and, on the other, by rice as a staple food. Obviously, climatic and topographic factors prohibited rice cultivation in northern regions before strains of rice adapted to cold climates were developed. Lowland varieties of wet rice did not grow in hilly areas where fields cannot be flooded.

But more importantly, recent findings point to a stronger tradition of nonrice cultivation (hi-inasaku bunka) than has hitherto been recognized. Proponents of the miscellaneous grains theory do not deny the importance of rice cultivation, but they realize that the hegemonic nature, in the Gramscian sense, of the ideology of rice agriculture (see chap. 6) prevented scholars from recognizing evidence of cultivation of plants other than rice.

Sasaki (1983; 1985), a cultural geographer cum anthropologist, has emphasized the importance in Japan of a type of slash-and-burn agriculture that is widespread in the *shōyōju* (East Asian or evergreen [*Lucido-phyllous*]) forests throughout Asia. He suggests that there was an intensive and extensive agriculture in the mountain areas of western Japan before the introduction of wet-rice agriculture. They cultivated upland rice varieties, various types of millet (awa, hie, *shikokubie*), beans (*daizu*, azuki), buckwheat (soba), as well as a number of other crops (Sasaki 1983:30–32). He argues that during the early and middle Yayoi period (350 B.C.–A.D. 350) more than half of the carbohydrate consumed came from crops other than rice (Sasaki 1985:56; see also Miyata 1990:66–76).

Amino, a historian, is a leading proponent for the miscellaneous grains theory for the Medieval period. To him, the excessive importance accorded to rice in past scholarship is a result of the projection back to the Medieval period (1185–1602) of the model based upon the data from the Early Modern period (1603–1867) (Amino 1980:32). After examining the records of the land tax in the Medieval period, he argues that although rice was used as a land tax in the manors (*shōen*) of regional lords and the public (government) estates (*kōryō*) in western Japan, it was rarely used for this purpose in eastern Japan (Amino 1980:32–34) where other goods, such as silk and cotton, were used to pay taxes. Furthermore, although people in western Japan cultivated rice for tax purposes, they relied on other grains for food. He cites a document, dated September 1347 (Teiwa 3), listing the confiscated property of a peasant woman who lived in the Tara manor in Wakasa (western part of present Fukui prefecture) in western Japan. It lists 90 liters of rice and 180 liters of awa (millet)—twice as much millet as rice. Since the land tax in this manor was paid with rice, Amino (1980:67–68) concludes that millet (awa) was the woman's staple food. Amino (1980:69) argues that even more than during the Early Modern period, the people during the Medieval period relied on other grains, often selling, if they had enough, the higher priced rice to buy cheaper grains.

Tsuboi, a folklorist,[5] likewise deemphasizes the importance of rice. His argument centers on the geographic distribution of the "New Year without rice cake" (*mochinashi shōgatsu*,) custom. Although scholars had assumed that New Year's offerings to the deities all over Japan were always rice cakes, he identifies a number of areas where this custom is not observed. In some districts, it is taboo to use rice cakes for the New Year; if the taboo is violated, villagers say that calamity will befall them. In other districts, though, there is no taboo against the use of rice cakes, yet the preferred offerings are nonrice food items, frequently taro (*satoimo*). Tsuboi, therefore, refers to this type of New Year's celebration as "the tuber New Year" (*imo shōgatsu*). In still other areas, foods made from rice, other grains, and tubers are simultaneously used as offerings with equal importance (Tsuboi 1984:88–90). Although he recognizes that in various parts of Japan[6] the New Year is celebrated with rice cakes, he contends that New Year's offerings exclusively of rice cakes are restricted to a relatively small area of Japan (Tsuboi 1984:152).

Because these foods are offered to the deities to seek their blessings to renew the agricultural cycle, in particular, and the cosmic order, in general, it follows that, in Tsuboi's interpretation, in many parts of Japan the rejuvenation of the world order was based on foods other than rice. In his view the common people of Japan subsisted on tubers and grains other than rice, while rice agriculture supported only the upper class.

Farmers as Rice Producers versus Consumers

The difference in interpretation of the importance of nonrice grains rests in part on whether rice farmers were rice consumers as well. The case of the peasant woman cited by Amino offers a prime example of how rice farmers probably ate millet and other grains as staple foods while they paid land taxes with rice. In general, however, evidence from the Medieval period is inconclusive.

More information is available for the Early Modern period. The implementation of a new policy by the shogunate requiring all samurai retainers to live in castle towns sharply separated the samurai and the peasant classes. In addition, the shogunate instituted a new system of taxation (*kokudaka*)—a taxation based on rice. Because the seigniorial class could not directly oversee the peasants' labor, it conducted detailed cadastral surveys of village farmlands to estimate rice production in *koku* (5.1 bushels, or 180 liters; *daka* in *kokudaka* is *taka* 'to yield').

The responsibility for the tax payment fell on the headman of the village (see Vlastos 1986:9). The headman's responsibility was delegated to a social group called *goningumi* (group of five)—a neighborhood group—rather than to an individual or one family. Scholars consider the system of assigning civil responsibilities to a social group to have been crucial in the formation of Japanese social organization and to have provided a structural basis for governmental control.

While it extracted agricultural products from farmers, the shogunate government during the Early Modern period took positive steps to promote agrarian productivity. For example, the government issued an ordinance in 1642 directing farmers not to eat or store large quantities of rice but to eat miscellaneous grains instead. The "ordinance of [the] Keian period" (*Keian no ofuregaki*) issued by the government in 1649 instructed farmers to rise early and work well into the night, forbade them to consume large amounts of rice on ordinary days, and encouraged them to cultivate miscellaneous grains for their own consumption (cited in Kitō 1983a:43; Koyanagi 1972:155–162; Tsukuba 1986:118–119). This shogunate policy had "a goal that Confucian moralists applauded as enthusiastically as the treasurer of the daimyo" (Vlastos 1986:31).

The effect this system of taxation and its practical application had on peasants as consumers of rice varied from region to region and from one historical period to the next. The putative practice was *shikō rokumin* (four for the government and six for the people), that is, 40 percent of the yield was taken as tax. Many argue that this rule was more often violated than practiced and that a higher percentage of the rice yield was taken as tax, leaving little for the farmers' own consumption (e.g., Tsukuba 1986:118). Although this is the commonly held view, Vlastos (1986:30–41) in a detailed examination of the Fukushima district, reveals that peasants "retained at least part of the increase in output" that resulted from an increase in arable land, improved technology, and more intensive labor inputs (1986:30). He points out that the shogunate government as well as the seigniorial class could not afford to oppress peasants until they abandoned farming (1986:33–41).

Certainly, there were variations in the people's diet during this time. Often cited in this connection is a passage from *Minkan Shōyō* (Survey of the people's lives) by Tanaka Kyūgū in which he describes the foodways of villagers near Edo (Tokyo) during the Kyōho era (1716–1735). Farmers near the fields ate rice cooked with other foods, whereas farmers in the mountainous areas did not eat rice, not even during the first three days of the New Year. Instead, they ate millet (hie, awa) and wheat along with a great many wild plants (cited in Kitō 1983:44).

During the Early Modern period peasants did not always enjoy a comfortable surplus of their products; peasant uprisings were numerous. More than twenty-eight hundred peasant disturbances occurred between 1590 and 1867, usually during famines, but especially in the 1730s, 1780s, and 1850s. During the well-known Tenmei Famine in the Tenmei era (1781–1788), two million people are reported to have died of hunger (Hane 1982:7; Wathall 1986:xi), which attests to the plight of farmers. Of 2,755 uprisings in rural Japan between 1590 and 1699, 158 (5.7 percent) were rice riots and in another 214 (7.7 percent) public laborers demanded rice (fushokumai); a total of 372 (13.1 percent) were related to rice issues. In cities during the same period, 241 outbreaks were rice riots, and in 34 the people requested rice, which accounts for 73.3 percent of the total city riots. Rural and urban uprisings included 372 rice riots during the Early Modern period (Aoki 1967:40–45).

Peasant uprisings were more numerous and more violent during the last years of the Early Modern period; 484 peasant protests (hyakushō ikki) and 353 village disturbances (murakata sōdō) were recorded although the latter did not directly involve the seigniorial class. Increased violence accompanied these outbreaks. Thus, in 1866 a demand for cheaper rice by the women of Nishinomiya near Ōsaka led to a riot that lasted two weeks and destroyed the property of 866 wealthy people. In the month following the Nishinomiya riot, poor peasants from the Chichibu district near Edo attacked four rice dealers, triggering 450 raids in several hundred villages (Vlastos 1986:159). The targets of these peasant uprisings were local authorities and local wealthy individuals, not basic social reforms or resolution of inequalities (Katsumata 1985) (for details of petitions, etc., see Walthall 1986; 1991; for a theoretical discussion of protest movements in historical perspective, see Pharr 1990:15–38).

The picture of peasant foodways during the Early Modern period is far from complete and only tentative conclusions can be drawn although far more information is available for this period than for earlier periods. Undoubtedly, the rice tax system affected peasants adversely in many regions. The peasant uprisings, however, evidence that rice must have been a significant part of the peasants' daily diet during this time, at least in some areas; there is no reason to assume that they demanded rice for ritual occasions alone.

Farmers' lives changed little during the Meiji and Taishō periods (Koyanagi 1972:162–189; cf. Yanagita 1982e:168), and peasant disturbances continued. In 1918 the wives of fishermen in Toyama Prefecture demonstrated against the high price of rice. By August the demonstrators in widespread rice riots attacked shops of rice and other merchants. Of about seven hundred thousand participants in these rice riots, 30–40 percent were burakumin, as were the leaders of rice riots in the 1920s (Hane 1982:160–161). The burakumin have comprised a minority group since the Early Modern period. The burakumin liberation movement was most active in the 1920s when the worldwide Marxist influence reached Japan. Whatever the precipitating factors may have been, it is noteworthy that the burakumin, whose ancestry derives from the nonsettled population toward the end of the Medieval period (see chap. 6), assumed leadership positions in riots involving rice, the symbol of the settled agrarian population.

During the late Taishō period, when Japan was striving hard to industrialize, companies in cities tried to entice rural women to become factory workers by guaranteeing rice three times a day (Koyanagi 1972:156–157); such luxury was not possible in rural areas. Needless to say, factory conditions were quite miserable. This incentive also suggests that rice was an important food for a rural population that did not have enough of it.

The Question of Rice as the Staple Food for the Japanese?

If rice was not part of the Japanese diet throughout history, when did it become the staple food, either in terms of the quantitative value or its being the defining and thus indispensable feature of Japanese meals. Scholars' opinions vary widely on this issue. According to Sasaki (1983: 292), urbanites began eating rice three times a day only in the middle of the Early Modern Period (1603–1868). Tsukuba (1986:106) holds that the majority of Japanese started to eat rice during the Meiji period (1868–1912).

In addition to greater yields from improved varieties and technology, two major events made rice available as daily food for a greater number of Japanese. First, the military draft (*chōhei*) adopted by the Meiji government provided rice daily for soldiers from areas that relied on miscellaneous grains (*zakkoku*) and, therefore, had not eaten rice as an everyday food. Obviously, this policy affected only the male population, a point not mentioned by these scholars. Second, the 1942 Food Control Act (Shokuryō Kanrihō), which regulated food provision and the rationing system (*haikyū*), brought rice to islands and remote regions where only miscellaneous grains were grown (Tsuboi 1984:68).

Watanabe (1989:083) claims that most Japanese began to eat rice as a staple food in 1939 when food rationing was adopted. He also believes that 90 percent of the population during the Early Modern Period (1603–1868) daily ate some rice and that 80 percent ate it three times a day; the remaining 20 percent of the people ate rice about half of the time, and a very small number of Japanese ate rice only occasionally. In Dore's opinion, by the 1930s, "white rice had come to be considered a part of the birthright of every Japanese" ([1958] 1973:58–59). Other scholars claim that in northeastern Japan, most people, except warriors and upperclass merchants, ate only millet (awa, hie) until the 1960s (e.g., Itoh, personal communication, 1990; Ōbayashi 1973:5–6).

During World War II, domestic rice was sent to soldiers while the rest of the population resorted to imported rice and other substitutes. The rice shortage enhanced the desirability of domestic rice in the mind of the Japanese. Kitagawa Hiroko, a fifty-eight-year-old housewife from Nagoya, recalled conditions in wartime Japan when her wish was to have a little more gruel, and, if possible, to eat "a bowlful of white rice" (*Asahi Shinbun*, June 30, 1990).

Rice in the Post–World War II Japanese Diet

During the postwar period, the Japanese eagerly sought rice, which remained a highly desired food in short supply. The rice shortage prompted a demonstration during which students carried red flags, symbolizing their affiliation with the Japanese Communist party, and demanded the release of rice stocks presumably in storage at the Imperial Household. As Japan began to rebuild from the ashes of the war, there was a brief period when most Japanese consumed a great deal of rice three times a day. The improvement in the economic status of the people in a farming community by 1955 was noted by Dore, who observes in amazement:

> One thing that remains unchanged is the central importance of rice in the diet. I still have trouble explaining to Shinohata people how it is that, if England's shushoku, staple food, is bread rather than rice, we do not consume a loaf or two of bread with each meal. Three times a day the centre of every Shinohata meal is a bowl of rice—several times refilled for hard-working men, and not quite so often refilled for hard-working women—to which all the other dishes are side dishes. (1978:86)

Dore's observation is familiar to most older Japanese today, and certainly some Japanese, especially in rural areas, still consume a sizable amount of rice.

If, however, one attempts to measure the relative affluence since the 1970s in terms of rice consumption, one encounters a paradox: affluence radically reduced rice consumption. Affluence thus tipped the balance between the amount of rice and the number of side dishes eaten so that a large amount of rice accompanied by few side dishes now represents a poor person's diet. Contemporary affluent Japanese, like wine connoisseurs (cf. Dore [1958] 1973:59), developed discriminating tastes: cooked rice must have luster (*tsuya*), stickiness (*nebari*), taste (*aji*), and be white.

But this pattern was already there before affluence. Dore, who was amazed by the quantity of rice eaten, also observed a feast in the same community in 1955:

> To be sure, on festive occasions, when saké [*sic*] or beer or (for women) the local wine is served, one eats only the side dishes as long as one drinks—until the host or his wife, perhaps observing that the guests are getting somewhat the worse for wear, says "shall we have the rice now?" The arrival of the rice signifies the end of drinking and even hearty eaters may by then have consumed so much from the plates of batter-fried vegetables and raw tuna and white cubes of bean curd, that they can manage no more than one small bowl of rice. *But still rice remains the king-pin of any real meal's architecture.* (Dore 1978:86; italics added)

When they could afford it, people used money for side dishes, and the amount of rice became proportionately smaller.

The influx of foreign foods has further reduced the amount of rice consumed by the Japanese. Among urbanites rice consumption fell from rice three times a day to only once or twice a day. The first meal to be "invaded" by foreign foods was breakfast as bread replaced rice. Dore ([1958] 1973:60) dates the beginning of the adoption of bread for breakfast in 1951. He found that the use of bread was welcomed by housewives, who no longer had to cook rice in the morning and, thus, could sleep a little longer.

In the 1990s lunch menus continue to feature traditional noodle dishes (menrui) as well as the spaghetti, hamburgers, and pizzas especially popular among young people. Many traditional Japanese dishes containing rice continue to be in demand, for example, sushi and *donburimono*, rice topped by side dishes such as chicken with vegetables served in a large bowl. Rice molded into various shapes with seaweed and other ingredients, called *nigirimeshi*, or *onigiri*, has made a remarkable comeback, and many of the popular Western dishes are those that to the Japanese go well with rice, such as steaks, hamburgers, and pork cutlets, and, thus, are served with it.

Most Japanese continue to associate the evening meal at home with rice; an evening meal without it would be equivalent to sandwiches for dinner for many Americans. But it is not the amount of rice that is important. During an ordinary evening meal, side dishes are eaten together with rice. On special occasions that, perhaps, include guests, many side dishes are served first. But no matter how many side dishes are served, a meal is not complete without rice, usually a small amount served at the very end. The woman of the house must ask guests toward the end of the meal, "Would you like *gohan* (rice) or *ochazuke* (rice in hot water or hot tea)?" Japanese, especially older Japanese who travel abroad, often complain that they do not feel satisfied after eating meals without rice; *manpukukan* (the full-stomach feeling) is not achieved without rice, no matter what else is eaten.

Traditional Japanese dishes (washoku) have made a remarkable comeback for special occasions. Many inns and restaurants try to attract customers with beautiful photographs of elaborate Japanese dinners, which have many courses served simultaneously. Most fashionable hotels and large buildings compete by having Western, Chinese, and Japanese haute cuisine. For example, on the ground floor of the commanding Tōshiba Building in the midst of Tokyo are seven elegant Japanese restaurants, two equally exclusive Western restaurants, a large, excellent Chinese restaurant, and a Wendy's fast food restaurant.

Quantitative and Qualitative Values of Rice

Amid disparate interpretations of rice and rice agriculture in Japan, scholarly controversy centers on whether rice was in the past a staple food among nonelite segments of Japanese society. These highly divided opinions do share several points of agreement. First, most scholars agree that dietary habits of the Japanese in the past varied considerably depending upon region, class, and so forth. Topographical factors were especially important: people who lived on the plains, in the mountains, or along the seacoast ate the plants that grew there; therefore, their reliance on specific foods, especially rice, differed.[7] Marked regional variations remain in foodways, including the treatment of rice, especially when one compares practices in eastern and western Japan. Second, most scholars also agree that rice was the staple food, qualitatively and quantitatively, valued by the elites—emperors, nobles, warriors, and wealthy merchants. The rice culture was *ryōshu bunka*, a culture of regional lords and elites in general.

Third, although rice has *not* always been the staple food of all Japanese, most agree that rice has been the major item of food for ritual occasions for most Japanese ever since rice agriculture was introduced to Japan (Amino 1980:69) even in some areas where the New Year was celebrated without it. Fourth, rice became central to the political economy, ideology, and daily life of most Japanese during the Early Modern period.

The quantitative value of rice is far more complex to determine. In a broad sense it seems safe to conclude that for a long period rice was not available in sufficient quantity for the nonelite of Japan, including rice producing peasants. During this long shortage, rice was so highly desired that the dream was to have a great deal of it. Then, perhaps, since sometime during the Early Modern period when improved technology made higher yields possible, a large quantity of rice with few side dishes became the poor people's diet, whereas the more affluent spent money on side dishes. The pattern continues in the 1990s. Thus, affluence brought to light a basic paradox—continued importance of the qualitative value of rice but a decisive decrease in its quantitative value. The quantitative value of rice, then, is a curious one: the presence of a small amount of rice is essential, but a large amount is desirable only when the standard of living is low.

I devote the remainder of this book to the qualitative importance of rice, that is, the *meanings* assigned to rice in Japanese culture.

Four

Rice in Cosmogony and Cosmology

CLEARLY, rice occupies a special place in the Japanese diet. Although rice has never been the staple food in a quantitative sense for all Japanese, it has always been the food for ritual occasions. Yanagita (1982d:159–160) points out that of all grains rice alone is believed to have a soul, and it alone requires ritual performances. In contrast, nonrice grains are called zakkoku (miscellaneous grains), a label that places them in a residual category.

I examine the cultural institutions and symbols primarily of ancient Japan, which show a gradual but decisive development of the powers and meanings was assigned to rice. The initial development of the supremacy of rice is closely associated with its symbolic equation with deities and its close relationship with the ancient imperial system. The earliest writings in Japan—the *Kojiki*, dated A.D. 712 and the *Nihonshoki*, dated A.D. 720—were commissioned by the Tenmu emperor (r. A.D. 672–686) who intended an official history of the imperial system. Whereas other grains are described as offerings to deities and of importance equal to rice, in a number of passages rice is assigned a special significance, which reveals how rice gradually gained primacy among grains during the time these myth-histories were compiled.

Rice in Cosmogony

The Ancient Imperial System

Almost six centuries had elapsed between the introduction of rice agriculture and the emergence of Japanese kingship at the end of the fourth century A.D. when the Ōjin emperor established his Yamato state near present-day Ōsaka (Waida 1975:319–320). Early Japanese kingship underwent significant transformation until its political, economic, and symbolic bases became firmly established. For example, according to Macé (1985), a sharp break in the funeral ritual for emperors occurred during the early eighth century. When the Empress Genmei died in 721, her body was cremated and buried one week after the funeral. This funeral contrasts sharply with the one for the previous emperor, Monmu; the temporary interment (*mogari*) lasted for six months before his body was buried. The mogari is the elaborate long mourning practice that lasted several months to several years (Macé 1985:58) during which a special hut was built for the corpse. Almost no description exists of how the corpse was kept, but apparently it was left to decay (Macé 1985:58). During mogari mourning horses and, possibly, humans, were sacrificed, and funeral attendants (*asobibe*) entered the mourning hut with weapons to fight symbolically against death. These features provide a sharp contrast to the harvest-ritual cum imperial accession ritual that developed later and is described in this chapter.

The eighth century myth-histories of the *Kojiki* and the *Nihonshoki*— replete with references to rice symbolism—reveal a gradual process whereby agrarian cosmology and ritual became the bulwark of the ancient imperial system. Although the Tenmu emperor compiled the myth-histories to establish an official history of Japan (see chap. 6), they were written over a period of time and do not represent a single official version. They include instead various versions of particular themes that reveal considerable variation in the myths and rituals among agrarian folk at the time. Rice harvest rituals, modeled after folk harvest rituals of the time, became the official rituals at the court; even the current version contains features from the folk cosmology of these early periods. (See Ohnuki-Tierney 1991b for fuller details of the Japanese imperial system.)

The Emperor as Shaman in Early History

The imperial system derives from the politico-religious leadership founded on a *rice* agriculture that gradually developed during the preceding centuries. These early agrarian leaders, including the early emperors, were magicoreligious leaders, shamans cum political leaders[1] whose political powers rested on an ability to solicit supernatural powers to ensure good crops. Thus, the annual harvest ritual served to legitimate a local political leader, ensure the leader's rebirth, and rejuvenate his power (see Murakami 1977:4–6). For this reason, many scholars (e.g., Akasaka 1988; Hora 1979; 1984; M. Inoue 1984; Miyata 1988:190–194; 1989; Murakami 1977; 1986; Okada 1970; Yamaori 1978; Yanagita 1982d) consider the emperor first and foremost as the officiant in rituals for the rice soul (*inadama no shusaisha*) who ensures the blessings of the deities for the new rice crop on behalf of the people. They argue that the religious-ritual focus of the Japanese kingship, a view held even by Marxist scholars like Murakami, emphasizes that the Japanese kingship was not exclusively political.

The religious cum political cum economic nature of the agrarian rituals of early leaders, including emperors, is clearly expressed in *matsurigoto*, the conceptual basis of the political system (*ritsuryō-sei*) at the time (cf. Kitagawa 1990:138–189). Advancing the interpretation by Mitsuya Shigematsu and Andō Seiji, Orikuchi (Orikuchi 1975a:175–177; 1975b: 160–161; 1983:275–277) proposes that the early use of the term *matsuri*, which in contemporary Japanese means festivals or ceremonies, meant *osukuni no matsurigoto*. Written in three characters that represent "to eat," "country," and "polity," this phrase denotes the country where food for the deities is made.[2] In other words, food and food consumption were an essential part of the polity at the time, and rice had begun to represent food in general.

Although other rituals were added in different historical periods, especially at the time of the Meiji "restoration" of the imperial system, the core imperial rituals officiated by the emperor all relate to rice harvesting: *niinamesai*, *ōnamesai* (*daijōsai*), and *kannamesai*. The annual harvest ritual of *niinamesai* becomes the *ōnamesai* at the accession of a new emperor and is held as the last of three accession rituals, following the *senso* (including *kenji togyo*) and the accession ritual (*sokui no rei*). Although the *niinamesai* and the *ōnamesai* are almost identical, the *kannamesai* is a ritual in which a new crop of rice is offered to the Ise Shrine, rather than at the Imperial Court itself (Orikuchi 1975a:183).

Until the late seventh century the *niinamesai* and *ōnamesai* meant the same ritual. Although interpretations of the term *niiname* vary, the predominant view is that it means the tasting of new crops (*name* 'to taste'; *nii* 'new'). Orikuchi (1975a:180–181) suggests that the term *ōname* derives from *nihe no imi* (*nihe* = *nie* 'offering to a deity'; *no* = possessive case; *imi* 'taboo'), which refers to the taboo observed by the officiant of the ritual (the emperor) in the period before the *ōnamesai*.[3]

In 1928 Orikuchi suggested that the *ōnamesai* was established before eastern Japan was under the control of Yamato leaders because no reference to eastern regions appears in the records of this ceremony, which always requires an offering of a new crop of rice from the two fields chosen from the regions lying southeast and northwest of Kyōto (Orikuchi 1975a). Following Orikuchi's suggestion, Yokota (1988) postulates that the basic structure of the ritual was established by the end of the Yayoi period (350 B.C.–A.D. 350) although others suggest much later dates.

The first reference to *niinamesai* occurs in the *Nihonshoki* (in the *Jinmu-ki*), which alludes to a performance of a harvest ritual by the legendary first emperor, Jinmu, who is said to have reigned from 660 B.C. to 585 B.C. In this reference, the *saishin* or deity to whom the ritual is addressed, is Takamusubi no Kami, one of the three major deities of creation when the Japanese universe came into being. A description in the

Nihonshoki of the twenty-second emperor, Seinei (r. A.D. 480–484), indicates that the imperial ritual of *niiname* had been formalized by this time. The emperor is said to have offered in *shimotsuki* (November of the lunar calendar) a new rice crop, which is referred to as *ōnie* (Miura 1988:143; Murakami 1977:12–13). Ueda Kenji (1988:32) suggests that the basic forms of the *niiname* were established by the time of the Tenmu emperor (r. A.D. 667–686). By the early Heian period (A.D. 794–1185), the ritual had been formalized and was far different from the folk harvest rituals that were the prototype of the imperial harvest ritual (Murakami 1977:12).

The question of when the ritual was established becomes more complicated if one examines the content of the imperial harvest ritual. The ritual may have originated as two separate rituals, each dedicated to a different deity and later combined into one ritual. The combination of these two rituals and the assignment of the central place to Amaterasu Ōmikami as the imperial ancestress seems to have taken place only after the Yamato state became well-established.

Furthermore, another accession ritual, introduced from China and independent of the *ōnamesai*, was performed early on. At the accession of the Kanmu emperor (r. A.D. 781–806) this accession ritual of Chinese origin was formalized as the accession ceremony (Murakami 1977:21). Consequently, the *ōnamesai* has come to be seen as a ceremony (*saiten*) rather than a political event. The earliest form of the *ōnamesai* included the rite of *senso* (*kenji togyo*) during which the three imperial treasures, the mirror, the sword, and the *magatama* jewel, were handed to the new emperor. These three items have been found in tombs of apparent aristocrats of the Yayoi period, indicating that these items were symbols for royalty or political leaders. *Senso* became independent of the *ōnamesai*. Thus, since the beginning of the Heian period the imperial accession has involved three separate rituals: *senso* (*kenji togyo*); *sokui no rei;* and *ōnamesai*. Of these, the *senso* is held immediately after the death of an emperor so that the three symbols of kingship are handed to the new emperor without any lapse of time. The timing of *senso* also is related to the fact that, unlike in China and Korea where the new emperor's accession took place immediately after the death of an emperor, the Japanese aversion to the impurity associated with death required that the accession ritual be held after the imperial funeral in which the impurity created by the previous emperor's death was ritually removed; only then could a new emperor be enthroned (M. Inoue 1984). Despite these changes, since the time of the Tenmu emperor in the midseventh century the *ōnamesai* has been essential for the accession of a new emperor (Murakami 1977:21–22), so much so that some shōguns contributed financially to ensure its performance by the emperor.

Because the three imperial rituals are all rice harvest rituals and share many essential elements, I confine my discussion to the *ōnamesai*, which, as part of the imperial accession ritual, is the most important.[4]

Ōnamesai: The Imperial Accession Ritual

The imperial harvest ritual, ōnamesai,[5] modeled after the folk harvest ritual in ancient Japan (Yanagita 1982a,133–134) evolved over time. Its earliest mention occurs during the reign of Seinei (A.D. 480–484) (Miura 1988:143). Only after the imperial system became established did the Sun Goddess (Amaterasu Ōmikami) become the deity addressed in the ritual (*saishin*); various deities of production and reproduction were addressed in earlier rituals (cf. Orikuchi 1975a:236–237).[6]

The preparation for the ōnamesai starts in the spring (February–April) preceding the major ceremony in the fall (Kōshitsu Bunka Kenkyūkai 1988) when the locations of two fields—*yuki* and *suki*—are chosen by divination.[7] Rice for the offering during the ōnamesai is grown in these fields with great care to prevent contamination by impurities. Situated southeast and northwest of Kyōto, respectively, these two fields symbolically represent the Japanese nation. The emperor and the Japanese people performed a series of purification rituals in preparation for the November ceremony. During the Heian period the entire process of the November ōnamesai lasted four days and consisted of eleven segments (Hida 1988:214; Kurabayashi 1988:37). Although the duration and details of the ritual have undergone historical changes, basically it consists of the following elements: the *mitamashizume*, the rejuvenation of the soul; *shinsen* (or *kyōsen*), offering of the new crop of rice by the new emperor to the deity; *naorai*, commensality between the emperor and the deity; and *utage*, commensality among the humans, that is, a feast hosted by the emperor (Orikuchi 1975a:239; Yoshino 1986:13–20).

Of these rituals, the most difficult and controversial to interpret is the *mitamashizume* (the rejuvenation of the soul), which takes place the night before the public ceremony and continues until dawn. It is a strictly private ritual during which the emperor lies in the sacred bed (*ohusuma*), which is placed on the sacred seat (*madoko*). Meanwhile, a court lady or, sometimes, two ladies (Miyata in Amino, Ueno, and Miyata 1988:52), perform a ritual to receive the emperor's soul that is departing from his body and renew it. Because the *mitamashizume* is a private (secret) ritual, little information is available about what took place during the ritual in different historical periods. Even today some refrain from discussing it openly.

There are three major lines of interpretation. First, the ritual rejuvenates the emperor's soul, enabling the emperor to perform the ōnamesai the following day at the height of his spiritual powers (Murakami 1977: 15–16). Second, the presence of a court lady implies that the emperor engages in sexual intercourse with her. Third, during the ōnamesai held when the previous emperor dies, according to some scholars, the deceased emperor's corpse is placed on the sacred seat. His soul enters the new emperor's body during the mitamashizume.

To understand the mitamashizume, one must understand the notion of "soul" in ancient Japan. According to Orikuchi (1975a:189–190), in the ancient belief the soul of a person or an object waxed in the winter and waned in the spring. It splits and easily detaches from the body. For a person to continue to live, another soul from outside one's body must attach to the body, an act called *tamafuri*, or, as conceptualized later in history, the soul must be recaptured, an act called *tamashizume*. The mitamashizume (*mi* is a prefix for the polite form) ritual, thus, first rejuvenates the emperor's soul, which might have waned or been ready to leave his body.

The sexual act thesis is not incompatible with the soul rejuvenation theory if one takes into account that in ancient Japan production and reproduction were seen as identical processes and both were conceptualized in terms of souls. The term *musubi* meant, on the one hand, encapsulation of a soul in a knot and, on the other hand, production and reproduction. Thus, the act of knotting (musubi) a string, twig, or piece of grass, as described in the *Manyōshū* and other literature of the time, was a ritual act to encapsulate a soul in a knot. During the mitamashizume, a cotton knot is tied as a ritual act to capture the soul of the emperor, which is ready to depart from his body (Matsumae 1977:96–97). But the term *musubi* also meant reproduction and production: *musu* meant reproduction and *bi* (*hi*) meant production or growth by the sun (Ebersole 1989:42, 56; Matsumae 1977:96–97). To suggest that the emperor sleeps with the court lady (or sacred lady) simply as a sexual act in a contemporary sense, therefore, grossly misrepresents its meaning in ancient Japan when sexual intercourse was conterminous with soul rejuvenation, which, in turn, was a necessary condition for agricultural reproduction.

The third proposition was originally advanced by Orikuchi (1975a: 194), who argues that the Japanese emperor is singularly characterized by the possession of what he called "the imperial soul." According to him, the ōnamesai ritually enables the imperial soul that is departing the previous emperor's body to enter the new emperor's body, thereby assuring the lineal transmission of the imperial soul, which is crucial to the Japanese imperial system. He is said to have remarked that a new

emperor used to bite into the corpse of the deceased emperor so the latter's soul could enter him (Miyata personal communication).[8] Orikuchi's
interpretation, although questionable, opens up an important problem in
comparative kingship—the continuity of kingship or the imperial system
irrespective of individual emperors—a point I return to in a later section.

Following this private ritual, the emperor offers various foods to the
deity (shinsen). The most important offerings are products of the new
rice crop grown in the aforementioned two fields: cooked rice, gruel,
white sake (shiroki), and black sake (made from sake colored with plant
ashes or, later in history, black sesame). Other food offerings include
cooked, freshly harvested Italian millet (awa), fresh fish, dried fish, fruits,
soup, and stew (oatsumono) (Kōshitsu Bunka Kenkyūkai 1988:104–
105; Murakami 1977:18). After these foods are offered during the ritual,
which lasts more than two hours, they are consumed by the deity and the
emperor together (the naorai). The ōnamesai concludes with an elaborate banquet in which the emperor and the guests feast together (the
utage). During the ōnamesai for the Shōwa emperor the feast lasted for
two days.

The Ōnamesai and the Myth-Histories

Unlike the Malinowskian claim that myths provide a charter for action,
including the performance of rituals, Saigō (1984) and others argue
that the two earliest writings in Japan—the Kojiki and the Nihonshoki—
represent attempts to validate the existing harvest rituals at the court ex
post facto.[9] A systematic comparison is difficult because these oral myth-
histories were set down in writing over a long period and contain many
different versions of what appear to be the same episodes and themes.[10]
Nevertheless, the two episodes are viewed as parallels to the imperial
harvest ritual.

In the episode popularly referred to as "the heavenly cave," (ame-no
iwaya) the Sun Goddess, Amaterasu Ōmikami, isolates herself in a building (cave)[11] because her younger brother has offended her with defiling
behavior. Myriad deities gather noisily in front of the building, laughing
and merrymaking. A shaman-deity, Ame-no Uzume no Mikoto, dances
seminude in front of the building, causing uproarious laughter. The deities hang an eight-handed mirror (a long, octagonal mirror) from a
branch in front of the building and tell Amaterasu that a deity superior to
her is in front of the building. Curious, she peeks and mistakes her own
image in the mirror for the superior deity. With her emergence from seclusion, the universe is again bright with the sun (Kurano and Takeda
1958:81–83).[12]

This episode is often interpreted as a symbolic enactment of the death and rebirth of the Sun Goddess (Saigō 1984:78–87; Orikuchi 1975a: 198) that, in turn, corresponds to what happens to the emperor's soul during the mitamashizume. Like Amaterasu in the myth, the emperor in the ritual goes into seclusion while his soul, "split" and is ready to depart from his body, returns and is rejuvenated. Likewise, the behavior of the court lady during the mitamashizume is thought to parallel the dancing by Ame-no Uzume-no-Mikoto in front of the building where Amaterasu is isolated (Matsumae 1977:119; Murakami 1977:15–16).

The second episode from the myth-histories that is thought to correspond to the imperial harvest ritual is the *tenson kōrin*—the descent of the heavenly grandson, Ninigi-no Mikoto, who, wrapped in the *madoko ohusuma*, the sacred bedding, is sent by the Sun Goddess to earth to govern.[13] This episode is perceived as corresponding to the scene during the mitamashizume when the emperor wraps himself in bedding.

Rice Deities in the Myth-Histories

Not only does the ōnamesai parallel episodes in the myth-histories but the myth-histories are replete with references to rice and its relationship to deities. Thus, the soul of the rice grain (*ina dama*, or *ina-damashii*) is clearly identified as a *kami* (deity) called *Uka no Kami*. There are various versions of the origin of this deity.[14] In one version of the creation myth for various grains in the *Nihonshoki* (Sakamoto et al. 1967:100–102), when Ukemochi-no-Kami, the deity in charge of food, turned his head toward land, *ihi* (the word for rice/meal at the time) came out of his mouth, and when he turned his head toward the sea, fish of various sizes emerged from his mouth. When the deity was slain, various foods came out of his corpse: rice emerged from his abdomen, millet from his eyes, and wheat and beans from his anus. Although the eyes and anus were important organs (Ohnuki-Tierney 1987:42–43), the abdomen (*hara*) has always been of crucial importance in the Japanese concept of the body and remains so even today (see Ohnuki-Tierney 1984:57–60). The soul was thought to reside in the abdomen, hence, the well-known cultural institution of male suicide during which a man cuts open his abdomen to release his soul. The abdomen, which houses the fetus, is where human life is thought to be located. Given the centrality accorded to the abdomen, it is significant that in the myth-histories, rice is depicted as originating from the abdomen—the abode of the soul and fetus—whereas other grains emerge from other parts of the body. This passage is at least suggestive of the special importance of rice among grains.

In another version in the *Nihonshoki*, the deity was born when Izanami and Izanagi, the creators of the Japanese universe, fainted from starvation immediately after the creation of *Ōyashima-no Kuni*, a name given to what later became Japan (Sakamoto et al. 1967: book 1, no. 1, 90; see also Itoh 1979:162–163; Ōbayashi 1973:8). In a version in the *Kojiki* the rice deity is an offspring of Susano-o-no Mikoto, the brother of the Sun Goddess and a notorious enfant terrible. In any case, the deity of the soul of rice (grain) is closely linked to the origin of the Japanese universe.

In the version in the *Kojiki* written after the Sun Goddess was established as the ancestral deity to the imperial family, Amaterasu Ōmikami is the mother of a grain soul called Masakatsu Akatsu Kachihaya Hiameno Oshihomimi-no Mikoto (Kurano and Takeda 1958:111, 125). Her famous grandson, Ninigi-no Mikoto, whom she sent from Heaven to rule the earth, is also referred to as Amatsu Hiko Hiko Ho-no Ninigi-no Mikoto which describes rice stalks with succulent grains (Kurano and Takeda 1958:125). At the time of his descent Amaterasu gives her grandson the original rice grains that she had harvested from the two fields in Heaven (Takamagahara) sown with the seeds of the five types of grains (*gokoku*) given to her by Ukemochi-no-Kami, the deity in charge of food (Kurano and Takeda 1958; see also Murakami 1977:13). The grandson of Amaterasu transforms a wilderness into a country of rice stalks with succulent heads of rice (*mizuho*) and abundant grains of five types (*gokoku*) with the original seeds given to him by Amaterasu.

As the *Kojiki* continues, Amaterasu's grandson (Ninigi-no Mikoto) marries a beautiful woman who gives birth to two sons—Hoderi-no Mikoto and Hoori-no Mikoto. The older brother (Hoderi-no Mikoto), who is also called Umi Sachi Biko (Sea-Bounty Lad), tends toward the sea and fishing, whereas the younger brother (Hoori-no Mikoto), who is also called Yama Sachi Biko (Land-Bounty Lad), tends toward land, and the hunting of land animals. The two brothers decide to exchange their tools and occupations for a while. The younger brother loses the fishhook while trying to fish. The older brother insists on having it back. The younger brother's search for the fishhook leads him to the palace of the Sea Deity at the bottom of the sea where he marries the Sea Deity's daughter. From the union is born the father of the legendary first emperor, Jinmu (Kurano and Takeda 1958:135–147; Saigō 1984:168), said to have been enthroned in A.D. 660.[15]

In this creation myth, then, it is the younger brother, the deity in charge of the land, instead of the sea, who becomes ancestral to the imperial line. Although the younger brother is described as a hunter, his alternative name, Amatsu Hiko Hiko Hohotemi-no Mikoto, means "a male child of the Sun Goddess and Lord of rice stalks with numerous heads" (Kurano and Takeda 1958:135). Thus, the struggle between sea and land ends with the latter's victory. The story also reveals, however, that the ultimate celebration of rice agriculture, expressed in his alternative name, must have been a gradual process because the great-grandson of the Sun Goddess also is described as a hunter.

Although there are a number of different imperial genealogies and versions in these myth-histories, the versions introduced here, both well-known, are not about the creation of the universe but about the transformation of wilderness (*ashihara-no nakatsu-no kuni*) into a land of abundant rice at the command of, according to the *Kojiki*, the Sun Goddess, whose descendants, the emperors, rule the country by officiating at the rice harvest rituals (Saigō 1984:15–29; Kawasoe 1980:86).

The symbolic supremacy of rice gradually developed during the Ancient period has been maintained even today. For example, in a folktale recorded in 1986 by Miyata (1988:193) in Kōfu City in Tottori Prefecture, Susano-o-no Mikoto, the brother of the Sun Goddess, visits a wealthy family who treat him coldly. Enraged, he orders the Smallpox Deity, who is under his command, to sneak into the house. When the Smallpox Deity tries to enter the house, he finds it surrounded by a rope made of rice stalks (*shimenawa*). Because a rope made of rice stalks is sacred and the space marked by the rope thus becomes sacred, the Smallpox Deity is unable to enter. Upon reporting back to Susano-o, the latter orders the Smallpox Deity to examine the rope closely because there should be a spot in the rope that is made of millet stalks. Upon finding this spot, the Smallpox Deity enters the house and decimates the family. The supremacy of rice is also revealed in a common expression, rice is the queen of five grains (*ine wa gokoku no ō*).[16]

Rice in Japanese Cosmology: An Interpretation

Deities and the Reflexive Structure

A predominant interpretation of Japanese deities among contemporary scholars is that from the earliest times they have been characterized by a dual nature and power: peaceful power (*nigimitama*), which is good and creative, coexists with violent power (*aramitama*), which is evil and destructive. These elements are referred to as the soul (*mi* = the prefix signaling the elevated register; *tama* = *tamashii* = soul), as is the case with the *inadama* (*ina* = rice plant; *dama* = *tama* = soul).

Orikuchi (1965a:78–82; 1965b:33–35; 1976a:303–17) first called attention to this aspect of the deity, *marebito*.[17] According to Orikuchi, the marebito was a god in ancient Japan who periodically visited the villages from a world located on the other side of the sea where aging and death were unknown. The god visited villagers to bring good luck although he was also potentially dangerous. Because deities are beings of nature for the Japanese, the dual nature ascribed to deities extends to natural beings and phenomena as well.

I propose that from the perspective of reflexivity, the marebito, or stranger-outsider deities who come from outside a settlement or outside of Japan, constitute the semiotic *other* for the Japanese, which is symbolically equivalent to their transcendental self, that is, the *self* perceived at a higher level of abstraction than a reflective self. The dual nature of marebito deities is, therefore, a projection of the dual qualities that the Japanese see in themselves. Japanese who ritually harness the positive power (nigitama) of the deities do so because of their awareness of the deities' negative side (aratama), which is also their own. From the structure of self and other, humans, to remain pure, must either fetch purity and energy—the nigitama—from the deities or remove impurity from their own lives by creating scapegoats (see Ohnuki-Tierney 1987). The purpose of ritual for the Japanese, then, is to harness the energy of the deities to rejuvenate their own lives, which otherwise would wither into a state of impurity.

That the marebito deities provide the basic model of the reflexive other is evident when one pursues further the symbolic relationships among purification, the rebirth of the self, and the reflexive process in the context of the metaphor of the mirror in Japanese culture. In the *Kojiki* and the *Nihonshoki* a mirror plays a significant role. In the episode in which Amaterasu Ōmikami (Sun Goddess, or "the heaven illuminating god"), ancestress of the Japanese in the creation myth, emerged from seclusion because of a mirror, that is, was reborn, and the Japanese universe was reborn with her light, she mistook her own image as that of a deity superior to her. The mirror represents, I think, her transcendental self. In other words, the rebirth of the Sun Goddess and the Japanese universe was facilitated by a mirror, which, in turn, symbolizes a self perceived at a higher level. The *Nihonshoki* also contains many passages that symbolically equate a mirror with a deity (Sakamoto et al. 1967:88, 146; see also 555, 570–571). For example, two deities are described as being born from white-copper mirrors (Sakamoto et al. 1967:88; Aston 1956:20).

Other ethnographic data describe mirrors or reflections in water as the embodiment of deities. The belief that supernatural power can be harnessed by a mirror is illustrated by the figures found in ancient tombs who hold mirrors on their chests. These figurines, called *haniwa*, are considered to represent ancient shamans (Yanagita 1951:94). Even today mirrors are installed in many shrines as the embodiment (*goshintai*) of the deity enshrined there. Throughout Japan, a number of valleys, ponds, mountains, hills, and rocks bear the word *kagami* (mirror) in their names; these are sacred places where supernatural powers are thought to reside (Yanagita 1951:94).

A Few Ounces of Divinity: Rice as Deities

The notions that each rice grain has a soul and that rice is alive in the hull are fundamental to the meanings assigned to rice in Japanese culture and in most other cultures that use rice as a staple food. Threshing, for example, was traditionally done shortly before consumption to prevent rice from losing its soul; hulled rice soon becomes lifeless rice, that is, "old rice" (*komai*).[18]

The belief in the soul of rice was further developed in agrarian cosmogony and cosmology expressed in the well-known versions of the myth-histories described. It was the mission of the grandson of the Sun Goddess to transform the wilderness into a land with succulent rice stalks. Rice constitutes Japanese deities whose names carry references to rice or to a bountiful rice crop. I suggest that the soul of rice grains is not simply equivalent to deities but is identified more specifically as the *nigitama*, the positive power of divine purity. It is relevant to note here that although most deities have dual qualities and powers, the Deity of the Rice Paddy has only the nigimitama, or peaceful soul. In fact, drought or flood, which destroys rice paddies, is an act of the Mizu-no Kami (Water Deity) rather than an expression of the *aratama* (violent spirit) of the Deity of the Rice Paddy.[19]

The following symbolic equivalents, therefore, are crucial to an understanding of the cosmological significance of rice:

rice = soul = deity = the *nigitama* (peaceful/positive power of the deity)

Production, Reproduction, Consumption, Ritual, and Polity

Human lives wane unless the positive principle replenishes its energy. Therefore, humans and their communities must rejuvenate themselves by harnessing the positive (nigitama) power of the deities. This can be accomplished in two ways: by performing a ritual or by consuming food. By consuming rice, the Japanese internalize the divine power of being, which then becomes part of the human body and its growth.

The divine souls objectified in rice grains do not stand for static objects. They symbolize "growth"—the dynamic energy for transforming the Japanese universe—and are the moving force in the dualistic universe. More concretely, they represent agricultural growth as well as growth of the human body that consumes them. Thus, the rituals of the folk and the imperial court that involve rice mark the growth cycle: planting rice seeds, transplanting seedlings, and harvesting.

In light of this argument on the symbolic nature of production, T. Sakurai's (1981) interpretation that the Japanese symbolic principles of the *hare* (sacred, special), *ke* (mundane, everyday) and *kegare* (impurity) arose out of agrarian life is convincing. Basing his argument on terms used by farmers, he proposes that the term *ke*, hitherto interpreted as "secular" and assumed to lack any power, refers to the vital energy in a seed that makes germination and growth possible. He explains that the daily life of farmers, as expressed in the term *ke* (the everyday), is characterized by this mysterious and *animistic* (his term) power. When the productive power of ke decreases, then, events of hare (the sacred) must rejuvenate the state. A state of decreased ke (the everyday), in his scheme, is kegare (impurity); *gare* comes from *kareru*, which means to wane or wither. According to Sakurai, this scheme radically departs from the hitherto accepted interpretation that kegare (impurity) represents the polar opposite of the purity of hare (the sacred). Instead, he argues that kegare (impurity) should be viewed as a state of waning ke. Sakurai's interpretation is similar to my interpretation of the nigitama as the source of rejuvenation.[20]

In ancient Japan the term *musu* meant both reproduction and growth stimulated by the sun. In Japanese cosmology the sun—the source of agricultural growth—is female, unlike the Sun God in many other cultures of the world.[21] Thus, the soul rejuvenation is equated with sexual intercourse, and production and reproduction are symbolically synonymous. Other evidence also testifies to the close association between rice and reproduction. As with a number of other deities identified as *kokurei* (souls of grains, not exclusively rice), this deity is female. Yanagita sees a parallel between the gender of grain deities and a ritual, first recorded during the tenth century and still observed today in some parts of Japan, in which rice grains are scattered in the parturition hut. The parallel led to Yanagita's well-known statement that the birth of grains and the birth of humans were once thought to be identical.[22] Again, production is equated with reproduction.

From the emperor's perspective, the harvest ritual is an important personal and political rite of passage that ensures the renewal of his soul and his political power as expressed in the notion of matsurigoto in which polity is defined as producing the food for deities.

From the perspective of the structure of the Japanese self, rice consumption, polity, rice production, the harvest ritual, and human reproduction are all equivalent in meaning: they facilitate the rejuvenation of the Japanese collective self by incorporating the divine power of nigi-tama. These activities, then, are conterminous with ritual. This interpretation can be summarized in the following symbolic equation:

$$\text{food consumption} = \text{ritual} = \text{agricultural production} =$$
$$\text{human reproduction} = \text{polity}$$

The Harvest Ritual as the Exchange of Self

If rice is a deity, however, rice production and consumption are not mere activities. Rice consumption is a religious act and, thus, requires a proper ceremony in order to make rice appropriate for human consumption. As noted, the basic theme of the imperial harvest ritual and the myth-histories is the reenactment of the way the original seeds of rice were given to humans, represented by the emperor/shaman, by the deities. In turn, humans offer the new crop of rice at harvest time and share it through an act of commensality not only between the emperor/shaman and the deities but also with the guests present at the feast.

On one level, the harvest ritual is a cosmic gift exchange in which a new crop of rice—a few grains of divinity—are offered to the deities in return for the original seeds given by the deities to the first emperor. The mode of exchange takes the form of commensality—co-eating—between deities and humans, including the emperor.

On another level, the harvest ritual constitutes a cosmological exchange of the soul and the body. Because rice embodies the nigitama, or the peaceful soul, of the deities, by offering rice grains to humans, the deities offer a part of themselves—not any part, their souls. This is, as Hocart ([1936] 1970:203) claims, "the body politic," deeply embedded, I emphasize, in the soul. Rice production, therefore, is not an economic activity as such but a system of gift exchange—the original gift of rice seeds from the deities and the countergift of the new rice crop at harvest. Ultimately, the soul and the body that are embodied in rice are exchanged in this cosmological system of exchange.

The gift exchange, then, is not a gift exchange in the ordinary sense. No separate gift is being exchanged. It is not a sacrificial ritual—no sacrificial victim is involved. Instead of a gift or a sacrificial animal, Japanese deities initiate the gift-exchange cycle by offering themselves to humans, who return their trust by growing the seeds to full maturity, *nurturing* the deities, as it were. This exchange is, therefore, not a simple "generalized exchange," an exchange "on credit" based on trust (Lévi-Strauss 1969a:265), it is a generalized exchange of souls and bodies between the deities and humans; they give their selves as an expression of their trust, just as in the classical Maussian sense "a man gives himself" (Mauss [1950] 1966:45).[23]

Yet on another level, given the symbolic equivalence of agricultural production and human reproduction, the harvest ritual enacts the cosmic cycle of production and reproduction facilitated by the flow of rice seeds, the soul, and semen. Semen is involved here because of the symbolic equation of production and reproduction, regardless of whether or not the shaman/emperor, in fact, engages in sexual intercourse during the harvest ritual.

Rice as the Food for Commensality

The cosmological exchange of the divine soul and power embodied in rice does not exist in the abstract in myths and the private ritual of the emperor. In fact, it is enacted by the people in their daily lives as well as during their folk festivals as presented in detail in chapter 7. Rice and rice products such as rice cakes and rice wine have been the food for commensality between humans and deities, on the one hand, and among humans, on the other (Yanagita 1982d). The three essential components of most Japanese rituals and festivals, whether folk or imperial, are shinsen (or kyōsen), offerings to the deities; naorai, commensality between the officiant of the ritual and the deities; and utage, the feast with the host and the guests. Although other food items are also used, rice and rice products are indispensable for all three.

Japanese Kingship and the Divine Kingship

The Japanese imperial system and the accession ritual described in this chapter call for a brief discussion of the divine kingship and sacrifice— two interrelated themes that have been of perennial interest to anthropologists. A systematic discussion of these topics, however, is beyond the scope of this book.

Some scholars have interpreted the Japanese imperial system as constituting the divine kingship. In Orikuchi's view the foundation of the imperial system was laid by myth-histories and the rituals that enabled the imperial system to transcend the problems of the emperor as a person and his or her biological humanity, or the "king's two bodies" as Kantorowicz (1957) puts it. Contemporary followers of Orikuchi's interpretation include Ebersole (1989) and Yamaori (1990a; 1990b). Like Orikuchi, Ebersole believes that the imperial soul is transmitted from one emperor to the next, guaranteeing the continuation of the imperial system regardless of individual emperors, and specifically links "the descent of the heavenly grandson" episode to the problem of "king (emperor)" versus "kingship (imperial system)" (Ebersole 1989:96).

Many anthropologists today see little utility in the notion of the divine kingship originally developed by Frazer (1911–1915) and elaborated by Hocart ([1927] 1969; [1936] 1970). Frazer's original formulation was based only on the classical example of the slaying of the priest-king of Diana at Nemi but was used as the universal model by Frazer himself and by others, as Ray (1991:22–53) most systematically reconstructs or, in fact, deconstructs, this unfortunate "history" in anthropology.[24]

There are several difficulties in interpreting the Japanese imperial system as the Frazerian divine kingship. Briefly put, God in the orthodox Judeo-Christian tradition, which provided the model for Frazer, is, in comparative perspective, "unique" as the sacred, as Redfield (1953:102) points out (for a detailed discussion on this point, see Ohnuki-Tierney 1981:108–111). Thus, the imposition of the divine kingship model conceals, rather than elucidates, the nature of the kingship in relation to the concept of the sacred in each culture.

Indeed, despite radical transformations of the imperial system through time, what has remained constant, at least until recently, is the emperor's identity as a deity (kami), but only in a Japanese sense. The kami (deity, deities) is radically different from the God of the ancient Hebrews. To give but one example, dramatic instances revealing the recognition of the power of kami by the warriors, who stripped the emperors of their political power since the end of the Ancient period, occurred when they demanded their own apotheosis. Thus, Toyotomi Hideyoshi, the military leader who in 1590 succeeded in uniting Japan for the first time, asked the imperial court to deify him as Toyokuni Daimyōjin. His life as a deity was short, and his descendants were unable to enjoy his divine status. Upon his death, his rival, Tokugawa Ieyasu, defeated the Toyotomi clan and asked, or more appropriately, ordered the imperial court to deny the divinity previously granted to Hideyoshi. Furthermore, as the most powerful of all shoguns, Tokugawa Ieyasu, in his will requested the imperial court to deify him as Tōshō Daigongen and his divinity became the bulwark of shogunate power for the next 250 years (K. Inoue 1967:258–259). Indeed, Napoleon's pontification of himself seems quite modest by contrast.

From the perspective of power, the hierarchy of beings in the universe consists of humans, shaman-emperors, and deities in ascending order. If one assumes this hierarchy is permanent and linear, then the orders by

Hideyoshi and Ieyasu to the emperors to deify them constitute an inversion of the hierarchy. It means that these humans willfully bestowed upon the emperor the power to create deities out of mere humans, quite an extraordinary feat. Likewise, the human architects of the imperial system during the Meiji period assigned themselves—mere humans—the power to create a bona fide deity out of an emperor. Such inversions of the hierarchy are embedded in Japanese religions in which the hierarchy of supernatural beings is neither fixed nor linear. Thus, in Japanese religion, an ordinary human can assign divinity even to a toothpick (Miyata [1970] 1975).

These individual instances expressing the dynamic characterization of the kami in Japanese religion are paralleled by the fluid ease with which the Japanese adopted various foreign religions. When Buddhism was introduced from India via China and Korea it was embraced eagerly by the elites, including the imperial family. But "most people in Japan at that time [the sixth and seventh centuries] probably thought of the Buddha as just another kami" (Kitagawa 1990:136). Officially, the Japanese tried to reconcile the two religions, by claiming that the kami are manifestations of the Buddhas and Bodhisattvas, a theory known as *honji suijaku*. With equal ease, the Tokugawa Japanese, especially the elites, adopted Neo-Confucianism with its emphasis on natural law and the Way of Heaven (Kitagawa 1990). Astonishing as it may be from the perspective of Western religions, the Meiji government concocted "'non-religious Shintō' which was to be adhered to by every Japanese subject, regardless of his or her personal 'religious' affiliation" (Kitagawa 1990:161). As I elaborated elsewhere (Ohnuki-Tierney 1984), most Japanese today are at least nominally both Buddhist and Shintoist simultaneously and, usually, without personal conviction.[25] To understand Japanese religiosity is to abandon the false dichotomies of magic/religion, and primitive/civilized (modern). How else could one explain the profusion of what I call "urban magic" among educated Japanese today?

If the Japanese have shown a fluid attitude toward individual deities as well as individual religious systems, so did they toward both individual emperors and the imperial system. From the perspective of the Japanese folk, neither the emperor nor the imperial system is divine, if the term implies an ascription of absolute divinity to the kingship. Feeley-Harnik (1985:276) reminds readers that divine kingship has existed mostly in the imagination of anthropologists and not in African and other kingships.

The trials and tribulations of the Japanese imperial system since the end of the Ancient period certainly do not indicate the presence of the divine kingship in Frazer's sense. From the perspective of the people, individual emperors have always been kami. As with all other deities, they are without almighty power and, thus, are susceptible to human manipulations yet capable of exercising power over humans (for historical and ethnographic details, see Ohnuki-Tierney 1991b). The Japanese imperial system and the harvest ritual cum accession ritual offer additional support to a recent critique of the divine kingship that identified the theoretical limitations and ethnographic applicability of the model developed by Frazer.

The classical model of sacrificial ritual developed by Robertson Smith ([1889] 1972) and Hubert and Mauss ([1898] 1964)—the ritual as integral to the kingly accession or the divine kingship—also has similar problems in cross-cultural perspective. The harvest ritual cum imperial accession ritual of ōnamesai shares the basic theme of the exchange of the self with the model of sacrifice. Purification and commensality are definitional elements shared between the two. The Japanese case, however, does not involve atonement. Most important, it differs radically from the classical model in that animal sacrifice and the violent death either of the king or the sacrificial animal are not features of the Japanese case.

In the original model of sacrifice, only animals are emphasized, for two reasons: violent death and food for commensality. In the divine kingship model (Frazer 1911–1915; Hubert and Mauss 1964), a violent death, either of the sacrificial animal or as regicide, is the most critical element because it is identified as the precondition of the rebirth of the divine king. Furthermore, animal food is considered the only food possible or appropriate for commensality following the sacrifice. Robertson Smith, a major architect of the model, makes a critical distinction between animal sacrifice and the cereal oblation. Animal sacrifice, according to him, is essentially an act of communion between the god and his worshippers, whereas a cereal oblation is a tribute paid to the god. The animal victim, thus, becomes holy; only ceremonially clean individuals may eat its parts. The cereal oblation, however, makes the entire crop "lawful" but not holy; anyone, clean or unclean, may freely consume it (Robertson Smith [1889] 1972:236–243). In fact, Robertson Smith ([1889] 1972:242–243) relegates to a footnote his reference to Wilken's work in which, Wilken, on the basis of information provided by J. G. Frazer, his friend, states, "A true sacrificial feast is made of the first-fruits of rice," and the act is called "eating the soul of rice."

In the Japanese case, instead of an animal violently sacrificed, plant food, rice, occupies the central role as the gift of self without an emphasis on the killing of it. Rice serves as the food for commensality. Far from being insignificant, rice among the Japanese is more than an offering to the gods for consecration; every grain of rice *is* a god. Rice consumption is not seen as a violent death or the killing of deities.[26] Thus, the rebirth of the Japanese emperors does not rest on violent death.

The Japanese imperial accession ritual does not refute the ethnographic import of violence in the ancient Middle East and other areas. In fact, before the agrarian harvest ritual became established as the accession ritual, the imperial funeral was, as noted earlier, altogether different and may have involved "violence," if one can document that the animals and, possibly, the humans buried with the deceased emperor were thought by the ancient Japanese to have been "violently killed."

A range of interpretations exists about the animal and plant offerings, and "killing" and "violent death" are only two of them. Most important, violent death as the precondition for the rebirth of a new king cannot be seen as a universal theme.

The Japanese case also prompts one to rethink the nature of kingship. The Japanese case is a reminder that the divine or the sacred in the orthodox Judeo-Christian tradition is a radically alien concept for many religions in the world, and, thus, the label "divine kingship," if applied, often misrepresents kingship in other societies. The Japanese imperial system has always held some symbolic power, but successive military leaders held the political and economic power. It is worthwhile to note here Bellah's (1967) well-known pronouncement that the Japanese emperor must be seen as a mother figure. The Japanese case is not unique. In Hindu kingdoms, the division of labor, as it were, is not exactly the same as the Japanese situation, but their kingship is equally complex. The king was equated with hunting, and the *ksatriya*, the prince and warrior, who remained meat eaters contrast with the brahman, who held the religious and symbolic power that were equated with nonviolence (Zimmermann 1987:180–194). Indeed, the kingship is often more complex than Frazer envisioned.

Five

Rice as Wealth, Power, and Aesthetics

To FURTHER understand the symbolism of rice, which served as the primary form of wealth for many centuries, I explore the concepts of wealth in the context of Japanese cosmology and the related notions of power and aesthetics of rice.

Wealth in Japanese Folklore and Folk Religions

Acquisition of wealth is a dominant motif in the folklore of various parts of Japan, past and present (Yanagita 1951:371). Tales in this genre, referred to as "tales of a wealthy person" (*chōjatan*), share common themes: (1) a stranger, sometimes in the form of an animal, brings fortune to a person; (2) the stranger lives somewhere outside the village, sometimes at the bottom of a river, sea, or pool, or in the mountains; (3) a person becomes wealthy as a reward for a virtuous personality trait, such as honesty, mercy for animals, and so forth. Two of the best-known tales, which remain favorite children's tales today, are *Shitakiri suzume* (A sparrow whose tongue was cut off) and *Tsuru no ongaeshi* (A crane who repaid its gratitude).

Shitakiri suzume is about an old man who loved a sparrow and fed her (the sparrow is always depicted as female) every day. One day, the sparrow ate the rice paste that his wife had made to use as starch for her laundry. The old woman became angry and cut off the sparrow's tongue. In tears, the sparrow flew away to her home. Without his sparrow, the old man was very sad and set off to the mountains to find her. After many failed attempts, he finally found her in a bamboo bush. The sparrow and her relatives and friends joyfully welcomed the old man with feasts, songs, and dances. When he was ready to go home, they gave him a small trunk. After returning home, he opened it to find, to his surprise, all sorts of treasures. The greedy old woman wanted treasures for herself and visited the sparrows. She returned with a large trunk, but when she opened it, out came ghosts and goblins (Muraki n.d.).[1]

Tsuru no ongaeshi begins with "Long, long ago, an old man and an old woman lived." They were very poor but very kind. One day the old man placed firewood on his back to take to town to sell. As he crossed a mountain to get to town, he saw something struggling in the snow—a crane caught in a trap. Feeling sorry for it, he released the crane, which spread its wings and cried happily as it flew into the sky. He returned home that evening after selling his firewood. As he was talking with his wife, someone knocked at the door. When they opened the door, a beautiful young woman was standing in the snow. She told them that she had lost her way in the snow. They invited her to stay until she became warm. She stayed on with them. One day she said she felt like weaving and asked to purchase some threads. She asked them not to look at her while she wove. Behind a screen, she wove for three days and nights without food or sleep. She then emerged from behind the screen with a beautiful brocade and gave it to the old man to sell in town. When the old man went to town, even the lord was pleased with the brocade's beauty and paid a high price for it. The young woman was pleased to hear the story and wanted to weave more. She again wove three days and nights without food or sleep. The old woman became so concerned about the young woman's health that she looked behind the screen. There she saw a crane picking her own feathers and weaving a brocade. The crane-maiden emerged from behind the screen and told them that she was the crane rescued by the old man and that she wanted to repay him for the mercy he had shown her. She then flew away into the sky. The old man and his wife lived happily ever after thanks to the wealth she bestowed upon them (Koharu n.d.).[2]

Although minor variations are found in various versions of these stories, depending on the historical period and the region, they share basic features (Yanagita 1951:258, 382).

Underlying the Buddhist moral message of mercy for all beings, I find in these tales important themes in Japanese cosmology. Because the mountains have been the abode of deities in Japanese cosmology, I interpret the animals in these stories as deities or their messengers. Birds have been messengers from the deities to humans ever since the eighth-century myth-histories. Either directly or via messengers, deities reward humans for their virtuous acts. These deities are "stranger deities" who live outside of human settlements in places like the mountains. Wealth is bestowed upon a person because of good nature and behavior and not as a result of hard work.

Another genre of folktales contains explicit references to the symbolic equivalence of rice and wealth given by the deity. A number of folktales that Komatsu (1983:25–26) classifies as Untoku (the name of the central figure) tales are found in various parts of Japan. Although there are variations, some themes are shared; below the boy is called Hyōtoku.

Somewhere lived an old man and his wife. The old man went to the mountains every day to fetch firewood. One day, while gathering firewood, he found a large cave in the ground. Thinking that such a cave was a residence of an evil spirit, he decided to fill it with firewood. He inserted one bundle of wood, but it was not enough. He continued until finally he used up all the firewood that he had gathered for the past three months. At that moment, a beautiful woman emerged from the cave. She thanked him for the firewood and urged him to visit the cave. Upon entering, he found a splendid mansion, beside which all his firewood was piled. As he entered the mansion at her request, he encountered a dignified old man with a white beard who entertained him with a feast. As he was leaving, the bearded host offered him a very ugly lad named Hyōtoku who was playing with his navel. The two returned to the old man's house. The boy continued his habit of constantly picking his navel. One day the old man poked the boy's navel with an iron tong used for the *hibachi* [portable heater], whereupon a gold grain came out of his navel. After that, the old man poked the boy's navel three times a day, and the old man and his wife became very rich. The old woman, however, was too greedy to settle for that amount of gold. While the old man was away, she poked the boy's navel forcefully to get more gold grains, whereupon the boy died. The old man was very sad, but the boy appeared in a dream and told him: "Please do not be so sad. Make a mask that looks just like me. Hang it on the pillar in front of the hearth where you look at it every day. Then, wealth will accumulate."

It is said that in this village even today people make an ugly mask from clay or wood and hang it on the pillar near the hearth.

Although there are other themes in this story, the central themes parallel the two folktales introduced earlier: wealth is a gift from a Stranger Deity offered as a reward for good behavior. The old man did not get rich as a direct consequence of his difficult work gathering firewood. Instead, the white-bearded man, that is, the Stranger Deity gives him a fortune because of the old man's generosity in offering the firewood without anticipating any return and his lack of greed for the gold grains. His spontaneous altruism is rewarded by the Stranger Deity with wealth.

The Hyōtoku genre of folktales has two additional themes that are important for understanding the meaning of wealth in Japanese cosmology. First, wealth is described as gold *grains*. Because ripe rice grains are referred to as "golden grains" and rice paddies full of ripe heads of rice are thus referred to as golden waves, I suggest that the gold grain coming out of the lad's navel is wealth in the form of rice. Second, gold is coming out of the abdomen—the abode of the soul and fetus—as in the eighth-century myth-history that describes rice originating in a deity's abdomen.

Folk religions are replete with the theme of wealth as a gift from a deity. Since the Medieval period, even today, Daikoku and Ebisu have been popular as the deities of the kitchen. They are two of the seven deities who bring fortune to people (*shichifukujin*). In paintings and statuettes made of porcelain, wood, or metal, that are still popular, Ebisu is depicted as a jolly fisherman with a fishing rod and a catch of fish on his shoulder, whereas Daikoku is depicted as a jolly man with fat cheeks, a hood on his head, carrying a large bag on his left shoulder and a mallet in his right hand, and with his foot on a bundle of rice (for details of Ebisu and Daikoku, see Yanagita 1951: 68–69, 338–339). A popular theme in folklore, the special mallet called *uchide no kozuchi* would produce fortune when struck. The fortune that Daikoku produces with his mallet is rice as iconographically represented by the bundle of rice (*komedawara*) upon which he places his foot.

These folktales, some of which are still told today, share the theme in the version of Japanese cosmogony in which the origin of rice—wealth par excellence—is explained as a *gift* from the deities in heaven. Seen in this light, a contemporary saying *tana kara botamochi* (a rice cake accidentally has fallen from a shelf) takes on a rich cultural meaning. Today, this saying refers to "luck" in a secular sense, a fortune received accidentally, without working for it. But, if a rice cake embodies the soul of a deity and rice originally was given by the deities in heaven, this ordinary saying is apparently embedded in cosmology and offers evidence that contemporary Japanese continue to think that wealth can sometimes be a windfall.

In folk cosmology as expressed in folktales and folk religions, wealth is bestowed upon a human by a Stranger Deity in the form of a sparrow, a crane, or a white-bearded man cum ugly boy because of the recipient's generosity, mercy, or other virtue, especially altruism. As a gift from a deity, wealth receives religious sanction. Being sacred, it takes the form of golden rice or gold itself.

The wealth as a divine gift described in these folktales often constitutes a part of the body of a deity—a feather of a crane or grain from the abdomen. In other words, wealth is portrayed as a part of the divine body in both the origin myths of the eighth century discussed in chapter 4 and in the folktales and folk religions found in many parts of Japan even today.

The folktales and folk religions clearly share common themes with the myth-histories and the imperial harvest ritual. Thus, the cosmology propagated by the imperial system during the Ancient period and the folk cosmology of later periods do not constitute or derive from separate systems of thought. In all these folk and imperial tales and religions, fortune is depicted as a gift from a Stranger Deity, who may be an agrarian or a nonagrarian deity who resides somewhere in heaven, in the mountains, the sea, and so forth.

Rice as a Sacred Tax and Sacred Currency

Rice as a Sacred Tax

During the Early Modern period a taxation system (kokudaka) was instituted in which the tax was based on the putative yield of rice in the territory of each regional lord. The kokudaka system has usually been discussed solely as an economic and political institution, especially as an instrument of oppression against the peasants. Recent scholarship, however, points to its religious nature. Amino (1983, 1987) has uncovered important evidence to demonstrate that markets, taxation, and interest in Japan's Ancient and Medieval periods were essentially religious institutions. At that time, the government, shrines, and temples gave peasants unhulled rice seeds (*tanemomi*) for planting in the spring. In the fall, at harvest time, they repaid the "loan" with the new crop of rice (*hatsuho*) in amounts that included "interest" (*ritō*). This practice of loaning seed with interest, called *suiko*, originated during the Ancient period (see also Oda 1986; Yoshimura 1986). According to Amino, this transaction derives from the custom of offering the new crop of rice (hatsuho) and the first catch of the sea (*hatsuo*) to deities and Buddhas. These offerings then became the properties of the deities and Buddhas and could not be handled carelessly by humans. This practice, called *jōbun*, is the prototype for the seed loan (suiko) and both practices, according to Amino, should be viewed in religious terms. Amino emphasizes that the jōbun provided the model for all monetary transactions, which were handled by religious specialists during the Medieval period.[3] The myth-histories and the imperial harvest ritual follow the same model as the jōbun.

Rice as Pure Money

Rice as the item of gift exchange between deities and humans is closely associated with the way rice was used as a medium of exchange in general. The strong tradition of a barter system and the use of rice as currency slowed the development of a cash economy based on metallic currency after its introduction from China. Thus, despite government encouragement of a cash economy, the Japanese continued the barter sys-

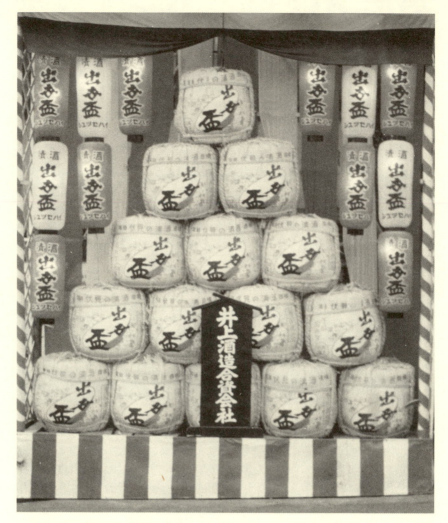

5.1. Containers of Rice Wine as Offerings to a Shrine in Kōbe, Japan, 1990. These containers are empty but symbolize cash donations. Photo by the author.

tem using rice, cloth, and other goods as items of exchange. Only with the beginning of the Medieval period, did the cash economy gradually make inroads into the Japanese economy. The percentage of coins and rice in the payment of a land tax during the Medieval period, quoted in Morisue (1953:125) delineates this gradual shift (table 5.1). The shift from the barter system to metallic currency took place gradually between the twelfth and fifteenth centuries (Reischauer and Craig 1978:63). By

TABLE 5.1
Land Tax Payment in Coins and Rice during the
Medieval Period (*Chūsei*) (percentage)

	Kamakura Period (1185–1392)			Muromachi Period (1392–1603)
	Early	Middle	Late	Early
Coin	39.7	69.9	84.2	93.2
Rice	60.3	30.1	15.8	6.8

1300 perhaps ten times as much metallic currency was in circulation as one century earlier (Sansom 1961:184). At the beginning of the Medieval period coins were imported from China, but by the fifteenth and sixteenth centuries, copper, silver, and gold mines had been discovered in Japan, enabling the Japanese to mint their own currency (K. Inoue 1967:206).

Despite the presumed switch from a barter to a cash economy, rice as a means of exchange and as a form of tax did not disappear. Thus, even though the *kandaka*, the tax collected in copper coins, was adopted during the midsixteenth century, the *kokudaka* system returned during the early seventeenth century only fifty years later (Yamamura 1988). The kokudaka system returned, according to Yamamura, because of the economic and political advantages of the rice tax system over the cash system although others argue that farmers often found it difficult to convert their rice into money to pay taxes. Many reasons were likely for the resistance to a monetary tax, but there is no question that the religious/symbolic meaning of rice had much to do with it. Rice continued to be the medium of exchange for special occasions and remains so today at least in its symbolic forms as discussed later.

From a cross-cultural perspective, a special character of rice as a medium of exchange should be noted. Precious objects, money and quasi-money are all mediums of exchange, but they all change hands. Salt money of the Baruya of the Eastern Highlands of New Guinea is more important for intergroup exchange than for intragroup exchange (Godelier 1977:127–151). The Ainu of southern Sakhalin eagerly sought goods from neighboring populations, but their use was limited to offerings to their bear deities; such goods had no use or exchange value among themselves (Ohnuki-Tierney 1974).

Rice as a medium of exchange differs from both salt money and the Ainu trade goods in that, in addition to being the most important offering to the deities, it had both use and exchange value among the Japanese. It was *not*, however, a medium of exchange with non-Japanese social groups. "Japanese rice" was exclusively for the Japanese, who, during most historical periods, did not have enough to export and refused for the most part to accept other peoples' rice precisely because Japanese rice serves as a metaphor for the collective self of the Japanese—the theme of chapter 6.

Pure Money and Impure Money

In a discussion of state-issued money in Western scholarly discourse, Parry and Bloch (1989) identify two disparate views that are part of Western cultural tradition. In the tradition from Aristotle, Thomas Aquinas, and Marx, money is condemned. Aristotle (1958:25–26) sees "the exchange of commodities," which is "limitless," as "the unnatural form of acquisition," in contrast to household acquisition with limits that are "natural." Like Aristotle, Marx views money as a commodity fetish par excellence. An opposite view of money is represented by Mandeville and Adam Smith, for whom money provided the means for the individual pursuit of happiness and prosperity. A third view, represented by Simmel ([1907] 1950), takes an intermediate position that regards money as an instrument of freedom for the individual, on the one hand, and a threat to the moral order of the community, on the other hand.

With regard to social relationship, like Marx, Simmel ([1907] 1950: especially 283–354) links money to the development of individualism and the destruction of communal solidarity. Parry and Bloch (1989:4) summarize Roberts and Stephenson's (1983:13) argument: Independent communities become dependent and dependent individuals become independent (see also Gregory 1982:71). To put the contrast between money and commodity crudely,

> Gift exchange = an exchange of inalienable objects (gifts) between interdependent transactors; creation of social bonds
>
> Commodity exchange = the exchange of alienable objects (commodities) between independent transactors; absence of social relations

Gift exchange and commodity exchange, however, are never clear-cut in practice. Discussing the origins of home industry in India between 1700 and 1930, Bayly notes, "What is striking here is the way in which the formal apparatus of markets and a monetized economy modeled themselves to and were accommodated by mentalities that still viewed the relationships between men, commodities, and other men in terms of good (pure) and evil (polluting)" (Bayly 1986:316). Thus, the Indians tried to accommodate both systems of transaction with an elaborate double-entry accounting system.

What Bayly observed among the Indians in these centuries, I think, pertains to even the most advanced capitalist societies of today, such as the United States and Japan. In practice, a sharp distinction between alienable and inalienable objects and between independent and inter-dependent human agents seems to obliterate human transactions in which, except in extreme cases, these structural oppositions are inter-twined in complex ways. Money can be both inalienable and alienable, and the agents of transaction can be independent of each other or inter-dependent.

Both "dirty money (metallic currency)" and "clean money" have been used in Japan. Since its introduction from China money has been impure, dirty, degrading, and "unnatural to human nature." The following state-ment about money in the twelfth century strikes a sympathetic cord even today:

> One of the first clear mentions of the growth of monetary transactions is a passage in the *Hyakurenshō* under the date 1179, which says: "There is a strange sickness going round the country nowadays. It is called the money disease." In conservative Court circles the use of coins was thought (not with-out some reason) to upset the price of commodities, and even so grave a states-man as Kujō Kanezane, writing in the 1180's, said that the decay of govern-ment at this time was due entirely to these coins. (Sansom 1961:184)

During the Medieval and Early Modern periods rice was preferred to money as a medium of exchange because rice was considered pure whereas money was impure (Amino personal communication). There were serious discussions in the Early Modern period about the definition of productivity. Should merchants "be considered productive" or should the definition of productivity be restricted to agrarian labor? (See chapter 6.) The rationale for locating the merchant class at the bottom of the four-class/caste system during this period was based on the idea that merchants dealt with dirty money. Even today, many Japanese demon-strate an intense aversion to "dirty" money. The Japanese who come to the United States often find it difficult to hold a sandwich in their hands after paying for it at the cash register because their hands have just touched "dirty money" that "you don't know who might have handled." Japanese children are often taught to wash their hands after handling money, even though except for a few items, it is taboo to use hands for eating; instead, one must always use chopsticks, which are "by definition clean," from a cultural standpoint (Ohnuki-Tierney 1984).

Money in Japan can, indeed, be clean, and even religious in nature. As shown in the folktales, a fortune, including gold currency, may be a di-vine gift. For example, in the crane story, the crane/deity weaves the bro-cade for the old man to *sell* for money. "Clean money," in fact, has been a major gift item in Japan throughout history, and even today gift-offerings to the deities must be money. People toss coins (*osaisen*) into a wooden box in front of a shrine and pray to the deities.

On many annual gift exchange occasions in Japan today money rather than an object is the prescribed gift. The *otoshidama*, a New Year's gift to children from adults, must be money. For funerals, rice and/or rice products used to be the main gift (*kōden*), but they were replaced by money (Itoh 1984:103; Ishimori 1984). Money is also the gift for weddings in contemporary Japan. On occasions for which money is the prescribed gift, there are commonsense "fixed prices" depending on the occasion and the relationship between the donor and the recipient. For example, in the 1980s and 1990s in urban Japan, ¥ 50,000 is appropriate if the person is equal or superior in social standing to the *parents* of a groom or a bride, but ¥ 30,000 is proper if given by a social inferior although friends and co-workers of a groom or a bride may follow a recent trend and opt to give a gift worth about ¥ 30,000. The money must be new bills and must be put in appropriate envelopes, properly and elaborately decorated. On some of these occasions, especially funerals, the family must keep a record of names and the amount of money each person gives to the family. The record enables the family to determine an appropriate return gift in the future.

Dirty money can be purified. During the Medieval period, people buried a money box (*senryōbako*) in the ground with a word *bukku* (offering to Buddha) in a belief that anything buried in the ground loses its ownership identity and becomes the property of buddhas and deities (Amino 1987). People could then lend the money and receive interest for it. This practice derives from the aforementioned ritual during which the new crop of rice and the first catch from the sea offered to the Buddhas and deities as *jōbun* became sacred and belonged to them. Burying money follows this tradition of consecration by offering it to the buddhas and deities. The oblong gold coins (*ōban* and *koban*) during the late Early Modern period bore an embossed picture of rice stalks with succulent rice grains, which made them symbolically equivalent to pure money.

How "pure money" became equivalent to rice is succinctly expressed in the way red rice (*sekihan*) and other rice products, which used to be the prescribed gifts for funerals, were replaced by money in the mid-nineteenth century. Ishimori (1984:276) analyzed the records of funeral gifts received by one family in Nagano Prefecture that covered seven generations, beginning in 1846. In table 5.2 I summarize the number of gifts of each type and combine all the rice products in Ishimori's table into one category that includes red rice (*sekihan*), rice wine, glutinous rice, rice cake, and *ohagi* (sweets made of rice). A dramatic shift occurred between 1846 and 1861. In 1861, 64 percent of donors gave money gifts, 76 per-

TABLE 5.2
Rice and Money as Funeral Gifts

Year	Money	Money Coupons	Rice Products	Other Gifts	Number of Donors
1846	6	13	31	9	59
1861	59	11	16	6	92
1867	37	4	13	1	55
1880	73	1	27	2	103
1898	65	0	26	1	92
1905	82	0	18	1	101
1938	184	0	1	0	185
1939	132	0	3	0	135
1961	215	0	0	0	215

Source: Ishimori 1984:276, table 1.

cent, if money coupons are combined with money. By 1961 money became the only gift item at funerals.

Metallic currency is equivalent to rice in that both are forms of exchange. But, although money can be dirty or clean, rice as an item of exchange has always been "sacred" in the past and remains "clean" today. Equivocal money, however, can be as clean as rice if the money is consecrated in precisely the same way as rice: by offering it to the deities and Buddhas, by prescribing it as a gift from the deities as in the folktales, identifying money with rice in a specific way as in the gold coins embossed with a rice motif, or giving new bills at culturally prescribed occasions, such as funerals and weddings.

The crucial difference between money and rice, then, is that money is equivocal whereas rice is unequivocal. Money, thus, can be an important inalienable gift or devilish fetish, whereas rice as an item of exchange is always an inalienable gift exchanged among interdependent individuals; there is no dirty rice currency. The meaning of rice as a medium of exchange retains its original religious, or, to put it more broadly, cosmological meaning: the soul of rice embodies the peaceful soul of the deities.

Japanese culture is far from unique in this respect. Among many peoples in the world—the Chinese, the Greeks, the Romans, the Vedic Indians, the Samoans, the Tongans, and so forth—money originated as a sacred object (Hocart 1952:97–104). Hocart identifies the origin of money with the fee paid to the priest who represents the god; the priest "is presented with some objects in which the nature of that god abides" (Hocart [1936] 1970:103). In Greece, for example, mints were housed in temples, and forgery was considered sacrilege. The word *money* comes from Juno Moneta, a temple on the Capitoline Hill where a mint for silver currency was set up in 269 B.C. (Hocart 1952:100). Having originated as an offering to the deities, money gave rise to trade, which was also sacred, according to Hocart, whose memorable sentence epitomizes the sacred spirit of the trade: "[a] little of it [gold] was given away in exchange for quantities of their stuff because *a few ounces of divinity were worth pounds of gross matter*" (Hocart 1952:101; italics added). Likewise, the origin of taxes is religious because "the Lord loveth a cheerful giver" (Hocart [1936] 1970:202).[4]

The Power and Aesthetics of Rice

Rice as Power

Because it embodied the sacred power of nigitama, rice was for a long time considered to provide sacred energy and power. Thus, many contemporary practices derive from the notion that rice gives a person sacred energy although today most Japanese observe these practices without believing in the sacredness of rice. Traditionally, rice cakes are eaten when people need strength, such as at the height of the agricultural season and the start of the New Year, a seasonal rite of passage. Even those Japanese who do not normally eat rice cakes do so on New Years, and until very recently, it was an important family affair in many regions of Japan, including urban areas, to prepare large numbers of rice cakes at the end of the year for the New Year when they were offered to the deities and shared among family members, relatives, and all other visitors (for details of New Year, see chap. 6). Rice cakes were also fed to women after childbirth (Yanagita 1982b:240–258). As a source of rejuvenating energy, even today rice gruel (*okayu*) is *the* food for the sick and the weaning food for babies, as well as for young people participating in sports as noted earlier. Shops sell rice cakes labeled "rice cake for strength (*chikara mochi*)." In other words, in a secularized form the symbolic power of rice remains significant in contemporary Japan, although its meaning and power may be recognized only at times of crisis, such as discussion of the rice importation issue today.[5]

Although the political dimension of rice is not a focus in this book, I should mention that the cosmological or religious power of rice underscored the political power. The rice tax system (kokudaka) was based on the putative yield of rice in the territory of regional lords. The putative yield of rice then became an important expression of wealth and power of the lords. A lord whose territory yielded one million *koku* of rice (*Hyakumangoku no otonosama*), for example, of Kaga-han (presently in the Ishikawa Prefecture), conveyed an image of fields of golden rice stalks, which symbolized wealth and power, underscored by their aesthetic beauty.

5.2. Contemporary Postage Stamps. The fragrance of the succulent heads of the early crop (*wase*) is praised in a poem. (Photo by the author)

Rice as Beautiful

Rice, both in raw and cooked forms, is not only powerful but also beautiful. Ripe heads of rice grain are described as having a golden luster. The association is between their color and "rice as money" because the character *kin* (or *kane*) refers both to money and gold.

The aesthetics of rice is expressed in poems, essays, and visual arts, which, in turn, further promoted the beauty of rice. Motoori Norinaga (1730–1801), a nativist scholar of the Early Modern period, emphasized in his chauvinistic way that Japan's superiority over other countries is epitomized by the rice grown in Japan, which is superior to that grown in other countries; its *beauty* is derived from the superiority of the country (Motoori Norinaga, *Kojikiden*, cited in Watanabe 1989:089).

Even today, the aesthetics of rice is extolled. A pair of ¥ 60 stamps, one with a picture of succulent heads of rice and the other with a poem written in calligraphy praising the fragrance of new rice grains were issued recently (see figs. 5.2, 5.3). The visual message of these stamps is powerful: rice is not only beautiful but its beauty is as quintessentially

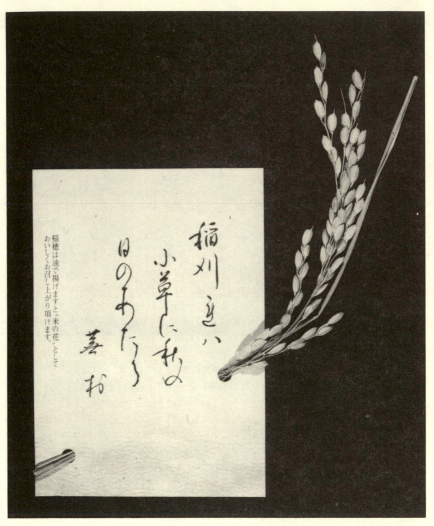

5.3. Insert in a Container of Rice Crackers. An illustration of succulent grains of rice with a poem by the famous poet, Buson, in which he describes rice harvesting in aesthetic terms. Photo by the author.

Japanese as the brushstrokes with which the Japanese often choose to present/represent their culture to outsiders.

As for the beauty of cooked rice, the most important characteristics are the related qualities of luster, purity, and whiteness. In his *In-ei Raisan* (In praise of shadows), Tanizaki Junichirō, an important novelist of this century, extols the beauty of cooked rice: "When cooked rice is in a lacquer container placed in the dark, shining with black luster, it is more aesthetic to look at, and it is more appetizing. When you lift the lid [of the lacquer container], you see pure white rice with vapor rising. *Each grain is a pearl.* If you are a Japanese, you certainly appreciate rice when you look at it this way (in a lacquerware container placed in the dark)" (Tanizaki [1933] 1959:17–18; translation by this author; italics added). This passage illustrates the aesthetics of rice as developed perhaps most highly among the elite but shared also by the folk.

Even today, "pure rice" (*junmai*) or "white rice" (*hakumai*) has aesthetic quality. The two kinds of rice preferred by most Japanese today are koshi*hikari* and sasa*nishiki*. The term *hikari* means light or luster in Japanese, and *nishiki* means gold. Both labels, thus, emphasize the luster of rice, its aesthetics. Like the deities embodied in mirrors, the aesthetics of rice must lie in the luster, whiteness, and purity.[6]

It is easy to see how the aesthetics of rice are closely related to the self-representation and perception of the Japanese and thereby become susceptible to a dangerous transformation into the chauvinistic value seen in the writings of Motoori Norinaga and Tanizaki Junichirō.

Rice as Good Life

In addition to beauty and power, rice also stands for "good life." In the folktales people who are rewarded with wealth (rice) live happily ever after. The purpose of many rituals, including the imperial and folk harvest rituals, is to guarantee an abundant crop of rice and a good life. Many other folk religions and millenarian movements share the same goal. For example, inari shinkō, a folk religion that celebrates the Deity of Rice Paddies (Ta-no Kami) and the fox, the messenger from this deity (Matsumae 1988; Yanagita 1951:35–36), concerns exclusively the rice harvest.

Ethnohistorical descriptions of peasant rebellions, which often took the form of millenarian movements, portray a utopia with abundant rice. Throughout the Early Modern period uprisings both in rural and urban areas were endemic. Most were expressions of peasant dissatisfaction with local people—local officials who failed to be benevolent, money lenders, sake dealers, and priests and monks at shrines and temples who hoarded wealth. During these riots peasants often targeted the storehouses of wealthy local people. The utopia portrayed in their demand was a community under a good government that eliminates unequal distribution of wealth and unfair accumulation of wealth by certain individuals (Katsumata 1985). These uprisings, therefore, had the characteristics of millenarian movements. When staging these uprisings, peasants donned rice-straw coats and carried straw bags of rice on their shoulders; their banners were also made of rice straw (Katsumata 1985:127–131). In other words, all the important symbols used in the peasant uprisings were made from the rice plant.

The message of these symbols is quite significant: Japanese deities are iconographically depicted as wearing rice-straw coats (Orikuchi 1975a: 202). Thus, according to Katsumata (1985:131), peasants symbolically carried deities on their backs when they staged their rebellion and demanded a utopia with "economic egalitarianism" among fellow villagers.[7] But the power to bring forth this utopia rested on rice, whose products were used for attire and banners during the uprisings. In short, the peasants aligned themselves directly with the agrarian deities in their protest by using rice products for their symbols.

A vision of utopia as a world with abundant crops, especially rice (Miyata 1970:89, 169–170, 195; 1987:28–44), is detailed in a well-known work by Miyata (1970) who offers a detailed historical and ethnographic account of the cosmology underlying a folk religion cum millenarian movement known as the "Miroku Shinkō" (The belief in Maitreya). Although the Buddha Maitreya derives from Indian Buddhism, it has been thoroughly transformed in Japan and become closely aligned with the rice rituals (Miyata 1970:169–70). Miyata argues that this utopia is shared by a number of millenarian movements, some spread across wide areas, toward the end of the Early Modern period and afterward, particularly after 1867. People began to realize that something was drastically wrong with the Tokugawa regime. For example, in a millenarian movement known as Eejanaika (It's all right), which was closely related to the Miroku belief, people took to the street where they danced and sang in a frenzy to express a desire for world renewal (*yonaoshi, yonaori*). The world they envisioned and hoped for emphasized a low price for rice and an abundant rice crop; their songs and dances often derived from harvest songs and dances (Takagi 1983:221–231; Miyata 1987). During the nineteenth century, villagers in many regions held a ritual called "longing for the good world," during which some villagers chanted, "Give us a pleasant world and a peaceful world, give us a world that is full of rice and millet" (Scheiner 1973:586).

The utopian vision portrayed in the rebellions and millenarian movements testifies to the acute shortage of food, especially rice. It is highly significant that the people who participated in these movements not only upheld the symbolic importance of rice but, in fact, intensified it by using symbols made from the rice plant, rather than challenging or subverting the cosmology based on rice agriculture.

Rice as Sacred Gift

The characterization of rice as wealth, money, and the source of power and aesthetics shows some cross-cultural parallels as well as meanings specific to Japanese culture. In contrast to the Protestant ethic introduced in chapter 3, which justified forcing farmers to work from dawn to dusk, there is another altogether different and equally important cosmological meaning of wealth—a gift from the Stranger Deity (marebito), a deity from a far-off land who brings good fortune to the people, just as the origin of rice was explained as the gift of self from the deities in heaven.

Anthropologists have been acutely aware that multiple, often competing if not contesting, world views are held either simultaneously by people or by different social groups within the same society. To find the theme of the Stranger Deity as the source of wealth alongside the notion of wealth as a result of hard work is not surprising. The former is nonformalized, whereas the latter is formalized, just as the male-centered, formalized world view of the Ainu is expressed in their bear ceremony, whereas the nonformalized world view, celebrating the symbolic power of women, is expressed in their shamanistic ritual (Ohnuki-Tierney 1981).

The notion of a "stranger" is widespread in Africa, Oceania, and many other parts of the world. Originally pointed out by Simmel ([1907] 1950:402–408), the "stranger" is simultaneously far and near, or belongs to and yet does not belong to the community in which he or she is in a position to exercise considerable power, including material and nonmaterial blessings. Although the specific nature of the power of the stranger varies from culture to culture, the Stranger Deity has been used by a number of scholars as a powerful analytical tool to explain cultural dynamics, including historical changes.[8]

In many societies, precious goods originate as a medium of exchange between deities and humans, thereby assigning religious meaning to these goods and to "economic" transactions. Because the sacred is often perceived both as powerful and beautiful, art and religion are inseparable in almost every past culture. Although the aesthetics of rice may be difficult to understand for nonrice-eating peoples, it is celebrated and appreciated almost as a piece of art would be. Some contrast must be noted here, however. Wheat and bread—the latter as the metaphor for the body of Christ—have not found their way into aesthetics as much as rice has, owing, perhaps, to the fact that, unlike rice, which is a deity, they themselves are not deified.

Equivocal metallic currency and unequivocal rice present us with a significant problem for students of symbolism. One knows that behavior or an object does not cry out with a specific meaning. Historical actors assign meanings to their own symbolic behaviors and objects. Yet one sees the basic cultural framework to restrict the actors who are not altogether free to assign meanings after all: the basic cultural meanings of rice and metallic currency, respectively, exercise some constraints. Money can be pure or dirty, whereas rice can be insignificant in the secularized world today but it can *never* be "dirty."

Six

Rice as Self, Rice Paddies as Our Land

HISTORICAL PROCESSES whereby "rice as self," that is, rice and rice paddies, have become dominant metaphors of the Japanese self must be examined in order to understand why this particular mode of representation has been accepted as *natural*, or self-evident, for so long. Because I argue that it is not as a result of a simple "mystification" process, I examine cultural institutions, including artistic representations and other expressive cultural practices, to show how agrarian cosmology cum ideology has penetrated the day-to-day lives of the Japanese. Equally important is to explore the social dimensions of the "cost" of this representation, which at the symbolic level denies the presence of non-rice-agrarian folk. That is, because symbolic representations are always embedded in the social life of the people, one must question what happened to the lives of the nonagrarian folk as they became excluded from "agrarian Japan."

Agrarian Japan: A Representation

If one takes a purely quantitative approach to time, the period during which Japan's subsistence economy was primarily agricultural lasted a mere two thousand years, much shorter than the preceding periods, during which Japan's subsistence economy was hunting-gathering: the Palaeolithic period (50,000 B.P.–11,000 B.C) and the Jōmon period (11,000 B.C.–250 B.C.) (see table 3.1). The relatively short duration of the agricultural period does not negate the importance of agriculture because it provided the economic base for the development of Japan as a nation-state. In fact, as discussed in chapter 4, the very foundation of the imperial system was based on an agrarian economy and agrarian cosmology.

It is one thing to celebrate the development of agriculture, but it is another matter to maintain an agrarian identity when the country's economy has diversified or has been urbanized and industrialized, as was the case with Japan. Yet, the "agrarian Japan" image of rice paddies, often featured on the covers of books on Japan, has been predominant until recently.

In the past, academics both Japanese and non-Japanese played no small role in the characterization of Japan as an agrarian society. The beginning of the Yayoi agricultural period has been much celebrated; discoveries of Yayoi sites with large-scale remains of rice paddies have been major events not only among archaeologists but for the Japanese in general and have received extensive media coverage. The Toro site, excavated in 1943 in Shizuoka Prefecture, for example, was heralded as evidence of the splendid agricultural beginning of the Japanese nation and resulted in numerous publications (see Ōtsuka and Mori 1985). Its "remarkable" rice paddies covered 70,585 square meters (Otomasu 1978).

The thesis that "rice has been the staple food for all the Japanese throughout history" had also been accepted by scholars as a historical fact until recently, as noted earlier. American anthropological studies of Japan began at the end of World War II with the "village Japan" concept. Although Japan was more rural at that time, the "agrarian Japan" image no doubt played a role in the selection of "village" ethnography and, in turn, propagated this image.[1]

Researchers are increasingly aware that Japanese culture and society have never been homogeneous as once claimed. The representation of the entire nation as "agrarian Japan" denies the heterogeneity of Japanese society throughout history by portraying the Japanese as a monolithic population consisting entirely of farmers.[2] "Agrarian Japan" has been equated with rice agriculture, thus denying the presence of nonrice agriculture, which has been equally, if not more, important for the production of staple crops for a long time.

An "agrarian Japan" concept leaves no place for the nonagrarian population. Recent scholarship not only stresses nonrice agriculture but other occupational diversities, offering a complex picture of Japan as comprising heterogeneous social groups: agrarian and nonagrarian populations; settled and nonsettled populations (Amino 1984); populations who rely on resources from the fields, from the mountains, and from the sea (Ōbayashi et al. 1983). Occupational diversity cuts across other classifications of people, such as those based on gender, class, and caste; together these classificatory principles have created a complex mosaic of Japanese society throughout history that is far from the simple image projected by the monolithic representation of an "agrarian Japan" and "Japan as a rice culture."

It is alarming that such a simple picture held sway for so long. One of the most exciting developments in scholarship in contemporary Japan is the burgeoning interface between history and anthropology in which prominent scholars are challenging the representation of Japan as agrarian, especially with the emphasis on rice agriculture. I focus in this chapter on two dimensions. First, how was "agrarian Japan" defined and redefined in different historical periods to represent Japan? My historical accounts are quite brief. Details of the complexity of Japanese society and culture and its historical transformations are presented in my study of the historical processes whereby minorities in Japanese society have been formed (Ohnuki-Tierney 1987). The development of "agrarian Japan" is the flip side of the marginalization of nonagrarian people who, since the end of the Medieval period, have come to form minorities.

Second, how has "agrarian Japan," as *the* Japanese self, been formed and reformulated again and again in dialogue with other peoples as the Japanese encountered them?

The Ancient Period (300 B.C.–A.D. 1185)

The myth-histories of the *Kojiki* and the *Nihonshoki* were compiled on orders from the Tenmu emperor (r. 672–686)[3] who set out to establish a Japanese identity in opposition to Tang China, whose influence had been pervasive (Kawasoe 1980:253–254). Not only had the accession ritual (sokui no rei) been imported from China and retained Chinese elements but the basic framework and rules for the Japanese imperial rituals were modeled after the Tang prescription for rituals (M. Inoue 1984:9–11).[4]

Ironically, however, rice agriculture introduced from the Asian Continent was chosen to establish *the* defining feature of the Japanese identity as distinct from that of the Chinese. To reconcile this apparent contradiction and to appropriate rice agriculture for the Yamato state, the imperial court "selected" (cf. Vansina 1985:190–192) from competing oral traditions the "myth" that contended that their own deity grew the first crop of rice and that this deity—first a deity of production and reproduction, later the Sun Goddess—was the ancestor of the imperial family and, hence, the Japanese people.

As noted in chapter 5, the basic structure of meaning underlying the myth selected by the imperial court and the imperial harvest ritual was shared by the agrarian folk as well. In all these symbolic expressions, good comes from outside—rice as wealth comes from deities in heaven. Thus, the contradiction is more apparent than real; the Chinese, like deities, were situated outside the Japanese villagers' world and were their benefactors, offering features of Chinese civilization.

The ōnamesai is a ritual equivalent of the myth-histories; it legitimated the rice-ruler theme for Japanese emperors. It reaffirmed at the time of each emperor's accession the emperor's religious, political, economic power while it reaffirmed the distinctive identity of the Japanese as defined in relation to the "other," that is, the Chinese and their culture. For this reason, the ōnamesai—a harvest ritual lacking explicit political pronouncements—has been kept as the major ceremony of accession although the sokui no rei (accession ritual) alone would suffice for political purposes.[5]

A strong emphasis on rice is coupled with scarce references to a hunting-gathering economy in the myth-histories (Ōbayashi 1973:4) and the ritual. A hunting-gathering economy preceded rice agriculture and had been practiced by the people on the archipelago for almost fifty thousand years by the time the Yamato state emerged. Hunting and gathering remained important activities in many parts of Japan, but especially in the east and the northeast, at the time the chronicles were compiled. As noted earlier, contradictions such as the Deity of the Land, whose name refers to succulent rice heads although he is described as a hunter, indicate that rice agriculture gradually replaced hunting and its symbolic importance.

Archaeological records indicate that Yamato society had been stratified since prehistoric times (Ninomiya 1933:60–64). Not until the Taika Reform of A.D. 645, however, did society become *legally* stratified. Through this reform, the population was divided into *ryōmin* (good people) and *senmin* (base people). The senmin, who constituted 10 percent of the total population of five to six million at that time (Ueda Kazuo 1978:80), were divided into five clearly delineated strata: the *ryōko*, who guarded and maintained the mausoleums of the imperial family; the *kanko*, who cultivated government official lands; the *kenin*, who were servants of individuals, shrines, and temples; the *kunuhi*, who were public slaves owned by the government and ordered to carry out miscellaneous labor; and the *shinuhi*, who were the slaves of private individuals (Ninomiya 1933:70–71).

There were renowned artists among the senmin, such as Hieda-no-Are, the narrator of the aforementioned *Kojiki*. Likewise, Kakinomoto-no-Hitomaro, one of the most celebrated poets of the *Manyōshū*—the first collection of poems in Japan, compiled in the mid–eighth century—is believed to have been an itinerant poet of senmin status as indicated by the inclusion in his name of *maro*, a title used for senmin (Orikuchi 1976b:464). During the Ancient period, music and dancing had religious significance. Although these people were of low social status in the formalized social structure, they, as religious specialists, had access to the center of power, including the emperor (for details, see Ohnuki-Tierney 1987:77–81, 111).

The imperial system developed during the Ancient period has lasted, then, for more than two thousand years. Yet political power had been stripped from the imperial system shortly after the eighth century. In other words, the Ancient period proved to be the only period in Japanese history when the imperial system was powerful. As Kitagawa (1990:140) remarks, "Never before or after in the history of Japan did the monarchy reach such a zenith as in the eighth century."

The Medieval Period (A.D. 1185–1603)

Dynamic dialectics between the introduction of a cash economy and other influences from the Asian continent and internal developments inaugurated the Medieval period (1185–1603), which was characterized by an unusual degree of fluidity and increasing complexity, including further occupational specialization. From the perspective of polity, the Medieval period signaled the beginning of hegemony by military governments, which lasted until the end of World War II.

Significant for an understanding of agrarian representation is Amino's interpretation that Japanese society until the end of the Medieval period had consisted of two systems: one governing residents and the other governing nonresidents (Amino 1980; 1983; 1984). Residents, called the *heimin* (common people), were warriors and farmers—segments of the Japanese population who, after the Medieval period, represented *the* Japanese. Residents were full-fledged members of society; they were free in that they were not owned by other individuals and were allowed to carry arms and to move freely. They were, however, obligated to pay taxes. At the margin of the structure governing the residents were slaves (*genin* and *shojū*) who were owned by other individuals and were "not qualified to be taxed" (Amino 1980:22–23).

Nonresidents comprised two categories: the *shokunin* (professionals) and the special status people, loosely called *eta hinin*. The professionals enjoyed the legally and socially sanctioned privilege of being partially or wholly exempt from taxes.[6] In addition to having the right *not* to pay regular taxes, some professionals were able to cross regional boundaries freely without being checked or taxed as residents were. Therefore, they were able to engage in cross-regional trade. In western Japan, the emperor himself granted these privileges to them because he directly controlled all boundaries between regional lords' territories. In eastern Japan, although some professionals received these privileges from the emperor, many received them from Minamoto-no-Yoritomo, then the shōgun (Amino 1980:133–145). At any rate, professionals apparently enjoyed many freedoms and privileges not accorded residents.

The other group of nonresidents, the eta hinin, were people with special—both positive and negative—statuses at the time. Their occupations were varied; some were artists, artisans, religious specialists, and enter-

tainers, and some worked in occupations that dealt with culturally defined impurities incurred by, for example, the deaths of humans and animals. Although many special status people had no permanent residence,[7]
those who resided in a settlement did so at its boundaries, such as along
riverbanks, under bridges, or near slopes. Because rivers, hills, and
mountains provided natural demarcation lines between settlements,
these locations symbolized spatial marginality, away from the central or
main part of the settlement, where no taxes were levied on them. During
the Medieval period, the term *kawaramono* (people of the river banks)
was applied to people who resided at these places where no tax was as-
sessed (Yokoi 1982:335–339). Another term, *sansho*, referred both to
these marginal areas and to the people who occupied them. The sansho
people held no land, and no land tax was levied against them (Noguchi
1978:89). *Sansho* 'the scattered place' contrasts with *honsho* 'central' or
'real place' (Yokoi 1982:337–339). Hayashiya (1980:130–131) maintains that sansho means "nontaxable." In the Japanese society of the
time "nontaxable" also meant "marginal" or "not mainstream" because
taxes were levied against land and earnings. Yet during most of Medieval
period, these people were not assigned radical negativity as they were
later.[8] The elite members of this group continued to be in close proximity
to the centers of sociopolitical power, including shoguns and emperors,[9]
as they did during the Ancient period.

The Early Modern Period (1603–1868)

The establishment of Tokugawa society—well-known for its oppressive
character—at the beginning of the seventeenth century signaled major
changes in Japanese culture and society that continued for the next three
hundred years. Externally, the government enforced national isolation
by restricting trade and closing ports to most foreigners. It tried to eliminate outside influences and effectively proscribed Christianity. Internally,
the Early Modern period witnessed the development of a caste society[10]
divided into four castes (warriors, farmers, manufacturers, and merchants, in descending order) plus two social categories outside the system—the emperor at the top and the outcastes at the bottom, both marginalized (see Ohnuki-Tierney 1991b for the marginalization of the
emperor).

The unitary social structure of the Early Modern period was radically
different from that of the Medieval period. Instead of multiple structures
of stratification, the structure governing nonresidents was *legally* subor-
dinate to the structure governing residents, which by this time had become the core of Japanese society, perhaps the only social structure. One

sees here the establishment of the social and legal foundations of "agrarian Japan."[11]

An important ordinance separated farmers and warriors. In 1588, just before the Early Modern period, Toyotomi Hideyoshi, the first lord to unify Japan, issued an ordinance known as "the confiscation [hunting] of swords" (*katanagari*). Consisting of three articles, it prohibited the possession of weapons by farmers and was intended to suppress the frequent peasant rebellions toward the end of the Medieval period. Before this ordinance, even within the settled sector, warriors (*bushi*) were part-time farmers, and farmers fought when necessary.[12] The peasants' right to land was at least nominally guaranteed by the government through registration, and peasants became well-defined members of society (see also Kurushima 1986: especially 274–277). The ordinance, nevertheless, deprived peasants of the right to use arms to protest or to defend themselves even when necessary, although during the Early Modern period warriors lived in castle towns and were unable or unwilling to defend the peasants in the villages from whom they extracted rice taxes.

It was during this long period that "agrarian Japan" became the dominant representation and "agrarian Ideology" became hegemonic, completing the picture of an "agrarian Japan" whose social and legal foundation became well-established. The rice taxation system likely played a significant role in the construction of agrarian ideology. Some elites took an active role in its construction although with varying degrees of conscious intent.

Agrarian Japan and the Nativists

Scholars of the nativist school (*kokugakuha*) of the late Early Modern period were most influential in the construction of agrarian ideology. Bellah emphasizes that a functional ethic with a strong emphasis on productivity, which he (1970:114) calls economic rationalization and aligns with the Protestant ethic, came to govern the moral system of the period. Occupations that were nonproductive in the agrarian sense were devalued. But the interpretation of productivity was not a simple matter. Although some scholars devalued merchants and, to a certain degree, artisans because they were nonproductive in the agrarian sense, others, including prominent kokugakuha scholars, such as Ishida Baigan (1685–1744) and Motoori Norinaga (1730–1801), considered merchants, "who did not produce from their sweat," productive. The interpretation rested on whether merchants were seen as making profits for themselves alone, or whether they performed services for others and for the economy of the nation at large (Bellah 1970:107–132).

Harootunian (1988) also details discussions among the nativist scholars who, during the eighteenth century, sought to establish a distinct and sacred Japanese identity. These scholars attempted to counter the strong influence from China upon Japanese culture. They sought the sources of pure "Japaneseness" in agricultural values and the ancient Shinto religion; Buddhism and Confucianism were both introduced from the Asian continent, from India via China and from China, respectively. These scholars reconstituted agricultural work and valorized it as the ancient way, that is, the pure Japanese way (Harootunian 1988:23). In their formulation, agricultural practice as well as consumption of agricultural products became religious practices. Thus, Hirata Atsutane (1776–1843) insisted that the worshipping of Toyouke, the agricultural deity, should consist not only of daily rituals but also of hard work in the field and proper consumption of agricultural products (Harootunian 1988:212). In short, agriculture introduced from the continent was again called on to define the presumed uniqueness of the Japanese in the discourse of self and other.

Agrarian Ideology in Everyday Life

The degree to which agrarianism successfully penetrated the thoughts of the elites as well as the people is evident in various forms of popular culture. For example, the following *haiku* poems by Issa (1763–1827) confirm that rice planting songs had become a familiar symbol of spring, even for those far removed from farming, and that people felt uncomfortable or, at least, were made to feel they were not "working" as much as rice farmers:

A midday nap	Motainaya
The song of the rice planters	Hiruneshite kiku
Makes me ashamed of myself[13]	Taue uta

(Kobayashi Issa 1929:508)

A midday nap	Tanohito o
Worship in mind	Kokoro de ogamu
The people in rice paddies	Hirune kana

(Kobayashi Issa 1929:473; my translation)

Sayings dated to this time also illustrate the sacred quality of rice, and some are still familiar to contemporary Japanese. For example, if one steps on a rice grain, one's leg will become crooked. In another, the diner will go blind if he or she leaves even a single grain of rice in a rice bowl. Agrarian productivity received primary emphasis, and hard work on the farm became not only virtuous but also was assigned an aesthetic value.

The pervasiveness with which rice agriculture and an agrarian image came to represent *the* Japan is well illustrated in woodblock prints of the masters of the *ukiyoe* (paintings of the floating world) of the Early Modern period, although these masters were more likely agents of consumption and dissemination of agrarianism than of its construction. I offer my own interpretation of three series of woodblock prints. First is the series of woodblocks executed by Katsushika Hokusai (1760–1849), entitled *Hyakunin Isshu Uba ga Etoki* (Pictures of one hundred poems by one hundred poets, explained by the wet-nurse). They are illustrations of the well-known collection of one hundred poems (*Hyakunin Isshu*; one hundred poems, one poem each) selected and completed in 1235 by Fujiwara no Teika (1162–1241) as Hokusai interpreted them from the perspective of the mid–eighteenth century. Hokusai, who started to work on this series at age seventy-six, completed prints for only twenty-seven of the one hundred poems but left many line drawings. Eighty-nine of them are reproduced in the collection by Morse (1989). The most common motif by far relates to rice and rice agriculture and appears in twenty-six prints.[14] Some have only sheaves of rice stalks somewhere in the scene, others are more focused on rice agriculture, including rice farmers at work (no. 14); flooded rice paddies in the background (no. 19); a sheaf of harvested rice on top of a pole in a scene from the Gion festival in Kyoto, which used to be held at harvest time (no. 22); rice harvesting (no. 39); a scene of the full-moon ritual (*jūgoya*), which is celebrated with rice wine (in the print) and rice cakes (not included in the print) (no. 68); winnowing rice (no. 71); making rice wine (no. 78); and pounding rice to make rice cakes (no. 79) (numbers are Morse's and appear at the top of the pages opposite the prints.)

This contrasts with the way the sea and the mountains are portrayed in the prints. Mountains, especially Mt. Fuji, appear often but never with any activities—no hunting, no lumbering, and no plant gathering in the woods. The sea also appears but only occasionally with fishermen. The sea appears twice as background (nos. 20, 21), twice with boats sailing at a distance (nos. 4, 7), four times with people crossing water in a boat (nos. 27 [sea], 36 [river?], 37 [pond?], 76 [sea]). Others involving the sea include one of a large boat with lovers in hiding peeking through an opening (no. 18) and another of people digging for clams (no. 92). One print depicts a salt-making scene (no. 97) but no sea in the background, and another shows workers repairing a boat (no. 33). Only one scene includes fishermen (no. 3), and one has abalone divers (*ama*) (no. 11). In sum, in sharp contrast to the agrarian activities that are common themes in these prints, the sea and activities related to it appear far less frequently.

Similar motifs of harvested rice fields, flooded rice paddies, bundles of rice (komedawara), and rice sheaves appear in the woodblock prints by Andō (Utakawa) Hiroshige (1797–1858) in his "Tōkaidō Gojū-San-Tsugi" (Fifty-three stations along the Tōkaidō) (Gotō 1975). The prints in Kiso Kaidō Rokujū-Kyū-Tsugi (Sixty-nine stations along the Kiso road) (Gotō 1976), which contains prints by both Hiroshige and Keisai Eisen (1790–?), contain similar motifs.

The recurrent motifs of rice and rice agriculture in these woodblock prints represent not rice and rice agriculture per se but something far more abstract. At the most obvious level, they signal seasons of the year. Flooded rice fields, like rice-planting songs, are the most familiar sign of spring or early summer; it is the time of birth and growth. Rice harvesting scenes, including sheaves of rice stalks—the most frequently used motif—represent fall and its joyful harvest but also the end of the growing season.

What is striking from the perspective of representation is that these cycles of rice growth have become markers of the seasons for all Japanese. For urbanites, fishermen, and all other nonagrarian people, life became marked by rice and its growth.

At an even more abstract level, travelers are often depicted against these agricultural scenes, suggesting that the scenes of rice and rice agriculture are a backdrop for an unchanging Japan, in contrast to the transient and changing Japan epitomized by Edo (Tokyo) where both roads (Tōkaidō and Kisokaidō) lead. There is no need to repeat a well-known anthropological discussion that travel constitutes a liminal experience that takes place "between and betwixt" ordinary time and place (cf. V. Turner 1975). Thus, against these travelers who seem not to belong to the scene, rice sheaves, fields, and farmers represent "agrarian Japan"— Japan in its pristine unchanging form. Far from the "reality" of mud, sweat, and fertilizer, rice agriculture, like rice itself, was valorized into aesthetics as were the "English countryside" and peasants in the French impressionists' paintings discussed in chapter 8.

Agrarian Occupational Identity and Nonagrarian Income in the Late Early Modern Period

Paradoxically, just as the agrarian ideology was intensifying, Japan was becoming increasingly urban and nonagricultural. As the Early Modern period progressed, more than half of the income of an "agrarian village" derived from nonagrarian activities, as pointed out by T. Smith (1988) in his study of the 1840 survey of Kaminoseki District of Chōshū in western Japan. On the one hand, the villagers in this county identified their occupations as agrarian:

> Most districts had a heavy preponderance of the latter [farming]; even Murotsu and Hirao, the two districts with the largest proportion of nonagriculturalists, had nearly as many farm as nonfarm families. Occupational figures therefore give the impression of an overwhelmingly agricultural county. (T. Smith 1988:78)

On the other hand:

> Yet, the ways in which income was earned give a very different impression. Income came about equally from farming on the one hand, and industry, transport, fishing, wage remittance, and central government expenditures on the other. Nonagricultural pursuits supplied 55 percent of the income of the county, and the proportion was over 70 percent in four districts. Thus Kaminoseki's population was predominantly agricultural but earned rather more than half its income from nonfarm work. (T. Smith 1988:79)

Thus, even during the Early Modern period, "agrarian Japan" ironically meant "predominantly agricultural" in occupational identity but "predominantly nonagricultural" in income activities—a truly important finding to show that in farmers' perceptions of themselves, an agrarian image was important, just as rice has been important for practically all Japanese, whether or not it was a staple food. Frequently cited figures, such as 50 percent or 80 percent of the population being farmers during the Early Modern period, must be seen in this context.

The Modern Period (Kin-Gendai) (1868–Present)

Even though the Early Modern period was far less agrarian than hitherto understood, without doubt when the Meiji period began, Japan was still heavily agricultural (Rosovsky 1966). Further depopulation of rural areas occurred as Japan began to rapidly industrialize. While Japan was becoming more urbanized and industrialized, "agrarian Japan" persisted, and successive governments continued as agents of this construction and representation. True, as T. Smith (1959:213) observes, the architects of modern Japan were ambitious fellows from rural Japan. Yet, the cultural landscape was too complex to attribute responsibility to a few politicians.

The intensification of agrarian ideology was echoed in the trajectory of the research career of Yanagita Kunio (1875–1962), the founder of the

Japanese folklore cum anthropological school. As did Malinowski in British social anthropology, Yanagita introduced fieldwork to this discipline. Through extensive fieldwork throughout Japan, Yanagita and his students gathered detailed ethnographic data. They focused on the *jōmin*, the ordinary people.[15]

Earlier in his career, Yanagita painstakingly studied various people in the mountains, including woodcraft workers and other artisans, street entertainers, noninstitutionalized religious specialists, and women and children.[16] The best ethnographic and historical information on the artistic and religious specialists who had been defined as "outcasts" since 1572 is found in his thirty-six volume collected works. Ōta (n.d.,12) captures Yanagita's contribution: "Against the hegemony of political authority that derived its legitimation only from written documents and religious establishments, Yanagita's folklore was the effort to represent the alienated, silenced 'common people' (jōmin) whose history had not been recorded." Yanagita and his students studied these people in a search for "the original pure Japanese culture," which at that time Yanagita (e.g., 1981b) believed had been preserved in the way of life of the people who lived in the mountains.

Yanagita's common people (jōmin), however, gradually were transformed into farmers (*nōmin*), especially rice farmers. Miyata (1990:37) believes that Yanagita's notion of the common people had shifted by 1935.[17] A well-known statement by Yanagita is that one cannot understand Japanese culture without studying rice although research on rice does not exhaust studies on Japanese culture. Yanagita, who was a bureaucrat in the Ministry of Farming, Lumbering, and Trade (Nōshō-mushō) from 1900 to 1902, contributed to the creation of the agrarian myth in the years following the Russo-Japanese war (Gluck 1985:180–181). Harootunian emphasizes Yanagita's rural Japan as a construction: "But Yanagita's countryside was an imaginary, constructed from a discourse aimed at conserving and preserving traces of a lost presence" (Harootunian 1988:416). I do not find Yanagita free of the ideology prevailing at the time, but I think there is more than a rice grain of truth in his statement about the importance of rice in Japanese culture although in a very different sense from what he intended. The value of his massive ethnography, gathered through painstaking fieldwork, about people written off from the official history of Japan, cannot be questioned; no matter how faulty this work may be, it cannot be dismissed purely as construction.

Gluck succinctly captures the major characterization of "agrarian Japan" during Meiji Japan: "For an industrializing economy they reinvigorated an agrarian myth, and in an urbanizing society they apotheosized the village" (Gluck 1985:265). Productivity, as a form of worship, became the highest virtue, even after it meant industrial rather than agrarian productivity.

"Modern Japan" inaugurated by the Meiji "Restoration" soon plunged into militarism and the catastrophe of World War II. During this time, especially during World War II, the agrarian ideology was ruthlessly used by the military government. White rice, that is, domestic rice, was constructed to represent the purity of the Japanese self. The government told the civilians that the Japanese rice was sent to soldiers at the front to give them energy to win the war; Japan's victory would guarantee abundant domestic rice rather than the "distasteful" foreign rice whose consumption epitomized the suffering of the Japanese.

During the military era many foodstuffs, especially rice, were cleverly used for nationalistic purposes by the military elite who tried to establish Japan's national identity and promote patriotism among the people. "Rising sun lunches (*hinomaru bentō*), appeared, typically, a box lunch with a red pickled plum (*umeboshi*) in the center of white rice (for a nationalistic account of the rising sun lunch, see Higuchi 1985). Variations included rice in a cone, shaped like Mount Fuji, with a paper rising sun flag on top that was served to children in restaurants.

Contemporary Japan

"Agrarian Japan" is alive and well in contemporary Japan, as noted in chapter 2, even though full-time farmers are becoming so rare that they may soon be designated "human national treasures" (*ningen kokuhō*).[18] Some attribute its continuing strength to the work of prominent politicians from rural areas. Of the sixteen prime ministers since the end of World War II, for example, only two are from the northeastern rice country.[19] Thus, agrarianism is far more complex and deeply rooted in culture than the creation of a handful of elites.

Although the transition from Shōwa to Akihito emperor nearly coincided with the California rice issue, and a considerable furor arose about the imperial rituals, the emperor and the imperial system were rarely mentioned in the controversy over the California rice issue. A surprising aspect of the interrelationship between ideology, economy, and polity in relation to the imperial system unfolds. When Japanese opposition to the importation of California rice was voiced (see chapter 7), it was couched in the language of "rice as self"; rice remained a powerful metaphor of self. In contrast, in contemporary Japan the emperor has ceased to be a metaphor for the Japanese. In fact, most Japanese would strongly oppose the idea that the Japanese people are represented by the emperor, whether Shōwa or Akihito.

Many contemporary Japanese are unaware of the connection between rice and the imperial system; when the Shōwa emperor was ill, television reported that the emperor had asked about the rice crop, and some young Japanese learned for the first time that a connection existed between the emperor and rice. Until the mass media began to discuss the *daijōsai* (ōnamesai), even older people scarcely recognized the term let alone knew the content of the ritual. Probably, no Japanese today believes that the emperor is the officiant of the rice harvest rituals whose power ensures a good rice crop. Some Japanese oppose both the imperial system and the importation of California rice. If the rice/emperor connection were recognized, opponents of the imperial system should welcome the importation of foreign rice. But even for these people, rice remains a metaphor of a post-industrial Japan in which rice agriculture has little economic value.

The California rice incident revealed that the imperial system had lost its connection with the rice symbolism. But the association between the two was never close except during the Ancient period. Rice symbolism does not presuppose, as scholars once assumed, the exclusive engagement of the people in rice agriculture or the quantitative importance of rice as food. The association between the imperial system and rice symbolism has been only partially retained during subsequent periods through the performance, at times intermittent, of rice rituals at court. Until the Meiji period, the imperial court was far removed from the people. Without the modern mass media, it is doubtful that the imperial harvest rituals had much impact on the people. As Taki (1990) observes, the visualization of the emperor began with the Meiji emperor when photography was introduced to Japan. Consequently, the imperial system and rice symbolism seem to have taken semi-independent historical courses.

Rice as Self in Everyday Life

Without question agrarian cosmology was systematically developed by the imperial court during the Ancient period and was used later by successive military governments as agrarian ideology. But "Japan" as a "rice agrarian nation" was not simply a construct by the elites, imperial or military, trickled down from the top. The cosmology based on rice agriculture as described in chapter 4 retained its importance to the people through their religions, folktales, and daily customs.

The importance of rice for an individual Japanese begins early in life. Rice gruel was a substitute for breast milk, symbolically linking rice to the most basic human relationship—the bond between mother and offspring. The association between mother and rice as the food for daily commensality among family members is also expressed in the symbolism of the wooden spatula (*shamoji*) used to scoop rice into individual bowls, which was, until recently, considered a symbol of the *shufu*. Shufu refers to the female *head* of the household, rather than simply "house*wife*," and the term reflects the considerable power that the Japanese shufu has over household affairs. Therefore, the transference of the spatula is a significant event that marks the time when the position and role are vacated by the current shufu and transferred to the next shufu (Yanagita 1951: 264–265). The event is especially important when the new shufu is the wife of the firstborn male who carries on the family line—the primogeniture system prevalent before the end of World War II. Examining the custom of transferring the spatula in various parts of Japan, Nōda (1943:52–56) emphasizes the central role played by the shufu as the central pillar (*daikokubashira*) of the household. In some regions the event is marked by a ritual. The time of the transference varies from region to region, in some cases occurring twenty years after the marriage of the "new" couple. A folk song from Sado Island and Shinshū, recorded by Nōda (1943:53), describes the custom in that region: "It has been six years since they got together [in marriage] and they are raising children; it is time to hand over the rice spatula to the daughter-in-law (*yome*)."

Even today, when the rice spatula has lost its symbolic significance and no longer represents the rights of the female head of the family, in most households, rural or urban, the female head of the household scoops rice into individual bowls for the family and guests at the table. Until the electric rice cooker appeared, cooking of rice was the most important task for women and their cooking skill was judged by their ability to cook it well. Whereas side dishes are served on individual plates ahead of time in urban Japanese households today, rice alone remains the common food to be distributed by the woman of the house. Commensality within a household is symbolized by the act of distributing rice from a single container, and it is objectified in the rice spatula. The collective self of the family—the most basic unit of Japanese society—is constructed through the sharing of rice during daily meals.

As an expression of commensality between the living family members and the deceased, the daily offering to the family ancestral alcove continues to be rice. Today, whenever rice is cooked, not necessarily in the morning as was the custom, it must be offered to the ancestors before the living partake of it. When I presented a paper on rice in May 1990 in Hokkaidō, some scholars insisted that the Japanese diet had changed to such an extent that white rice was no longer essential. When I asked, however, if they could envision a day when the Japanese would offer something other than white rice, perhaps fried rice, to the ancestral alcove, everyone emphatically agreed that it would never happen. I was able to drive home my point, white rice, "Japanese rice," is symbolically important even today.

In 1989 I heard an expression from a Niigata farmer, "Komenuka sangō areba yōshi ni dasuna" (If you have enough rice to produce three gō [.18 liters] of rice powder you should not give up your son for adoption). Rice and rice powder (made from bran and other rice-by-products while brown rice is polished), are measures of wealth as well as metaphors for the family as a corporate group, *we*, whose members should not be given away to *they*.

Expressions commonly used today even by urban Japanese, such as *hiyameshi o kuu* (to eat cold rice) and *tanin no meshi o kuu* (to eat someone else's rice) refer to a situation in which people no longer are surrounded by the warm comfort of their families. Because rice must be served hot (unless used as sushi or onigiri [rice balls]), these expressions refer to ill fortune and going through hardships among strangers.[20]

Reseeding by individual farm households also contributes to rice as a metaphor of self. As noted in chapter 2, until recently, farmers kept some of their own crops for next year's seed so that there were innumerable varieties of rice in Japan, each family producing its own version. Such reseeding practices are not confined to Japan. Gudeman and Rivera (1990:12–13, 118) describe the importance of reseeding by individual families in Colombia and also use the house metaphor—keeping the crop "inside the doors."

Beyond individual families, the members of a rural community also share rice and rice cakes as the food for commensality in rituals when relatives residing elsewhere return to dine and drink together. Today, these are often the only occasions when young family members working in cities return home to rural areas.

Rice has been an important food for commensality for urbanites as well. Today's New Year celebration is a nationwide ritual that involves the same types of commensality between deities and humans and among humans as the agricultural rituals. Both rural and urban Japanese offer mirror-rice cakes (*kagamimochi*) to the deities for the New Year.[21] Two mirror-shaped (round) rice cakes are placed on top of each other. On January 11, the date of *kagamibiraki* (the opening of the mirror), the hardened rice cakes are broken up, and the pieces are distributed to all members of the family and eaten. Because a mirror represents the deities, these rice cakes embody the souls of rice and, thus, are thought to give power to those who consume them (Yanagita 1951:94–95). Offering and consuming them are acts of commensality—both between deities and humans and among humans.

Although rice and the rice spatula symbolize commensality within the household, wine (sake) is the most important item of commensality in social settings, especially among men. It introduces an element of social exchange. A basic rule of social sake drinking is that one never pours sake for oneself; one pours it for someone else who, in turn, pours sake into one's own sake cup in a never-ending series. The word *hitorizake* (drinking alone) is an expression for loneliness—nothing is lonelier than having to pour one's own sake.

Rice and rice products are also the foods used to establish and maintain the most important human relationships. Not only during ritual occasions but in the day-to-day lives of the Japanese, rice and rice products play a crucial role in commensal activities. Rice stands for *we*, that is, whatever social group one belongs to. "To eat from the same rice-cooking pan" (*onaji kama no meshi o kuu*) is a common expression for close human relationships that emphasizes the strong sense of fellowship arising from meal sharing. If you eat together, you are members of the same social group; you become *we* as opposed to *they*.

The metaphoric association between rice and a social group does not stop at small social group face-to-face interactions. It extends to larger social groups, including Japan as a whole. Here rice paddies take on a crucial role. As discussed in connection with the nativists and the woodblock prints, rice paddies stand for Japanese space, time, and ultimately "our land."

Agrarian Cosmology, Agrarian Ideology

Rice agrarian cosmology has remained more powerful than both the imperial system and agriculture itself. The symbolic structure based on wet-rice agriculture was the basis of the ancient imperial system. The political and economic foundations were soon stripped away from the imperial system in subsequent periods by military elites who developed it into agrarian ideology and successfully propagated it to the rest of the population quite to the advantage of the military elites. Thus, a structure of meaning that was relevant only for early rice agriculturists was adopted by the rest of the people throughout history, most of whom were engaged in nonagrarian occupations.

That the symbolism of rice has remained more important for the Japanese than rice agriculture itself is quite remarkable. Japan was not as agrarian as sometimes portrayed even during the Early Modern period, the period considered most agrarian in Japanese history. In today's high-technology era, rice agriculture quantitatively is not important. Yet valorization of the village, the countryside, and agriculture continues through the government, mass media, and tourist industry—a common phenomenon in many parts of the world.

The success of the representation of Japan as agrarian did not rest on the imperial system. The skillfulness with which political elites mystified and naturalized agrarian ideology during subsequent periods is only partly responsible for its success, which owes in large measure to the symbolic significance of rice and rice paddies in day-to-day practices through which they became powerful metaphors of the collective self. Commensality binds together people who interact face to face in almost all societies to establish a sense of community, or *we*. The food chosen for commensality, therefore, often becomes identified with the social group, that is, becomes a metaphor for them.

No less powerful as a metaphor are the rice paddies. They stand for "our ancestral land" for the individual farm family who, until recently, raised their rice from their own seeds. Their collective self is reinforced by the twin metaphors of rice and rice paddies. Ultimately, rice paddies also stand for the Japanese nation itself with its quintessential beauty and changing colors marking "the Japanese seasons."

The representation of Japan as agrarian marginalized the nonagrarian population. For example, the well-known *Suwa Shinkō* (Suwa belief) represents a vestige of the beliefs and rituals of hunters (*matagi*) in which animal sacrifice was once practiced. The deity addressed in their ritual is said to have resisted the Yamato hegemony (Yanagita 1951:310). Even more victimized in this historical process were the special status people who became scapegoats. They were assigned the impurity of the dominant Japanese, who objectified their own impurity by creating "the internal other."

If rice farmers rebelled against their local power holders using symbols made of rice plants, thereby identifying themselves with the rice deity, nonrice agrarian and nonagrarian people, too, have shared the daily practices and annual rituals based on the symbolism of rice to a great degree. Conversely, the symbolism of rice and rice paddies has been so thoroughly embedded in folkways that, ironically, it has become fertile ground for any political leader to manipulate for chauvinistic purposes.

Seven

Rice in the Discourse of Selves and Others

THROUGH historical processes rice and rice paddies have come to represent the collective self of a social group within Japanese society from the smallest unit, of a family, to Japan as a whole. The collective self of the Japanese has undergone historical changes, changes that are almost always intimately related to historical developments outside of Japan.

In anthropology, the classical formulation of the person/self by Mauss ([1938]1985) is quasi-evolutionary—the transformation of the *personnage* (role) in primitive holism into the *personne* (self) characterizing modern individualism, with the *moi* (awareness of self) as a human universal. Dumont's ([1966] 1970, 1986) argument rests on a complex comparison along the two axes of holism/individualism and the hierarchy/equalitarianism. A plethora of publications on the self and personhood includes an important collection edited by Carrithers, Collins, and Lukes (1985).

Of a number of approaches to a study of personhood, the tradition advocated by G. H. Mead, Charles Taylor, and others views the self as an agency. Scholars of postmodern persuasion have alerted to the importance of Bakhtin's "polyphony," which derives from a set of assumptions about the "negotiated realities" that is "multisubjective, power-laden, and incongruent" (Clifford and Marcus 1986:14–15). Kondo's work for Japan, most appropriately entitled *Crafting Selves* (1990), is an example of this approach. Kelly (1991) offers an extensive overview of publications on the personhood of the Japanese published in English. From the perspective of psychological anthropology, Shweder and his co-authors (Shweder and Miller 1985; Shweder and Sullivan 1990) have been influential.

My concern in this book is the self-identities of social groups. When a social group is juxtaposed against another, each group often constitutes a collective self. Here the "context" shifts to the "negotiation" between two social groups, often power laden whether the social groups are within a nation-state or comprise an entire population against another. Thus, various individual identities within a population become usually, although not necessarily always, irrelevant when they conceptualize themselves in relation to other peoples, as one has seen all too frequently in recent decades with the rise of nationalism and ethnic identity.

The two approaches to the self—an individual self in a given social context and the collective self of a social group defined in relation to another social group—are, needless to say, not contradictory or in conflict (see chap. 1, n. 4). The Japanese conceptualization of the person and humans has given a conceptual framework with which the Japanese have interpreted others in their historical encounters.

The Personhood in Japanese Culture:
A Basic Framework

The Japanese conception of the person as a *socially* interdependent person is succinctly expressed in the two characters that form the word for *humans—ningen*. The character for *nin* means humans, and the character for *gen* means among. The ningen is relationally defined in reference to other persons in a social context and dialectically defined by both humans and a social group to which one belongs (Watsuji 1959).[1] In this view, a social group does *not* consist of atomized individuals, each making his or her own decisions.[2]

Some Japanese daily practices articulate the interdependency or, more accurately, relational definition of the self and other. For example, in daily discourse, personal pronouns and their possessive cases often are not used, but the inflections of verbs, auxiliary verbs, nouns, and so forth express the persons—both the speaker and the addressee—as they are *related* in the context of discourse. If, for example, someone says, *okuruma*, which consists of *o*, the honorific prefix for a noun, and *kuruma*, which means car, then without question the car belongs to the addressee who holds a higher social status than the speaker in this particular discourse context (for details, see Ohnuki-Tierney [in press]; see also Martin 1964; Miller 1967; Shibamoto 1987:269–272).[3]

Needless to say, Japanese are not always reverent toward the social other nor do they always interact harmoniously with each other and sacrifice themselves to the goals of their social groups. In fact, in a type of discourse that presupposes sensitivity and an understanding of finely tuned rules, they can effectively insult or ridicule their social superiors by strategically choosing inappropriate speech levels or transgressing other rules of discourse, without ever using curse words—very few exist in Japanese. Gilbert and Sullivan lyrics capture how an inappropriately used superpolite form can be devastatingly ridiculous.

The relational construction of self at the individual level in a given social context is paralleled by the construction of the Japanese identity in relation to other peoples. At this level, the important cosmological principle of the Stranger Deity comes into play. As noted, the Stranger Deity who possesses dual natures and powers—the benevolent, pure energy of nigitama and the violent, destructive energy of aratama—constitutes the reflexive self of humans, who, likewise, have dual qualities. For humans to remain pure, they must harness the pure energy of the Stranger Deity.

The structure of self and other as defined in the cosmological scheme has been translated into historical discourse in which foreigners are symbolically equivalent to the Stranger Deity. Contrary to the stereotype of Japan as an isolated country tucked away in the northeast corner of the world, Japan's history actually comprises a series of conjunctures that have been interpreted through the lens of the Japanese structure of self and other, and they, in turn, have forced the Japanese to reconceptualize their notion of the self. Thus, the desire to reach for the other has propelled the Japanese to imitate and then surpass the superior qualities of the Chinese and Westerners, whether a writing system, the arts, or technology and science. In the flow of history, the Japanese collective self must be continuously redefined as Japan's position in relation to other nations undergoes changes.

Of all the conjunctures, the two that sent the most profound and lasting shock waves throughout the country were Japan's encounter with the highly developed civilization of Tang China between the fifth and seventh centuries and the encounter with Western civilization at the end of the nineteenth century. In both cases, the Japanese were overwhelmed by the civilizations "out there" and hurriedly and earnestly attempted to learn about and imitate them. The heretofore illiterate Japanese adopted the Chinese writing system in its entirety, even though the two spoken languages were totally unrelated and, thus, not transferable without considerable difficulty. Likewise, metallurgy, city planning, and a range of features of Chinese civilization were eagerly adopted by the Japanese, who, nonetheless, strenuously resisted Chinese civilization in a chauvinistic effort to protect their own culture and collective self as detailed in Pollack (1986).

When the country reopened at the end of the nineteenth century after three centuries of isolation, it again painfully encountered a "superior" civilization, this time the West, with its scientific and technological advances. Again, the Japanese avidly adopted aspects of this civilization while guarding their Japanese identity and self. By this time, China had suffered internal and external conflicts and had declined in international standing. The West thus replaced China as the transcendental other. As Pollack (1986:53) succinctly puts it, "During the last century and a half the West has been the antithetical term in the dialectic, and as always it has been in that 'other' that Japan has sought its own image, peering anxiously for signs of its own identity into the mirror of the rest of the world."

Although this view of Japanese history is, admittedly, oversimplified, it highlights how the internal developments in Japanese society resulted from Japan's interactions with the rest of the world. These interactions also had a significant impact on the Japanese concept of the collective self—who they are as a people—because the Japanese, or for that matter any other people's, concept of the self, individual or collective, is always defined in relation to the other.

In the discourse of self and other, rice has served as a powerful vehicle for the Japanese to think about themselves in relation to other peoples.

Domestic Rice as Self and Foreign Rice as the Other: Japanese versus Other Asians

Rice, the dominant metaphor for a social group within society, surfaces again and again in Japanese deliberations of self at crucial historical junctures. Rice has been a critical metaphor by which the Japanese have defined and redefined themselves through interaction with other peoples throughout history.

As noted in chapter 4, the two myth-histories of the eighth century and the imperial ritual represent a strenuous attempt to appropriate rice agriculture as the defining feature of Japanese culture in opposition to Chinese culture from which rice agriculture was, in fact, introduced. The Japanese, who had not previously developed a writing system of their own, adopted the Chinese writing system in its entirety and wrote down a Japanese version of the origin of rice agriculture, thus using another marker of Chinese "civilization." Furthermore, they adopted the Chinese designation for Japan, *Nihon* (the base where the sun rises); from the Chinese perspective Japan is situated at the base where the sun rises (Amino, personal communication). Although some people have adopted other people's religions, or even language, and the Japanese case is by no means unique, these are striking examples of how the Japanese concept of self was born in the encounter with the Chinese who were interpreted through the conceptual scheme of the Stranger Deity.

Despite the eagerness with which the Japanese adopted features of Chinese civilization, the Japanese self could not simply merge with that of the Chinese. In an effort to redefine the Japanese identity, in addition to appropriating rice agriculture and other features of Chinese civilization as their own, the Japanese distinguished items imported from China linguistically. Thus, objects with the prefix *kan* (Han) designated things from the Han, or Chinese, including *kanji* (Chinese characters) and *kanbun* (texts written in Chinese characters). Likewise, the character for Tang, read either as *kara* or *tō*, also signals a Chinese origin, *karafū*

(Chinese style), *karatoji* (a book bound in the Chinese style), and *kara-mono* (imported goods from China; imported goods in general).

Although the phrase *wakan secchū* meant a combination of Japanese and Chinese ways, a most revealing expression for the relationship between self and other is *wakon kansai* (the Japanese soul and Chinese knowledge). Referring to the best of both worlds the phrase represents a Japanese effort to preserve their identity as "the Japanese *soul*."[4] As noted, in ancient Japan rice was symbolically equivalent to the soul, which, in turn, was conterminous with the deity. Highly important is that the phrase "the Japanese soul and Chinese knowledge" reveals Japanese insistence on their own identity in the soul cum rice introduced from China. Furthermore, in the Japanese concept, humans are distinguished from animals not through their rationality, as in the Western concept, but through the capacity for emotion, which is generated by the soul (Ohnuki-Tierney 1987:200). Therefore, a seemingly simple expression like wakon kansai is derived from one of the basic conceptual foundations of Japanese culture that has undergone significant transformations.

As long as the Chinese remained a well-defined other, the Japanese task of defining themselves vis-à-vis the Chinese was relatively easy. It became more difficult, however, when the world of the Japanese no longer consisted solely of the Japanese and Chinese. By the eighteenth century, the Japanese had become acutely aware of various Western civilizations. The Portuguese brought firearms, soap, and other goods while the Dutch impressed the Japanese with their medical system, which was, to some Japanese, more advanced than the Chinese medicine introduced to Japan earlier. The Germans, the English, and the Americans awed the Japanese with their science, medicine, and various technological skills. All were usually seen collectively as "Westerners" without distinguishing nationalities or individuals. By this time, Chinese civilization—once the mirror for the Japanese—was no longer at the apex of its power, culturally or politically. To further complicate the matter, the Japanese had to face the fact that Westeners lumped the Japanese indiscriminately as Orientals, just as, ironically, the Japanese lumped all Westerners together.

This more complex international scene required the Japanese to both distinguish themselves from the West, on the one hand, and to extricate themselves from other Asians, or "Orientals," on the other. Although the distinction between Japanese and Westerners could be readily made and expressed as rice versus meat (or bread), the distinction between the Japanese and other Asians was more difficult to identify. In particular, the distinction could not be expressed as rice versus some other food item because other Asians also eat rice. The distinction, therefore, had to be made on the basis of domestic rice grown on Japanese soil versus foreign rice.

Domestic rice (*naichimai*) as a metaphor for the Japanese as contrasted with foreign rice (*gaimai*) as a metaphor for other Asians surfaced toward the end of the Early Modern period. During the eighteenth and nineteenth centuries nativist scholars striving to establish the Japanese identity chose agrarian ideology and rice agriculture as the pristine Japanese way. For Hirata Atsutane (1776–1843), one of the four major figures in the nativist movement, rice cultivation was a critical concern; rice production and consumption were equivalent to the worship of Shinto deities and the repayment of their blessings. In his search for an exclusive Japanese claim to divine rice, he degraded Chinese rice as "inferior" and "begun by the mandate of men," and, therefore, "those who eat are weak and enervated" (Harootunian 1988:211–212). Since Hirata considered eating and working as religious acts, he demeaned other peoples who quarreled during meals "like dogs" and claimed that other peoples admired the Japanese because of their good table manners (Harootunian 1988:213). To Hirata, then, humans are to animals as Japanese are to other peoples. Most important, these "other peoples" who eat inferior rice and have bad table manners are non-Japanese Asians.

One of the ways in which nativist scholars of the late Early Modern period and Meiji scholars attempted to distinguish the Japanese from the Chinese was by objectifying China with the label Shina, a designation for China by other peoples. In Asia, the name Shina first appeared in an Indian sutra and was adopted by the Japanese during the mid-Early Modern period; it was used until the end of World War II. The Chinese designation for their country is *Chūgoku* (the Middle Kingdom, or, literally, the country at the center), which expresses the centrality of China (*chū* = center) in their view (cf. S. Tanaka n.d.). By adopting the label of Shina, the Japanese deliberately chose to ignore the significance that the Chinese placed on their own representation to the world.

The Japanese effort to extricate themselves from other Asians during the Meiji period continued to be expressed in the metaphorical uses of rice. For example, in the *Kōfu* (The miners), a novel by Natsume Sōseki, one of the best known writers of the period, a nineteen-year-old son from a "good family" runs away from home in Tokyo and is led by a dubious character to a mine. The miner's occupation is described: to ask if there is an occupation more inferior (*katō*) than mining is like asking if there are any days in the year after December 31. The novel, written as a first-person narrative, recounts the young man's experiences in a lead mine. When his first meal at the mine is served, he notices a rice container (*meshibitsu*). He has not drunk a drop of water or eaten rice for two days and two nights. Although he is depressed ("the soul has shrunk"), the sight of a rice container immediately awakens an enormous appetite. He scoops the rice into his rice bowl and proceeds to eat with his chopsticks.

To his surprise, however, the rice is too slippery to manage. After trying three times unsuccessfully, he pauses to figure out why; in his nineteen years of life, such an experience has never happened. As he pauses, the other miners, who have been watching this newcomer, burst into laughter. One of the miners shouts, "Look what he is doing" while another says, "He thinks the rice is 'the silver rice (ginshari)' even though today is not a festival." Yet another says, "Without tasting the Chinese rice (*nankinmai*), how can he assume he can be a miner!" (Natsume Sōseki 1984:560–561). He hurriedly shoves the rice into his mouth and finds that it does not taste like rice; it tastes like the mud used to build a wall. In another passage, a miner explains to the protagonist that he had gone to school, but his misbehavior resulted in "eating rice meals (meshi) in the mines" (Natsume Sōseki 1984:556).

Another index of his miserable living conditions is the presence of innumerable bed bugs, called *nankinmushi* (Chinese bugs) in Japanese. The novel ends with the young man summing up his experiences at the mine as eating Chinese rice and being eaten by Chinese bugs (Natsume Sōseki 1984:674).

An educated miner, who also had "fallen," urges the young man, "You are a Japanese, aren't you? If you are a Japanese, get out of the mine and find an occupation that is good for Japan."

The dismal life at the mine is symbolized by Chinese rice and Chinese bugs, whereas life outside is the proper life for Japanese. The symbolic opposition of /domestic rice: Chinese rice :: silver: mud/ represent the basic opposition of /Japanese self: *marginalized external other*," which the Chinese have become by this time in the Japanese view. Modernizing Japan faced a double process of identification to distinguish themselves both from the West and from other Asians.

Rice as Self and Meat as the Other:
Japanese versus Westerners

Toward the end of the Early Modern period, the Japanese were becoming acutely aware of the presence of Western civilization outside their closed country. Nativist scholars summoned "agriculture" and "the countryside" in their efforts to redefine and represent the pristine Japanese self. The valorization of agriculture, especially rice agriculture, was not confined to these scholars. The Japanese seasons and, even more, the Japanese landscape were represented by symbols of rice agriculture such as rice sheaves, sometimes with Mt. Fuji in the background, in woodblock prints.[5]

This pattern continued through the Meiji to the present. The transformation of the "common people" of Yanagita and other scholars from mountain people to farmers occurred during the Russo-Japanese War when Japan, for the first time, was pitched against a Western nation. At this time, the Japanese engaged in seemingly contradictory efforts to simultaneously "modernize/industrialize" their country while redefining themselves in terms of the rice agriculture of the distant past.

Not surprisingly, rice as a metaphor of the Japanese people surfaced conspicuously during the Meiji period, the period immediately after the opening of the country to the outside. Agrarian ideology was an important tool used by the Meiji government to unify the people, who were acutely aware that their country's "progress" in science and technology was far behind that of Western countries. They were in awe of the Western science and technology that had developed during the three centuries when the country was closed to most outsiders.

The discourse on the Japanese self vis-à-vis Westerners as "the other" took the form of rice versus meat. From a Japanese perspective, meat was the distinguishing characteristic of the Western diet. Shortly after the introduction of Buddhism in the sixth century, its doctrine of mercy for all living beings was translated into a legal prohibition against the consumption of land animal meat. The "official" diet of the Japanese since consisted of fish and vegetables.[6]

Some people favored unabashed imitation of the West and advocated the abandonment of rice agriculture and the adoption of animal husbandry. They argued that as long as the Japanese continued to eat only rice, fish, and vegetables, their bodies would never become strong enough to compete with the bodies of meat-eating Westerners (Tsukuba 1986:109–112). They also associated a diet dominated by rice with country bumpkins and uncivilized habits (Tsukuba 1986:113).[7]

Others opposed imitating the West and emphasized the importance of rice agriculture and the superiority of a rice diet. Thus, proponents of a rice diet staged an event in which *sumō* wrestlers were asked to lift heavy sacks of rice (komedawara) in front of foreign delegates, one of whom asked why "the Japanese" were strong. One of the wrestlers, Hitachiyama, replied that the Japanese were strong because they ate rice grown on Japanese soil (Tsukuba 1986:109–112).

Since the Early Modern period, but most dramatically during World War II, domestic rice came to stand symbolically for the collective self of the Japanese. More specifically, the *purity* of white rice (*hakumai*) or "pure rice" (*junmai*) became a powerful metaphor for the purity of the Japanese self. During World War II, white rice—symbolically the most powerful but nutritionally the most deficient—was saved for the most precious sector of the population—the soldiers. The rest of the population was motivated by the lack of Japanese rice to work hard for Japan's victory, which promised to bring back good times with plenty of white rice, that is, "Japanese rice," rather than foreign rice (gaimai).

Just as Japanese objects are distinguished from Chinese objects by prefixes, certain prefixes designate objects of Japanese rather than Western origin: *wa*, *hō*, or *nihon* designate Japanese origin and *yō* signify Western origin. Some examples are:

Japanese	*Western*
washoku (Japanese cuisine)	*yōshoku* (Western cuisine)
wagashi (Japanese sweets)	*yōgashi* (pastries and cakes)
washi (Japanese paper, so-called rice paper)	*yōshi* (Western paper)
wafuku (Japanese kimono)	*yōfuku* (Western dress)
nihonshu (sake wine)	*yōshu* (wine)
nihonkan (Japanese-style house)	*yōkan* (Western-style house)

At times foreign words are retained to distinguish them from the Japanese counterparts: *wain* (wine) refers to Western wines and not to Japanese *sake* (rice wine).

Although some expressions are self-explanatory, others, such as "*yokomeshi o kuu*" (to eat a horizontal meal), require some explanation. This particular phrase is a reference to the Western alphabet as horizontal writing; Chinese and Japanese writing is vertical. People often say, "I am poor at the horizontal writing (*yokomoji wa nigateda*)," meaning "I am not good at English." Thus, to eat a horizontal meal refers to the Western diet, which, in turn, means an adjustment to a Western life-style.

Today, Japan is inundated with foreign foods. Not only Big Macs, pizza, Kentucky Fried Chicken, Dairy Queen ice cream, A & W root beer, and bagels but also haute cuisine from every culture of the world is available and eagerly sought. In addition to, or, more precisely, because of the profusion of Western foods, Japanese cuisine, washoku, has made a phenomenal comeback. Streetcars and newspapers are full of advertisements by restaurants and inns featuring numerous courses of Japanese dishes.

Japanese cuisine, whose prototype is the cuisine for the tea ceremony (*kaiseki ryōri*) in Kyoto, is a conspicuous contemporary "construction" or "invention" of Japanese culture. From pictures of these colorful and aesthetically arranged dishes, contemporary Japanese "learn" what Japanese cuisine is about, even though these dishes are by no means a faithful reconstruction of the traditional cuisine for the tea ceremony. There never was a prototypical traditional Japanese cuisine in the first place. Ironically, Japan now imports most of the ingredients for these "Japanese dishes." Amid a flood of Western foods, contemporary Japanese continue to reaffirm their collective self by constructing their own foodway.

Rice is the defining feature of "traditional Japanese cuisine" but the amount used is usually small. The more *haute* a meal is, the more numerous are the side dishes and the less rice is included. Thus, although rice continues to be referred to as the main food (*shushoku*) and other dishes as auxiliary side dishes (*fukushoku*), the quantitative balance is reversed in haute cuisine, which emphasizes the side dishes and not the rice. What makes any dish washoku, however, whether *haute* or not, is the presence of rice, no matter how small. "Japanese style steak" (*washokushiki suteiki*)—a popular menu item in contemporary Japan—means steak served with cooked white rice. The symbolic hierarchy established by the words used, rice as *shu*shoku (*main* dish) as opposed to *fuku*-shoku (*side* dish), expresses the importance of rice as far more than a staple food.

Rice that accompanies a Western dish such as steak is often referred to as *raisu*, that is, rice, as in "rice hamburger" (*raisu hanbāgā*), which is a hamburger sandwiched between two layers of bun-shaped rice. Variations of "rice burgers" include those with *teriyaki*, salmon, *kinpira* (cooked burdocks), and so forth. Many Western dishes, such as pork cutlets, hamburgers, steaks, and omelets are served with rice. At restaurants, a waiter or a waitress usually asks, "Would you like raisu or *pan* (from the Portuguese word for bread, *pão*, adopted by the Japanese) with it?" The code switch from *gohan* (the Japanese word for rice) to *raisu* (the English word *rice* in Japanese pronunciation) is a significant semiotic marker; the use of *raisu* signifies that the dish belongs to a different culinary system and is not, to a Japanese, *washoku*.

In contemporary Japan, the food for the poor continues to be envisioned as a large amount of rice accompanied by a pickled plum (*umeboshi*) or pickles (*takuwan*), just as the poor in bread-eating countries rely on bread with soup or salt pork. But regardless of quantity, rice remains "the king-pin of any meal's architecture" in Japan (Dore 1978:86).

Western Short-Grain Rice versus Japanese Short-Grain Rice

When the United States, a powerful other, pressured Japan to import rice from California, the Japanese immediately defended domestic rice and Japanese agriculture. Scarcely any contemporary Japanese would hold, even as a collective representation without individual belief, that rice has a soul or that rice is a deity. Many are unaware of the connection between rice and the emperor system, which has very little to do with the Japanese identity today.

Furthermore, this is not the only time that Japan has faced the importation of foreign rice. Earlier, Japan imported rice from time to time and even cultivated "foreign rice":

> In the thirteenth century a strain of rice from Indo-China (Champa) was introduced by way of China. It was appreciated by growers because of its early ripening and its resistance to cold and to pests, and by the end of the fourteenth century it was widely grown in the western provinces. According to the records of the Daigoji manors in Sanuki and Harima, about one-third of their tax rice was this strain. It was a low-grade rice in colour and flavour, but it was consumed in quantity by the poorer classes. (Sansom 1961:183)

The domestic rice today, which contemporary Japanese identify as *the* Japanese rice, is, in fact, an "invention of a tradition" in that the original species of rice was radically different from any of the many species cultivated today. Furthermore, no single species of rice ever constituted *the* Japanese rice in the past. As we saw, each farm household cultivated its own version of "the Japanese rice."

In contrast to other rice that had been imported to Japan, California rice is identical with domestic rice. Unlike long-grain rice from China and other rice-consuming countries, short-grain California rice was cultivated from seeds originally brought from Japan and resembles Japanese rice. Yet symbolically it is just as different as any other food that represents the other because California rice is grown on foreign soil.

The powerful agricultural union, Zenchū, pointing out that Japan imports from the United States 77.1 percent of its corn, 88.5 percent of its soybeans, 58.7 percent of its wheat, and 53.7 percent of its grain sorghum (*Zenchū Farm News*, no.5, January 1987:2), issued the following statement:

> In Japanese agriculture, rice carries incalculable weight compared with other crops. It is no exaggeration whatsoever to say that the maintenance of complete rice *self-sufficiency* is the sole guarantee to agriculture and farming households in Japan. Rice farming in Japan, with a history of 2,300 years behind it, has greatly influenced all areas of *national life*, including social order, religious worship, festivals, food, clothings and housing, thus molding *the prototype of Japanese culture*. In addition, Japanese agriculture and its farming household economy have traditionally developed around rice, and other sectors of agriculture, such as livestock farming and horticulture, are actually based on rice. (Italics added)

Okabe Saburō, director of the Science and Technology Division of the Liberal Democratic party and a member of the House of Councilors, expresses a similar view about the role of rice agriculture in Japan.[8] To explain the benefits of rice agriculture, he calls attention to the frequent flooding of the Kanda River in Tokyo caused by the transformation of rice paddies along its upper banks into urban space. When rice paddies were there, 60 percent of the rainfall was absorbed by the paddies; without them 90 percent of the rainfall pours into the river, causing flooding. He argues that the role of rice agriculture goes far beyond the production of food. It contributes to flood control, soil conservation, preservation of underground water, purification of water, and land beautification. He concludes that rice agriculture is the best use of the land for every rice-producing country in monsoon Asia.

The statements by Zenchū or an LDP Diet member may be quite predictable, and if they were alone in expressing this sentiment, one could dismiss its significance. Of note, however, is that people in other sectors of Japanese society, including consumers, also use similar expressions that link rice with the Japanese self. In its editorial column, the Asahi newspaper (*Asahi Shinbun* June 13, 1990)—the most liberal major newspaper in Japan—reports that in 1988, of the 2,629 calories a day consumed by typical Japanese, only 49 percent comes from food produced in Japan. Of the 49 percent, 54 percent comes from rice. Based on the calculation of calories, then, Japan has the lowest self-sufficiency in the world. Therefore, according to this editorial, if domestic rice is threatened, the self-sufficiency of the Japanese diet is in severe danger.

Similarly, H. Inoue (1988) emphasizes how, according to estimates by the Agricultural Department of Iwate Prefecture, rice paddies function as dams which in northeastern Japan alone would cost ¥ 200 trillion to build (see also Shimogaito 1986:13–15). Rice production literally preserves the soil, the Japanese land. Not only the soil but also the vegetation and air of Japan benefit directly from rice production. Inoue echoes a common sentiment expressed in newspapers and other mass media, "American rice would not clear the air, nor would it adorn the scenery with beautiful green" (H. Inoue 1988:103). In these arguments, rice symbolizes *Japan itself*, its land, water, and air.

While opponents emphasize the positive features of domestic rice and rice paddies, they also stress the negative aspects of California rice. A frequently voiced charge against foreign rice is the extensive use of chemicals on agricultural products in the United States. Shimogaito (1988:76–78) lists a number of chemicals, both insecticides and postharvest preservatives, and stresses the benefits of chemical-free Japanese rice. The farm union (Zenchū) picked up on this fear and produced a video exaggerating the harm to people who consume chemically treated agricultural products. This extreme tactic was criticized even in Japan (*Asahi Shin-*

bun April 1, 1988; August 3, 1988), especially when not all Japanese products are chemical free. They discontinued the campaign.

At a symbolic level, the accusation about the chemicals on rice relates to the aforementioned structure of reflexivity in which the principle of purity and impurity is the single most important principle both cognitively and affectively. Chemicals symbolize *the impurity of foreign rice* and, thus, constitute a threat to *the purity of the Japanese self.*

The controversy over California rice clearly demonstrates that domestic rice serves as a metaphor of self for the Japanese and their land, water, and air, for all of which purity is the essential quality. Equating self-sufficiency (jikyū jisoku) with domestic rice is the most frequent expression in the discourse (see also Ōshima 1984:2–4). Other metaphors of self include lifeblood crop (I. Yamaguchi 1987:40); the life line (*seimeisen*); the last sacred realm (*saigo no seiiki*) (*Kobe Shinbun*, July 6, 1990); and the last citadel (used by the minister of Agriculture and Fishing, *Asahi Shinbun*, evening ed., June 27, 1990). The last two phrases express the Japanese fear that if they make concessions on the rice issue, they may have to concede to other impositions from the United States, such as nuclear weapons.

Historical Conjunctures and Changing Identities

Contrary to the stereotype of Japan as an isolated country and of the Japanese as chauvinists with closed minds, the Japanese identity has been formulated and reformulated through their dialogue with outsiders. The Japanese, thus, adopted rice and rice paddies, introduced from outside, as the marks of their identity during the eighth century. Remarkably, these dominant metaphors continue to have symbolic power even today.

Contemporary Japan is a postindustrial nation that is a far cry from a rice-paddy agrarian society. Government subsidies to farmers have been under attack from urbanites who now make up the majority of the population. With an increase in the use of side dishes, the amount of rice consumed by contemporary Japanese has been drastically reduced. Yet rice continues to be a dominant metaphor of the Japanese self. Many, but by no means all, Japanese view the California rice importation as a threat to their identity and its autonomy. Urbanites, many of whom resent the farm subsidies provided by the government and are antagonistic toward farmers, are still willing to pay for the *symbolic* value of domestic rice.

The rice issue has become the rallying point to defend *the self* when *the other* threatens it. Intriguingly, the California rice issue that coincided with the illness and death of the Shōwa emperor scarcely involves the emperor, whose symbolic relationship to rice has been almost forgotten and whose symbolic power to represent the Japanese has been radically eroded. Secularized rice, as it were, remains a dominant symbol of the self with a strong emotive resonance that surfaced dramatically when the United States, a powerful other, pressured Japan to open the rice market.

Why is there such a strong surge in support of agriculture and rice as metaphors *at this time in history* when Japan has achieved a so-called economic miracle? Japan's economic achievement has prompted an intense discourse on the self in relation to the other (Ohnuki-Tierney 1990a). Technology defined the superiority of Western civilization in the eyes of the Japanese when the country was reopened near the end of the nineteenth century. The native concept of the Stranger Deity provided the model for perceiving foreigners as superior to the self, offering an ideal mirror for the Japanese to emulate. The Japanese effort to excel in technology is explained by the symbolic position that technology occupied. By superseding Western technology, at least in some ways, the Japanese no longer feel inferior to the *other*. Their "conquest," as many Japanese see it, of the world market in high technology, the auto industry, and other economic-technological spheres should not be seen simply as an economic success. As a symbol of the superior other, technology and industry motivated the Japanese to excel in these areas. Their achievements, in turn, have had a profound impact on their concept of their collective self. It is a complex picture in which the internal logic of symbolic structure provides symbolic meaning to "external" phenomena, such as foreigners. The symbolic meaning of technology was partially responsible for the Japanese effort in technological advancement, which, in turn, has affected the structure of reflexivity.

From the perspective of the structure of reflexivity, therefore, the present is a new era for the Japanese who feel for the first time in their history that they have "mastered" the outside, the *other*, whose negative power devastated the country in 1945. The hierarchy between the *self* and *other* has been inverted. This inversion is a drastic change happening for the first time for the Japanese over whom the Chinese and Westerners had always claimed superiority.

The Japanese, however, are aware of how they were and still are placed within the Oriental framework. Dan Rather, a news commentator, went all the way to Japan to announce that 150 foreign delegates attended the emperor's funeral when there were 163.[9] Every delegate counted because to the Japanese the number of foreign delegates reflected Japan's newly gained stature in the world. To some Japanese his carelessness expressed that Japan had not, after all, achieved the recognition sought. They are also acutely aware of the resurgence of a great deal of anti-Japanese feelings and attitudes in the United States. It is time to re-define themselves. They summoned, as it were, rice agriculture, which has been on native soil long enough since its introduction from outside to become the defining feature of themselves; the Western origin of science and technology is too recent to claim as their own. The Japanese insistence on domestic rice is part of the process of redefining the endangered self of the Japanese.

What emerges from this picture is that although the Stranger Deity provided the Japanese with a model to conceptualize the superiority of the other, their view of the other could never be simple adoration. It has always been double-edged because the superiority of the other has brought ambivalence about themselves. To understand the Japanese relation with the other, especially toward Western peoples, one must keep in mind the ambivalence that many peoples—those politically and/or culturally colonized—must wrestle with in their relationships with the West (see chap. 9). The ambivalence toward the other may be responsible for an amazing chauvinism, on the one hand, and the historical continuity of the Japanese national identity, on the other. Eisenstadt (1978:144) points out that a structural and organizational pluralism—one not unlike the European pattern—has developed in Japan, but it did so only within the framework of the historical continuity of the national identity.

Throughout this complex dialogue with various others, then, rice and rice paddies have served as the metaphor, always representing the Japanese self, a self that nonetheless has transformed into various selves in Japanese encounters with others.

Eight

Foods as Selves and Others in Cross-cultural Perspective

A SYMBOLIC complex involving foods, agriculture, and nature serves as a metaphor of self in many other cultures. Some examples highlight both cultural specificities and cross-cultural parallels in the use of important foods as reflexive metaphors. Needless to say, the comparisons that follow are not meant to be systematic.

The Food versus Foods

Just as there are multiple voices of actors and social groups, there are diverse foodways within a single population. On the other hand, there is a striking cross-cultural parallel whereby people conceptualize a particular food as *the* food, that is, the epitome of *their* food. Across cultures *the* food chosen by the people for self-identity often is or used to be the food for the powerful, often men and/or upper class members of the society.

In almost all cultures, important foods are gendered and embedded in stratification and are assigned powerful symbolic meanings. Among the Ainu of southern Sakhalin, a hunting-gathering people until the turn of the century, both men and women considered bear meat to be *the* food. I recall vividly how my women informants glowed with joy when they talked about delicious bear meat, the best part of which, however, is consumed by men. Every activity concerning the bear is a male activity, and women must leave the site before the ceremony when the bear is killed (for details, see Ohnuki-Tierney 1974; 1981). I soon discovered that most Ainu had tasted bear meat only once or twice a year and several times if they were lucky (Ohnuki-Tierney 1976). The bear is a male deity, even though the biological sex of individual bears is distinguished. In other words, this masculine food is regarded as *the* food for all Ainu. Similarly, among the !Kung San, meat is far more valued than the plant foods that provide from 60 to 80 percent of the annual diet by weight. About twice as many calories as meat are supplied by *mongongo* nuts, which are also very high in protein (Lee 1968). In New Guinea, yams—the most prestigious food and, thus, the food distributed at feasts—are grown by men, whereas women grow sweet potatoes (Rosaldo 1974:19).

Among aboriginal groups in Australia, only meat is considered a proper food; it is also distributed by men (Kaberry 1939).

The disproportionately high cultural value assigned to meat is almost universal among hunter-gatherers (Friedle 1975:13). The value accorded meat over plant foods and the assignment of male gender to meat are not confined to hunter-gatherers but are among many meat-eating peoples. In the contemporary United States, men still carve meat such as turkey, ham, and roast beef at holiday dinner tables, and barbecue meat, especially steak, whereas other types of cooking have traditionally been the province of women. Despite the increasing popularity of vegetarian diets and aversion to red meat for health reasons, a strictly vegetarian cuisine is not usually considered appropriate for dinner parties when commensality takes on a highly significant social function.

In highly stratified societies class/caste structures also play a dominant role in food symbolism. Historically, Mennell (1985:64) considers the end of the Middle Ages a cultural watershed when significant changes in cookery took place in Europe. He locates the emergence of class differences in eating at the end of the eighteenth century when the haute cuisine of the upper and middle classes became pronounced—the trend initiated by a decisive break at courts in the cities of Renaissance Italy from the medieval style cookery that was common to the whole of Western Europe. In 1533 the cooks who accompanied Cathérine de'Medici on her journey from Florence to marry the future Henri VII introduced Italian cookery to France, where the French soon raised it to a height of elegance and "assumed for themselves the culinary hegemony of Europe" (Mennell 1985:63). This historical development was paralleled in many other parts of the world. Braudel (1973:125) boldly proclaims that "elaborate cooking" is "known to every mature civilization."

Bourdieu's emphasis on the *distinction* of taste in food lies in its mediation between the class and gender, on the one hand, and the body, on the other: "Taste, class culture turned into nature, that is, *embodied*, helps to shape the class today. . . . the body is the most indisputable materialization of class taste" (Bourdieu 1984:190). J. Goody (1982) examines historical processes and determinants of the development of "high" and "low" cuisines. In some societies, like Goody's West Africa, the primary mode of production (shifting cultivation) and communication (oral tradition) have prevented the formation of classes and, consequently, differentiated cuisines. Vansina (personal communication), on the other hand, argues that in the eighteenth-century Loango kingdom the banana was the food of the elite, whereas maize was eaten by commoners and slaves.

An intriguing cross-cultural parallel is the phenomenon whereby a "taste" for a particular "highbrow" food is disseminated throughout a population. Rice was the staple food only for the elite in central Japan, but ultimately it became the most desired food for most Japanese. White (polished) rice became *the* rice, and unpolished rice became the food of the poor. Bread in England has undergone a similar historical process. By the end of the eighteenth century, white bread, because of its status value, had gained prestige over dark bread to the extent that laborers who ate "wheaten [whole wheat] bread" were thought to "suffer from weakness, indigestion, or nausea" (Thompson 1971:81). The story of sugar—the symbol of Western colonial expansion—is remarkably similar to the stories of rice and bread. According to Mintz (1985), sugar, which reached England in small quantities by about A.D. 1100, from 1650 onward began to change from a luxury food for the elite to a necessity for everyone in many nations. Sugar also was whitened by processing. "Even in the case of societies that have been sucrose consumers for centuries, one of the corollaries of 'development' is that older, traditional kinds of sugar are being gradually replaced with the white, refined product, which the manufacturers like to call 'pure'" (Mintz 1985:193, see also 87).

As economic affluence reached segments of many societies, however, a reversal in taste occurred. As "natural foods" become popular, the preference for dark bread increased in England as well as the United States; unpolished rice is coming back on the market in Japan, but its popularity is still confined to a small segment of health-conscious Japanese. In Japan, far more popular than unpolished rice are various kinds of less-refined sugar, which is also preferred in some segments of the United States and many other countries. Foodways have come full cycle.

Striking parallels are found among rice, bread, and sugar. All three foods have been closely associated with political power, both within and outside of society. A particular food becomes the food for the people, no matter how differentially distributed it originally was among social groups and individuals. Ainu bears and other examples discussed in this section also point to a general phenomenon: the food considered most important is often the food with prestige, that is, the food for the powerful. Yet it is considered symbolically as *our food*.

Staple Food as a Metaphor of Food in General

As rice stands for food in general in both the Chinese and Japanese cultures, so does bread in the United States in expressions such as "Give us our daily bread," "breadwinner," "bread-and-butter issue," and "bread line." "Sliced bread" is a metaphor for a great invention because of the cultural importance of bread; "a bread box" is a colloquial measure of a small space. Similarly, "dough" is a slang expression for money, a dominant symbol of power and status in the United States. A Washington charity kitchen is named "Bread for the City." Equally numerous expressions include *pain* in French, which occupies three columns in Robert's dictionary (1962:67–68).

Bread scarcity signals a serious crisis. Just as there were rice riots in Japan, there were innumerable bread riots in bread-eating countries, for example, in the *ancien régime* in France. Most recently, in Moscow the shortage of *khleb* struck the nerve center of the people and was reported in American mass media as evidence of the Soviet economic and political crisis.

While discussing bread in eighteenth-century England, Thompson (1971) remarks that "next to air and water, corn [wheat] was a prime necessity of life" and that when the price of bread went up, the poor "do not go over to cake" but eat more bread to compensate for the absence of other foods (Thompson 1971:92, 91, respectively). In other words, bread was *the* food for the English, and other foods, even if available, could not substitute entirely for it.

Like bread for the English and rice for the Japanese, millet occupies the central place for the Bemba. "To the Bemba, millet porridge is not only necessary, but it is the only constituent of his diet which actually ranks as food. . . . I have watched natives eating the roasted grain off four or five maize cobs under my very eyes, only to hear them shouting to their fellows later, 'Alas, we are dying of hunger. We have not had a bite to eat all day.'" (Richards [1939]1961:46–47). Just as the term for rice means meals, millet porridge also represents food or meals. I have often heard my American colleagues who specialize in Asian studies marvel at informants who remark that they have not eaten until they have eaten rice. These staple foods are the focus of meals for these people, even though the quantities eaten may be insignificant.

Staple Food as a Metaphor of Self

It is a small step for a particular food that is *the* food for the people to become a metaphor for the people. The Japanese quibble over whether to eat short-grain domestic rice or short-grain California rice ceases to appear extreme if one recalls the careful distinction made among French bread, German bread, and Italian bread by the French, the Germans, and the Italians. Each nationality feels strong attachment to its own bread, which stands for *we* and not *they*. A new magazine for Asian-Americans is entitled *Rice*; all Asians in the United States are represented by the metaphor of rice, in contrast with bread-eating white Americans, tortilla-eating Latinos, and so forth.[1] In nineteenth-century central Africa, the Pende near the Kasai River were identified with their sorghum; the

Mbuun were known for their fields of maize (Vansina 1978:177). As with rice for the Japanese, these staple foods stand for *we* contrasted with *they*. As noted in chapter 1, not just the staple food but the entire foodways—cooking methods to table manners—is closely, and often passionately, identified as the collective self of the people.

Commensality

Symbolically important staple foods, such as rice for the Japanese, are the foods selected for commensality. The importance of bread for commensality is most powerfully expressed in the bread and wine taken during Communion for Catholics and many Protestants. For those who believe in transubstantiation, they become the body and blood of Christ. Christ distributed bread and wine at the Last Supper, and the Eucharist and the Lord's Supper always involve these two items. Even today, whether at a formal dinner or a family meal, bread is passed around the table while other foods are dished onto individual plates. Bread remains the food for commensality.

Millet is important for the Bemba because of its role in commensality: "The importance of millet porridge in native eyes is constantly reflected in traditional utterance and ritual. In proverb and folktale the *ubwali* (millet porridge) stands for food itself. When discussing his kinship obligations, a native will say, "How can a man refuse to help his mother's brother who has give him *ubwali* all these years?" or, "Is he not her son? How should she refuse to make him *ubwali*?" (Richards [1939] 1961:47). Millet porridge is *the* item of commensality, and its meaning and value for the Bemba come from these cultural practices rather than from its quantitative value to fill the stomach.

As a powerful means of nonverbal communication, in almost every culture commensality is symbolically equated with sexual union. In his description of communication through exchanges of goods, messages, and women, Lévi-Strauss (1969:269) calls attention to the near universal symbolic equation of food consumption and sexual union by using examples from South America: "All these myths present a sexual aspect. As is the case the world over, the South American languages bear witness to the fact that the two aspects are closely linked. The Tupari express coitus by locutions whose literal meaning is 'to eat the vagina' . . . , 'to eat the penis.' The Caingang dialects of southern Brazil have a verb that means both to 'copulate' and 'eat'." The Japanese imperial ritual of ōnamesai is not an exception then as it enacts the symbolic equations among food consumption, ritual, agricultural production, and human reproduction.

Commensality and sexual union are the fibers that weave human relationships into a tapestry of culturally meaningful patterns. Rather than a
quantitative value simply as food to fill the stomach, the symbolic meaning of staple foods often derives from their roles in commensality.

Plant Food for Commensality

Commensality has been of perennial interest among anthropologists;
both structural functionalists and structuralists have long pointed out its
significance. In anthropological discussions, however, meat, especially
big game meats often receive more attention than plant foods. One of the
most commonly cited explanations for the emphasis on big game is that
its size makes it an obvious item for the commensality that usually follows the sacrificial ritual. That is why, the explanation goes, Ainu males
go after dangerous bears and the !Kung San males embark on an arduous
and precarious trip to hunt giraffes[2] and call them *the* foods. Both Ainu
and !Kung San women, in contrast, gather tubers and mongongo nuts
that are "staples" in a practical sense but are never elevated to the prestige level of big game.

But rice and millet are perfectly capable of being the food for commensality. Neglect of the role of plant foods, I suggest, is in part because of
the higher value accorded meat by the people themselves. It is, however,
also the result of the low value assigned to plant foods in the Western
cultures to which most scholars belong. Both Greek mythology and the
Bible are replete with differential treatment of animal and plant foods;
the former receive more prestige and, thus, are assigned to men. In Greek
mythology Hercules is the prototype of "man the hunter," whereas
Deianira represents "woman the tiller." In the Bible the Lord's preference for Abel over Cain is symbolically expressed through his contrasting
treatment of the animal offering from Abel, a keeper of sheep, and the
fruit of the ground offering from Cain, a tiller of the ground. Abel and
Cain represent a highly complex structure of thoughts, but Cain's association with agriculture and plant food seems to be embedded in a culture
that values animals more highly.

Robertson Smith, a major figure in the study of ritual commensality,
insists, as I quoted in chapter 4, that animal sacrifice alone constitutes
communion between god and humans, and that cereal oblation is only a
tribute to the gods: "Those who sit at meat together are united for all
social effects; those who do not eat together are aliens to one another,
without fellowship in religion and without reciprocal social duties"
(Robertson Smith [1889] 1972:269).

As noted, he relegated to a footnote the information from Frazer that a true sacrificial feast can be made from the first fruits of rice and that people believe in the soul of rice. Thus, he failed to recognize that there is no "objective" difference between animal and plant foods in their capacity to become items of commensality. Rice is alive and has a soul among rice-eating peoples; it is even a deity for the Japanese. In his discussion of mortuary rites in north India, Parry (1985) points out that although cultivated grain is the "prototypical food," rice is "the food par excellence" for Brahmans and refers to the nineteenth-century practice of mixing the ground bones of the deceased with boiled rice.

The animal-centered view, or the prejudice against plant food, is found in the view of another major historian, F. Braudel. After explaining the caloric advantage of agricultural products, Braudel quite frankly expresses his prejudice:

> Now fields were cultivated *at the expense* of hunting-ground and extensive stock-raising. As centuries passed a larger and larger number of people were *reduced to* eating vegetable foods . . . *often insipid and always monotonous.* . . . In ancient Greece it was said that "the eaters of barley gruel have no desire to make war." An Englishman centuries later [1776] stated: "You find more courage among men who eat their fill of flesh than among those who make shift with lighter foods." (Braudel 1973:68; italics added)

Meat in many western European countries has been not only gendered but also class linked. Game meat was a symbol of the upper class in pre-industrial Europe. In the nineteenth century, wild animal meat remained prestigious while the bourgeoisie ate the meat of domesticated animals. Even today, prestige accrues to hunting, a very male activity. Food for the lower class in rural Europe continued to be dominated by dark bread, soup, eggs, and dairy products (Mennell 1985:62–63).

To reiterate, there is no objective reason for any food to be chosen as the food for commensality. Rather, it is high cultural valuation that underscores the food that is chosen for communal sharing.

Plant Food as Nature

A crucial dimension of rice symbolism in Japanese culture is the rice paddies that stand for agriculture, the countryside, and the past—all symbolizing nature with its soil and water and, ultimately, the Japanese nation and its people. These associations in Japanese culture are far from unique. The symbolic equation of agriculture with nature is found in diverse cultures—among agriculturalists of the Far East and among Europeans who eat meat and raise animals. This is intriguing because agriculture represents not only human mastery over nature but a thorough transformation of nature into cultivated land (Tuan 1989:82).

The representation of agriculture cum nature is usually assigned both positive and negative senses. The cultural construction of the "English countryside" is well-articulated by Newby, R. Williams, and others. R. Williams (1973:1) sees the dual nature assigned to the English countryside and the city as historical processes: "On the country has gathered the idea of a natural way of life: of peace, innocence, and simple virtue. On the city has gathered the idea of an achieved centre: of learning, communication, light. Powerful hostile associations have also developed: on the city as a place of noise, worldliness and ambition; on the country as a place of backwardness, ignorance, limitation."

This contrast between country and city not only holds today in England but also reaches back to classical times (R. Williams 1973:46–54). For Athenians, "life on the farm was missed as though it were a garden of the gods irretrievably lost" (Tuan 1986:34). In a similar vein, Newby (1979) tells how an eighteenth-century landowner commissioned his landscapers to rearrange nature to form what is now accepted as "picturesque natural beauty." Nature thus represented was "the antithesis of works of nature" for it was created by eliminating "unpleasant agricultural necessities" (Newby 1979:16). England's natural beauty was reified by a series of painters—William Kent, Lancelot ("Capability") Brown, and Humphrey Repton, among others—who painted this constructed nature. "To most inhabitants of urban England . . . the countryside supports a serene, idyllic existence, enjoyed by blameless Arcadians happy in their communion with Nature; or alternatively it is a backward and isolated world where boredom vies with boorishness, inducing melancholia and a suspicion of incest" (Newby 1979:13).

In the 1970s, "in contrast to the apparently unending gloomy news about conflict-ridden, strike prone, double-digit inflation, urban, industrial England," a *real* English countryside thrived in the minds of the people, especially middle-class English mostly ignorant of agriculture, and in a few calendars and chocolatebox lids (Newby 1979:14–18). The wealthy could enjoy "nature" in their own compounds as did Marie Antoinette who built a little farm in Versailles where she played at raising sheep (Berque 1990:122).

As in Newby's description of "the real English countryside," the nativist scholars of the late Early Modern period assigned a dual nature to the country and the city; the Meiji intellectuals exalted the simplicity and purity of the Japanese countryside and its farmers, but regarded them, nonetheless, as country bumpkins. These scholars eagerly supported the modernization and industrialization of Japan while lamenting the decay of the quality of life in Edo (Tokyo).

Like the eighteenth-century English artists and the Japanese masters who created woodblock prints, French impressionists saw "nature" in rural France. Countless painters, both major and minor, chose rural France as their artistic subject. The "grainstock" series by Monet (1840–1926) and the paintings of farmers (*L'Angélus, Des glaneuses*, etc.) by Jean-François Millet (1814–1875) are the most celebrated examples, but there are many others.[3] R. Brettell and C. Brettell write of primarily French but also other European representations of the peasants as living "outside time" in a state of purity (Brettell and Brettell 1983:8).[4]

In his comparative history of landscapes, Berque (1990:87) emphasizes that "nature" is a historical product, created in an era when humans became dependent on the products of their own labor rather than on products of nature. Berque stresses that the city created the countryside; the countryside did not originate among peasants (Berque 1990:110–112). Likewise, industrialization created the representation of agriculture.

Nature as the Past

Inherent in representations of landscapes and subsistence activities are temporal representations. The representation of the past in relation to the present shows a striking parallel to that of rural-agriculture in relation to urban-industry. "Whether recent or remote, the desired past exhibits strikingly similar traits: natural, simple, comfortable—yet also vivid and exciting. 'The old, gray, modern existence' had little to offer Robin Carson's hero compared with 'the new, colorful opulence' of Renaissance Venice" (Lowenthal 1985:24). Temporal representations also began very early. R. Williams (1973:47) cites a marvelous quotation from *Satire XV*: "But today even snakes agree better than men."

Both of these examples from the West parallel a longing for the pristine past by nativist scholars. The Meiji intellectuals focused on traditional Japan versus modernizing Japan and juxtaposed the rural in opposition to the city. A rural existence represented the purity of the Japanese who were in danger of being corrupted by the pressure of modernization epitomized in city life (Gluck 1985:178). The Meiji commentators contended that agriculture was the foundation of the Japanese nation and that its villages preserved the rustic, simple ways of the past, which, in turn, contributed to a stronger body; degenerate city life weakened the Japanese body (Gluck 1985:179, 181).

Gluck (1985:185) also points out that the characterization of rural life during the early twentieth century was not unequivocal; the country bumpkin (*inakamono*), according to some, destroyed life in Edo

(Tokyo). The first wave of country people moved the samurai from out-lying areas to Edo in the 1870s and the second brought villagers who came to work in the factories. Both groups were perceived as contribut-ing to a decline in the quality of life in Edo.

In Japan, despite these negative opinions, the valorization of the coun-tryside has been a far more dominant view. In a search for the "original" Japanese culture that presumably existed in ancient times, scholars, in-cluding some anthropologists, contributed, albeit unwittingly, to the construction of the "agrarian myth" (Gluck 1985:181). Today, the Japa-nese continue to search for *nature* in the countryside, now nostalgically referred to as *furusato* (old homestead, 'one's home region')—a romanti-cized image promoted by the government, the tourist industry, urbanites in postindustrial Japan, and "rural" people who reconstruct and invent their traditions to suit tourists' expectations.

Although the past may be idealized during ordinary times, a crisis often intensifies the longing for it in Japan and elsewhere. At critical times, peoples need to rethink their identities and their civilizations, that is, their selves—the self that is no longer sure of itself. Such times have included the classical *fin de siècle* in Europe and, in Japan, the end of the long reign under the shoguns or the beginning of a new era when the "economic miracle" necessitated a reassessment of Japan both by the Japanese and others. People seek salvation in the protoself, as it were, that presumably existed in the past or, more accurately, in "myth time," which is thought to be "retained" in the countryside and in peasants' lives.

Rice Paddies as Japanese Nature

Although there are remarkable cross-cultural regularities in the represen-tations of agriculture, countryside, nature, and the past, they contain sig-nificant culture-specific elements. Consider, for example, the character-ization of nature in each culture. "Wild nature" is important in Western culture and is fundamental to its fascination with hunter-gatherers. Simi-larly, pastoralism that idealizes "a simplified life in the country" (Frye 1971:43) has a far-reaching effect not only on the way people in various Western cultures think of nature but also religion, as exemplified in a series of metaphors such as Christ the lamb, the pastor and flock, and so on (Frye 1971).

In contrast, untouched nature seldom exists in the Japanese vision of "nature," which also lacks animals. Hunter-gatherers, although they once lived in the archipelago, and pastoralism, that never existed, do not hold much fascination. Their nature is with*out* nonhuman animals. This

8.1. Flooded Rice Paddies: Rice Paddies as *Our* Land and *Our* History. Photo by the author.

feature makes the Japanese representation of nature quite different from those of some European cultures in which grazing land was transformed into cropland, creating some tension between those who used the land through agriculture or pastoralism, as noted in the passage by Braudel. Although this is not the place for a full analysis, the importance that animals commanded in some European cultures has profoundly influenced various representations, especially because the opposition between animals and plants is often, beginning with the Bible, symbolically equated with the opposition between men and women. In these cultures, then, the representation of the past by agriculture must be situated in the broader context of the representation of the past, sometimes by hunting and other times by pastoralism.

In contrast, Japanese nature has also been inhabited by plants with souls. Thus, when the wilderness was transformed into a land filled with succulent heads of rice, plants became hegemonic, as it were, denying the hunting that preceded their agriculture a place in history.

Japanese nature is a culturalized nature, for example, a rock garden, which represents and presents "nature" that has been thoroughly transformed yet from which all traces of human agents of creation have been removed so that it looks "natural." Rice paddies, often without farmers, therefore, are Japanese nature par excellence. They represent agriculture without manure and sweat, which, in turn, represents the idealized past.

The cosmological significance of the Japanese emphasis on raw food and their deemphasis of long cooking methods derive from the same concept of nature. The ability of a Japanese chef is judged not so much by how the food is cooked as by his (usually not her) ability to choose raw food that is of excellent quality. For example, raw fish (*ike*, or *ikezakana*) is a highly prized item, and in many coastal regions chefs pride themselves on serving raw fish (*sashimi*) that still moves after being sliced. Chefs must demonstrate the ability to identify such food material. In addition, a Japanese chef's goal is to reproduce culturally defined nature by preserving the "nature" of the food in taste and appearance or even enhance them. They shape the food and choose and arrange containers, many of which are natural items, such as bamboo or iris leaves. Porcelain or pottery containers may be in the form of leaves, flowers, or other items that symbolize human interaction with nature, such as boats or wooden buckets used to scoop water.[5]

Given this conceptualization of nature, what is more appropriate than steamed rice—a cooked food that remains natural—to represent "nature"? The type of rice the Japanese choose for this purpose, however, is the one most removed from nature—polished rice.

Symbolic Importance of Agriculture for Highly Industrialized Nations

If agriculture represents nature, it is easy to understand agriculture's association with our land and our nation. For this reason, agricultural protectionism is a widespread policy in many countries, including the United States and the European Economic Community (EEC) except the United

Kingdom.[6] Progress on the creation of the EEC is also hampered by an inability to agree on a common agricultural policy; differentially subsidized food exports affect the common monetary system. P. Williams (1992), former chief of GATT, declares that the success of the Uruguay Round of GATT negotiations depends solely on whether an agreement on agricultural issues is achieved.

Note that "real agricultural nations," such as those in Latin America, do not have as extensive agricultural protectionism as highly industrialized nations do. The latter are reluctant to eliminate farms from their landscapes; they cannot afford to let "nature" go. Only plant foods become "natural foods" that, presumably, are healthy for the body. Yet the rhetoric defending agriculture often includes the functional argument of food to fill the stomach and satisfy the body. These arguments remain powerful even in countries in which the standard of living of most people rose above a subsistence level long ago.

Nine

Symbolic Practice through Time: Self, Ethnicity, and Nationalism

THERE IS a long tradition in symbolic anthropology of "food for thought" and, I would add, "for feeling." Theoretical dimensions of foods and food taboos have been discussed by a number of distinguished anthropologists; Douglas (1966), Leach (1968), Lévi-Strauss (1963, 1969b), and Tambiah (1969), to name only a few. Many others contributed to an understanding of offerings to deities. But the symbolic meaning of staple foods has escaped systematic attention.

In this book I have questioned an assumption, held at least by some, that so-called staple foods are primarily of quantitative value. I may have overemphasized the symbolic value of rice and other staple foods by using a construction from the perspective of urbanites and the affluent. I concur with Spence (1977:261) who insists on "the harsh backdrop of famine or the threat of famine" to understand food and eating.[1] In Japan many died of starvation during famines (see chapter 5). In France, Darnton convincingly argues that "to eat one's fill" was the "principal pleasure" for the peasants in early modern Europe who readily traded a promise to heaven after death for a "square meal" while alive (Darnton 1985:34, 33). I also think that there was a period when rice, bread, and other staple foods occupied a far more quantitative significance than they do now. The symbolic values of these staple foods, however, have always been important even during food shortages.

The cross-cultural parallels are striking in the social and cultural institutions in which the meanings of staple foods are embedded. Not to reify falsely the uniqueness of Japanese culture or its appropriation of rice, I have used some cross-cultural references, which have broadened the scope of a subject that is already enormous. I have raised more questions than answers in this book.

Symbolic Practice: Materialities and Meanings of Rice as Constituent

I have discussed rice as if it were an unchangeable object with a fixed meaning without stressing the plurality of both its materialities and meanings. When one examines the use of rice as a symbol, however, it is neither an unchanging object nor does it have a fixed meaning.

Although the meaning of rice as the self or the self-identity seems univocal, the Japanese identity has been redefined time and again during every historical encounter with the others. If the self has undergone changes, then its meaning, too, has changed. The Japanese identity in relation to the Chinese is certainly different from the Japanese identity contrasted with that of Westerners.

If the meaning of the self as represented by rice has changed through history, so has the materiality of rice. The original rice was a tropical or subtropical plant, an entirely different rice from the rices of later periods. Until recently, because of the tradition of home grown reseeding there were innumerable varieties, each representing rice as self at the family level. Even in the 1990s there are several kinds on the market. Thus, under the linguistic label of 'rice', innumerable rices have been thought of as *the* Japanese rice.

When rice is opposed to meat as the metaphor for the Japanese self vis-à-vis the Western self, the entire category (class) of rice is at issue. But it is short-grain rice, rather than generic rice, that stands for the Japanese self; the Chinese by contrast are represented by long-grain rice. When California rice is the issue, short-grain rice grown on Japanese soil is opposed to the short-grain rice grown on foreign soil, even though the California rice may be "objectively" similar to Japanese domestic rice.

Similarly, a small amount of white rice defines a meal as *haute cuisine*, but it can also be a cheap meal, depending upon how it is served. That is, the containers, ambience, and above all, the social context define the same or similar rices in radically different ways. It depends upon the use by a social actor.

In contemporary restaurants raisu or gohan presents a dramatic case of code switching that assigns the same rice to separate systems of cuisine, giving different meanings to each.

Or, to take the Goffmanian approach, rice may be used by an actor as a symbol for "the presentation of self." Thus, the man introduced in chapter 2, who boasted that he and his colleagues eat nonrice foods for lunch, such as spaghetti, is, in fact, using his nonrice diet to present himself as "modern." Similarly, Japanese who have spent some time overseas, especially in the United States, often nostalgically associate the California rice they ate while in the United States with their enjoyable stay. Some even ask someone to send California rice for their personal use (*Asahi Shinbun*, May 12, 1987).

The constituent nature of the meaning or meanings of a symbol has been pointed out by scholars. Often neglected is the fact that the materiality of a symbol, too, is constituted by social actors. From the perspective of symbols, an important finding of the study of rice in historical perspective is that "Japanese rice" has not always been the same item. Rice became a different rice each time the Japanese self encountered a different other—rice first introduced from Asia, rice as opposed to meat, short-grain domestic rice as opposed to long-grain foreign rice, short-grain domestic rice in contrast to short-grain foreign rice—each was or is "rice as self." Rice, then, is not a static object; both its materiality and meaning are constructed *in practice* by historical actors (chap. 7).

In semiotics and symbolic anthropology, in general, emphasis is on multiplicity of meaning; a symbol is almost always multivocal or polysemic. In my recent works (Ohnuki-Tierney 1990c; 1991a), I point out that, in addition to being polysemic, symbols are often polytropic, that is, they assume various tropic capacities—as metaphors, metonyms, synecdoches, or ironies—as actors use the symbols. In the findings in this book I point to yet another dimension of the symbolic process: objects, like rice, are also constituent.

Paradoxically, then, the Japanese collective self has both changed and not changed. Rice, too, has stayed the same while not only its meaning but its materiality has changed. Put the other way, rice has been simultaneously univocal and multivocal; it represents the Japanese self while that self undergoes various historical changes. Thus, this book is about the Japanese selves and rices examined through "Rice as Self" for the Japanese. Through a very dynamic process of symbolization rice represents a variety of objects—*many rices representing many selves*. The symbolization process is far more complex and dynamic than a simple semiotic notion of a signifier that has multiple meanings.

Actors, however, never have free rein. Criticizing the individual-centered model of historical change, Moore (1986:322) warns of "the crippling disadvantage of a limited conception of analytic field and of causality." Rice remained unequivocal, whereas the metallic currency was equivocal. Thus, depending upon the context and the use by a social actor, money can be pure or extremely impure. But rice does not provide such freedom for actors. With increased secularization, today's rice is sacred or pure only in certain contexts. But it cannot be impure, even though rice was once used as currency. Unrestrained celebration of the power of individuals, although inviting, does not help one understand human behavior.

Food: Metonym-Metaphor of Self

The power of food as a symbol of self-identity derives from the particular nature of the symbolic process involved. An important food as a metaphor of a social group involves two interlocking dimensions. First, each member of the social group consumes the food, which becomes part of his or her body. The important food becomes *embodied* in each individual. It operates as a *metonym* by being part of the self. Second, the food is consumed by individual members of the social group who eat the food together. Communal consumption of the food leads to rice as a *metaphor* of *we*—his or her social group and, often, the people as a whole.

The double layering of metonymic and metaphoric relations between a symbol and what it stands for is often the source of the cognitive and evocative power of a symbol. Lévi-Strauss, who considers contiguity and analogy as the two most important conceptual principles of the human mind, calls attention to the importance of the "transformation and countertransformation" between metonymy and metaphor (1966:150) as does Fernandez (1974:125–126; 1982:558–562), who has persistently expounded the importance of metaphor for anthropological interpretations (see also Fernandez 1991). Even those who hold metaphor to be the most central of all tropes emphasize that a metonymic principle is often involved in it. For example, de Man (1979) insists that a striking metaphor depends upon metonymic connections, and Genette (1972) emphasizes the coexistence and mutual support or interpenetration of metaphor and metonymy.[2]

Consumed food, then, embodies the biaxial principles of metonymy and metaphor or contiguity and similarity in practice by social actors. Whether a food represents an individual self, a social group, or a people as a whole, this symbolic process renders foods as powerful not only conceptually but also psychologically. For this reason "our food" versus "their food" becomes a powerful way to express *we* versus *they*. This is so not only for the representation of *we* through a food item but also for discriminating the other from *us*. Although I have already given some examples in chapter 1, it is worth quoting one more from the ancient Chinese, who defined themselves in terms of the two important principles of *their* foodway: the eating of grain and the eating of *cooked* meat. These were the important markers that distinguished them from the neighboring "barbarians."

> The people of those five regions. . . . The tribes on the east . . . had their hair unbound, and tattooed their bodies. Some of them ate their food without its being cooked with fire. Those on the south . . . tattooed their foreheads, and their feet turned in toward each other. Some of them ate their food without its being cooked with fire. Those on the west . . . had their hair unbound, and wore skins. Some of them did not eat grain-food. Those on the north . . . wore skins of animals and birds, and dwelt in caves. Some of them did not eat grain-food. (Cited in Chang 1977a:42; Chang's italics)[3]

The barbarians lack one of the two defining features of the culinary principles. The "food semantics" (Chang 1977b) reveals the social system succinctly and powerfully.

The beauty and purity of *we* are *embodied doubly in the body of the people and in the food that represents them*, and, conversely, the undesirable qualities of the other are embodied in *their* foods and foodway.

No such powerful embedment is involved for the emperor, whose ability to represent the Japanese has throughout history been tenuous, while the rice-Japanese association has remained intact. This is, however, by no means the only reason nor the causal factor for what happened in history to the imperial system.

The Primordial Self: Purity, Land, and History

Purity: Self, Ethnicity, and Nationalism

The study of ethnicity and nationalism is a burgeoning field in anthropology and related disciplines. In the post-colonial era ethnicity and nationalism intensified all over the world, well before the dissolution of the USSR. The symbolism of rice and rice paddies resonates with the symbolic dimensions of ethnicity and nationalism elsewhere in the world.

In his analytical comparison of the empire, nation, and ethnic group, Yalman (1992:1–2) sees an imperial system, such as the Ottoman empire, as one that "accepts and respects, on principle, the existence of diversity within its borders and devises political institutions which are responsive to diverse legal, religious and ethnic traditions." In contrast, ethnicity and nationalism both demand its *purity* and are intolerant of diversity.[4] B. Williams (1989) repeatedly emphasizes how "the invention of purity" is entailed in all nation building, both with a newly emerging nation as well as an established nation. Herzfeld (1987:82) describes the Greeks in their "search for the secular Eden of national *purity*." Handler (1988) points out that linguistic pollution and the search for purity are important concerns of recent Quebec nationalism. All these cases from a variety of societies testify that the notion of purity is deeply embedded in the concept of self, whether it is part of ethnicity or nationalism or independent of its political component. One of the findings of the long-term study presented here is that purity is an integral part of the concept of Japanese self and, thus, its presence did not have to wait until the rise of ethnicity or nationalism.

But, the purity of self is Janus faced. No one can forget the grotesque development of Hitler's Germany when this established nation strove for "racial purity." Japanese rice stood for the purity, or positive energy, of deities, whose consumption rejuvenates humans. But the purity of rice has been used for nationalistic purposes since the Early Modern period. The rallying cry during World War II was to win the war so that the Japanese could again eat the "pure white rice" that symbolizes their purity. In *symbolic practice* purity can be elevated to an aesthetic level without political implications; it can also be shackled with intolerance to serve as the handmaiden of a negative nationalism in which the marginalized sectors within the society as well as the external other become scapegoats in the name of achieving individual purity.

Spatiotemporal Representations

Recent anthropological studies have shown the importance of metaphors of time and space, or, more concretely, land (territory) and history, for nationalism. Sometimes they are represented in nature. In a comparative study of nationalism in Sri Lanka and Australia, Kapferer (1988) repeatedly points to the metaphors of space-time—embodied in "nature"—in Australian nationalism. Herzfeld's work (1991) on "the disputed ownership of history" in a Cretan town is entitled, *A Place in History*, a clever title using the space-time metaphors of contemporary Greeks who struggle to come to terms with their identity or identities. Architecture becomes the main focus of contestation because it embodys *histories* of these people in *place*.

The evocative power, as V. Turner would say, of rice rests in the simultaneous double layering of rice as a metonym—a part of the body through consumption by individual Japanese—and a metaphor for the Japanese through commensality and other collective activities. This symbolic mechanism, however, only partially explains the power of rice as a symbol because the same argument can be applied to various other foods and drinks.

What distinguishes rice from other candidates for symbols is its link to space and time, or more concretely, land and history. This dimension of rice symbolism is buried if rice represents only the polished grains eaten. But when the eighth-century myth-histories appropriated the rice agriculture introduced from the Asian continent as their own, their "creation myth" of the Japanese universe, or at least one version of it, was a transformation of wilderness into a land filled with succulent heads of rice. In short, rice paddies created "Japanese land." Rice paddies stand for "the ancestral land" at the family level, and seigniorial power was expressed through the image of golden heads of rice stretching across the lord's territory.

This double linkage to the Japanese self—representing its *body* and its *land*—may be a clue to the enormous power and resilience of rice symbolism which has *remained more meaningful and powerful than both the imperial system and agriculture itself*. No other food item, even tea, which is *not* mentioned in the myth-histories, has received such consistent attention throughout history.

The intimate involvement of space for the Japanese concept of self, however, does *not* derive from a need to demarcate Japan, which is surrounded by the sea. This situation contrasts with circumstances in which the ethnicity and nationalism of social groups in adjacent areas physically need territorial boundaries, as symbolized by the Berlin Wall.

One of the defining characteristics of B. Anderson's (1991:7) well-known thesis of the nation as the "imagined community" is that the nation is "imagined as *limited*" in that it is within national "boundaries." The Japanese case powerfully argues for the importance of recognizing the symbolic importance of spatial boundaries even in the absence of the physical or political need to do so. "Space" is essential in the self-identity of a people, and Japan's case testifies that the need is *symbolic*.

In addition to *our land*, rice paddies objectify *time*. It is the *Japanese nature* that tells them of the four seasons, beginning with rice planting in the spring, through its growth during the summer, its harvesting in the fall, and empty rice paddies with sheaves of rice plants covered with snow in winter. But, nature objectifies time in another significant way— a past that is pure, simple, imbued with pristine beauty, and uncontaminated by foreign influences. It embodies *our history*. It is, then, no wonder that the myth-histories of the eighth century were summoned again and again during later periods in the effort to construct *our* history.

Landlessness as Transgression

But the link of rice to land gains an even more profound cultural cum politico-economic significance during the formation of internal others in Japan. It was the *nonsettled* people (*hiteijūmin*) who became increasingly marginalized after the end of the Medieval period, and this process paralleled the transformation of agrarian cosmology into agrarian ideology. Seen in this light, the labels used to refer to these people take on additional meaning. The main difference between the settled population and the nonsettled was that only the settled population was taxed. But, the designations applied to the nonsettled population all referred to marginalized space—people of the riverbanks, scattered places, and so forth. The economic principle of taxed versus nontaxed status is expressed through spatial metaphors.[5]

Even in the agrarian sector, stratification is closely tied to the notion of land. Rice farmers are not necessarily rice consumers. Those who rose to the top in the stratification were landowners, who were thereby able to control the mode of production, the relations of production, and even consumption. The key was to own land.

Thus, the development of the collective identity of the Japanese, as expressed in "rices as selves" and "rice paddies as Japanese land," represents a historical process whereby those social groups who were not anchored to politically defined space became minorities—the *internal others*—whose presence was excluded both from history and from the representation of Japan as "agrarian." Within the agrarian sector, land-ownership became critical in the stratification. This is the other side of the development of the agrarian ideology, which accrued both symbolic and political centrality to the settled population (warriors and farmers). The process of *naturalization* of the agrarian cosmology-turned-ideology was accompanied by the devaluation of the nonsettled and their way of life. "The landlessness" became *transgression*.

To recapitulate, neither rice as food nor rice paddies as land them-selves engender negative meanings. Precisely because these multivocal symbols are powerful, however, they can also be mobilized effectively for political purposes, including as tools for discrimination and chauvinism, as well documented in Hardacre (1989) in her work on State Shintoism.

Contrary to Hobsbawm's (1992:7) claim that "the social disorienta-tion" is the key causal agent for the intensification of nationalism and ethnicity in the contemporary world, in the case of Japan, "social disori-entation" is a result of the development of the agrarian ideology that became the ideological backbone of Japanese nationalism later.

"Cultural Colonialism" in Historical Conjunctures

A major focus of this study has been historical confluences. The follow-ing quotation from Moore (1986:4–5) offers an unforgettable visual metaphor of historical conjunctures:

> When, at the foot of Mount Kilimanjaro, one meets a blanket-wearing, other-wise naked, spear-carrying Maasai man on a back path in the Tanzanian bush, one notices that he has a spool from a Kodak film packet in his earholes as an earring plug. That earring alone is sufficient to indicate that he is not a total reproducer of an integrated ancestral culture. His film spindle is made of ex-truded plastic manufactured in Rochester, New York, his red blanket comes from Europe, his knife is made of Sheffield steel. Dangling from a thong around his neck is a small leather container full of Tanzanian paper money, the proceeds from selling his cattle in a government-regulated market. The price of his animals varies with world inflation. The roads nearby have buses and tourists. The international economy has penetrated everywhere.

Although Moore's purpose in presenting this passage is to argue her point about historical reproduction and changes, the passage also articu-lates how every culture, past and present, has been changing as a result of dialectic between internal and external developments.

If the Maasai man objectified historical conjunctures in Africa, so do architectures of a contemporary Cretan town in Rethemnos. Herzfeld's (1991:112) caption for photo 26 reads, "A characteristic conjuncture: electric light pole, Venetian masonry, shattered Turkish window box." The material culture objectifies multiple histories, and "the choice of pasts is negotiated in a shifting present" (Herzfeld 1991:257).

In all these conjunctures, the discourse of self and other has been deeply embedded in a complex historical interplay of power inequalities. Selves and others are seldom equal partners in these conjunctures. It is far easier to recognize the political domination of the West over Africa and other former colonies. But an even more serious consequence is the cultural domination by Western civilization not only over their former colonies but over many other parts of the world. The attitude of the Japanese is double-edged toward the superior other—the Chinese and the Westerners. Today, feeling that they have conquered Western technological fields, some Japanese are still eager to prove their *distinction*, developed within their society, through a craze for Beaujolais nouveau immediately after its release in France (for more detail see Ohnuki-Tierney 1990a:202–203) while defending *our* (Japanese) rice.

In the Middle East, Yalman (1989:15) explains the amazing appeal of Khomeini to the Iranians as an expression of "the violent gut reaction against the penetration of the West into the Middle East" and evokes Ashis Nandy's powerful phrase "the colonized mind" to understand what S. Rushdie stands for—the complexity and ambivalence that the culturally/politically colonized peoples feel about themselves in relation toward the West (Yalman 1989:16). Occidentalism, therefore, can never be a simple inversion of Orientalism.

But the symbolic power inequality is not confined to the West versus the other. It works even within so-called Western civilization. Mischievously calling the Greeks aboriginal Europeans, Herzfeld identifies the ambivalence contemporary Greeks feel about themselves and toward others. The image of fallen Hellenism portrays both the holy and the polluted visions of modern Greece, where rural Greeks satirize the literate, at the same time grudgingly recognizing "the power that literacy confers" (Herzfeld 1987:49).

Even more important than the recognition of inequality in symbolic power in historical encounters between peoples is its further effects upon the culture perceived to be inferior. The power inequality between the self and the "superior" *external other* is in part responsible for the creation of a scapegoat—the marginalized self turned into minorities, internally, and, the marginalized other, externally. "Cultural colonialism," as I call it, can play havoc toward others as well as toward themselves when it is combined with nationalism. It is an unfortunate subtext of many inter-national discourses and an even more unfortunate subtext for the phenomenon of using scapegoats to create marginalized selves and others.

The theme of the Stranger Deity—the deity with positive and negative powers who visits from outside—has provided a powerful model for the Japanese to interpret historical encounters with the superior others— the Chinese and, then, the Westerners. The cosmological model of the Stranger Deity, however, embodies symbolic power inequality: the deity is superior to humans, who must harness the deity's positive power. In historical practice the Stranger Deity can turn into a politically or cultur- ally powerful other. Perhaps it is not surprising that the Stranger Deity is a theme found in many parts of the world (see chap. 5, n. 8); the model serves as an explanatory model for inequality, symbolic and political.

When the Stranger Deity is rejected and its energy and power are no longer harnessed for the rejuvenation of the self, the self must rely on its own source of purity for regeneration. To protect the last citadel—a metaphor for self-identity under threat as the phrase is used to oppose California rice importation, the *pure*, "chemical-free" domestic rice, rice paddies that *purify* Japanese air and represent the *pure* Japanese past without contamination from foreign influence, and the *pure* white rice *embodied* in the self, both individually and collectively, must be sum- moned for the self-rejuvenation. Or, the self purges itself by removing its impurity and placing it on the internal and external others.

The Japanese identity that was created in their discourse with the Chi- nese, the culturally superior other at the time, has since then gone through historical transformations as it encountered different others. In all these encounters between selves and others, the multivocal rice and rice paddies have served as the vehicle for deliberation about the self- identity as it transforms into selves and as the internal source of purity for the ever-changing self.

Notes

Chapter One

1. This phrase has been used too frequently and too superficially to retain its original explanatory power. The "invention" refers to something that is grounded in particular historical precedent, and not out of a vacuum.

2. Although the recent rapprochement between history and anthropology is phenomenal, it is also natural because the two disciplines share "distancing of self" (Braudel [1958] 1980:37) through a study of the temporal "other" by historians and the spatial "other" by anthropologists (cf. Cohn 1980; 1981; Lévi-Strauss [1958] 1967:17; 1983:36).

3. This scheme and each of these three approaches, quantitatively defined by Braudel, are embedded in his complex idea about history, which, in turn, arose out of scholarly debate about historiography inside and outside the *Annales* school in France. As a study of the historical process of a much shorter period than the *longue durée*, *conjuncture* also entails the historical confluence of transnational and transcontinental traffic, which influences historical developments in all the regions involved. He and his younger colleagues examined the general conjecture of the sixteenth century, which involved vast regions of the world, not only "Venice or Lisbon, Antwerp or Seville, Lyons or Milan, but also the complex economy of the Baltic, the ancient rhythms of the Mediterranean, the major currents of the Atlantic and the Iberian Pacific, Chinese junks, and even now I am omitting things" (Braudel 1980:13–14; see also Braudel [1949] 1972:462–642).

4. This emphasis gives a healthy antithesis to an overly rigid structuralism. Some extreme forms of this approach to culture have created a danger of uprooting individuals from their sociocultural and historical contexts. Advocating the midlevel approach and offering a detailed study of "customary" law in Kilimanjaro for one century, Moore (1986:322), nevertheless, points to "the crippling disadvantage" of the "individual-centered model of change," in which "the external context is all but ignored and the actors are treated as if they made their own fate." As Ortner (1989:11–18) in her characteristically succinct way puts it, structure or system is not in apposition to individuals and their actions. In fact, the original formulation of *dialogism* and *polyphony* (Bakhtin 1981) or *practice* (Bourdieu 1977)—two major influences on this recent development—are deeply embedded in these scholars' intellectual and *political* thoughts, which place individuals in the context of power inequalities in society.

I note here some profound differences among scholars in the use of the terms of *individual, actor, agent*, and so forth. In response to misunderstandings of his concepts, Bourdieu (1990:9–17) emphasizes that his concern is *not* subjects but agents, and his aim is "to reintroduce agents that Lévi-Strauss and the structuralists, among others Althusser, tended to abolish, making them into simple epiphenomena of structure." Similarly, Godelier (In press) emphatically distinguishes between society and individuals and the limit of the power of individuals: "Socie-ties are not individuals and cultural systems are like living languages; they are not invented by any one person. No one invented Chinese or Finnish." Society or culture cannot be reduced to a composite of as many views as there are members of the society. One cannot abandon either individuals as members of the society or the cultural structures/systems, however one defines them. The rela-tive importance one places on each, however, depends on the purpose of each project.

5. I do not subscribe to the Durkheimian notion of "society" that anthropolo-gists have superimposed upon other peoples (see chap. 6, n.2).

6. Both Augé (1982:10–11) and Cohn (1980:211) point out that the term *non-Western* defines the rest of the world as a residual category, whereas *West-ern* lumps many cultures with different traditions into one blanket category as do the terms *Oriental* and *Asian*.

Chapter Two

1. Rice produced in some Asian countries, notably Indonesia, is of different varieties.

2. Usually brown rice (*genmai* 'unpolished rice') is considered the same as black rice (*kurogome*), but Ishige (1985:132) argues that black rice was partially polished (*hichibuzuki*) and, therefore, should not be equated with brown rice.

3. The white rice only diet is linked to beriberi.

4. Tsuboi ([1982] 1984:63) cites 1966 as the year of rice overproduction.

5. Some report lower figures. For example, C. Smith (1987) quotes ¥ 380 bil-lion for government subsidies.

6. Japanese government surveys always combine farming with lumbering.

7. In addition to the wedding itself, they talked about the following rituals as part of the marriage ceremony: *okaotsunagi* (the introduction of the bride to the groom's relatives and the members of his village) and *yuinō* (the exchange of gifts between the groom's and bride's families officially to signal the engagement; those I interviewed estimated a cost of ¥ 100,000). Even after the marriage, the bride's family must continue certain annual rituals, for example, *harikuyō* (the "memorial service for needles," a fixed day on the calendar, although the exact date differs from region to region) when women abstain from sewing and ritually dispose of broken needles, sometimes offering them to a shrine, to pray for the souls of the needles. In some areas, the bride's family must distribute pastry (*omanjū*) to the couple's neighbors; an annual gift of *kanburi* (yellow tail) to the groom's family when the fish is in season (winter); and gifts to the children on the boys' and girls' days (*sekku*). Furthermore, life-cycle rituals require families to hold feasts and offer gifts to the guests: *yakubarai* (the ritual to expel evil spirits); the ritual for males at age forty-two, the most inauspicious year for males; the *kanreki* ritual, celebrating a man's sixtieth birthday (sixty-first according to the traditional way age is counted in Japan); during the ritual, he is clad in red, sym-bol of childhood, to announce his return to childhood (*honke gaeri*). In urban areas, usually only the wedding and the engagement ritual of *yuinō* are observed although the bride's family sends gifts to the groom's family during the two an-

nual gift exchange periods, and the groom's family sends gifts to the bride's family in return. A farmer I interviewed also pointed out that in rural areas residents spend more money on their houses to maintain family honor.

8. Of a number of farm unions (*nōkyō*), *zennō* has acted as the central agent for the opposition.

9. The irony is that arguments on *both* sides are essentially noneconomic. Japan, with its overproduction of rice, would not lose much by opening its rice market because demand is low. The United States would not gain much if it gained entry, not only because demand in Japan is low but because rice, unlike potatoes and corn, is not a significant agricultural product in the U.S. economy. Thus, if the Japanese market is opened, Thailand and the People's Republic of China—two major rice-growing countries—or Pakistan will likely capture a larger share of Japan's small rice market.

If so, U.S. pressure on the rice exportation issue may be understood only in relation to the broader picture of trade friction that has been going on for some time. Some, both in the United States and Japan, say that the United States has chosen the rice issue because it drives home how chauvinistic and irrational the Japanese have been on trade issues. In fact, as a part of the trade issue, Japanese multinational corporations prefer that California rice is imported to decrease trade friction.

Chapter Three

1. Although the role of agriculture in the development of nation-states is not to be questioned, many societies based on a hunting-gathering economy, such as the Ainu in parts of Hokkaidō and the Indians of the northwest coast of North America, have enjoyed what M. Sahlins has called "the Original Affluent Society" with permanent settlements (See Ohnuki-Tierney 1976).

2. Critics of their work claim that the *Hita no Gofudoki* was compiled by an official at a later date and that no evidence exists that villagers ate the foods listed in the record.

3. Both potatoes and sweet potatoes were introduced to Japan during the Early Modern period. The Japanese preferred sweet potatoes because they could eat them alone; regular potatoes were not tasty enough to eat by themselves (Tsukuba 1986:23).

4. The term *gokoku* ("five" grains), introduced originally from the Chinese, is also used, but it actually means many grains, not "five" grains. It includes rice (*ine*); wheat (*mugi*), Italian millet (*awa*), true millet (*kibi*), and beans (*mame*).

5. In contemporary Japan, the folklore school is distinct from ethnology, but both are referred to as *minzokugaku*. They use different characters for *zoku*; the one for the folklore school means "customs," and the one for ethnology means "people." In my view, differences between the two are more apparent than real although diversity within each approach defies simple generalizations.

6. He includes the following regions: *Tōhoku, Hokuriku, Chūbu, Kinki*, and *Kyūshū*.

7. This finding is not surprising; in China, another major rice-eating country, rice is not the quantitatively important food for all the Chinese: "Only in a few

very fertile alluvial plains of southeast China is rice the only staple food, and only in the alluvial valleys of south and central China is it a staple at all" (E. Anderson 1988:142). Today in China, rice provides only 40 percent of starchy staple foods (E. Anderson 1988:142).

Chapter Four

1. See Tsunoda and Goodrich (1968:14–15) for a description in the Chinese dynastic histories of a Japanese woman ruler, named Pimiko, who is said to have bewitched her people with magic and sorcery (see also Sansom [(1931) 1943: 29]).

2. Orikuchi further suggests that this notion involved the people's obedience to the order issued by the deity (1975a:178–179). The central government collected the new crop of rice from various parts of the country for offerings. The religious act of following the orders of the deity who gave rice seeds to humans and offering the deity their harvest in return involved the political act of collecting the rice crop from the people. The head of the nation, then, had an obligation to oversee the growth of rice. Most scholars accept Orikuchi's insight regarding *matsurigoto* and the concept of soul in ancient Japan. However, his inference of the Japanese emperor system as an absolute monarchy and his other nationalistic interpretations are rejected outright.

3. Although most scholars agree that the *niiname* and the *ōname* refer to the same imperial harvest ritual, some claim that both were called the *niiname* (T. Tanaka 1988:29), whereas others argue that they were called the *ōname* (Orikuchi 1975a:180–181; K. Sakurai 1988:33), and still others argue that *ōname* was simply a more elegant name for the harvest ceremony than *niiname* (Murakami 1977:13). After A.D. 673 (the second year of the reign of the Tenmu emperor, [r. A.D. 667–686), *niinamesai* referred to the annual imperial harvest ritual, whereas *ōnamesai* referred to the ritual at the time of a new emperor's accession (Murakami 1977:13; T. Tanaka 1988).

4. For an overview of the imperial rituals see Nihiname Kenkyūkai 1955; K. Sakurai 1988; T. Tanaka 1988; Ueda Kenji 1988; Yamamoto, Satō, and staff 1988:224–231; Yokota 1988. For descriptions of the imperial rituals in English see Ebersole 1989, Ellwood 1973, Holtom 1972, and Mayer 1991.

5. The pronunciation of *daijōsai* is more popular at present although I use *ōnamesai*, a customary pronunciation until recently. A more correct pronunciation was *ōname matsuri* (reading all the characters in *kun*) or *ōnie matsuri* (see Bock 1990:27).

The *ōnamesai*, the major ceremony for accession, is held in the year the accession occurs if the accession takes place before July, or in the following year, if the accession takes place after August. If the accession is necessitated by the death of the previous emperor, however, it is held in November of the following year to allow a period of mourning. The date of the ceremony used to be the *u* (rabbit) day of November in the lunar calendar; if there are three days of *u* in November, then it is the middle one (*naka no u no hi*) (Hida 1988:214). Since the adoption of the Gregorian calendar by the Meiji government, the date of the ceremony has been November 23. It has always been held in Kyōto, the capital of Japan before the capital was moved to Tokyo, except for the Meiji emperor, for whom it was held in Tokyo to highlight the restored imperial system at the new capital.

Orikuchi's article (1975a), indispensable for any discussion of the *ōnamesai*, was originally delivered as a lecture in September 1926 after the death of Taishō and preceding the *ōnamesai* executed by Shōwa. For descriptions of the *ōnamesai* in English see Bock 1990; Ellwood 1973; Holtom 1972.

6. Orikuchi (1975a:178) suggests that the *saishin*, the deity for whom the ritual is performed, is the Deity of Heaven (*amatsu kami*). Elsewhere he refers to the emperor as the divine son of the sun (*hi no miko, hitsugi no miko*) (1975a:194). Murakami (1977:19) proposes that Musubi no Kami, the creator of all beings (Shimonaka 1941b:332–333), was the original *saishin*. It is a female deity, personifying reproductive power as well as creative power in general. Murakami (1977:19) further believes that Musubi no Kami derived from the soul of grain as the latter became more explicitly deified. Although Murakami (1977:19) does not explicitly suggest that the *ōnamesai* ritual involves sexual union between the emperor and the deity, he claims that Japanese emperors have been male because the deity with whom the emperor is united during the ritual is female.

Matsumae (1977:105–106), however, suggests that two deities were the original *saishin* for the *ōnamesai*: Takami Musubi and Miketsu Kami. Takami Musubi was one of the three deities of creation when the Japanese universe came into existence (Shimonaka 1941a:426). He was also the early agricultural deity of production and reproduction for the imperial family (Matsumae 1977:97). Miketsu Kami was the deity of foods (Shimonaka 1941b:290).

Takami Musubi is a likely candidate because he was also the ancestral deity of the imperial family before Amaterasu became established. Amaterasu was originally a deity worshipped only by the people in the Ise region, a region regarded by the Imperial Court as the abode of the Sun Goddess because it is situated east of Yamato. Some scholars say she was originally the wife of the Sun God (e.g., Saigō 1984:87–90). The Imperial Court later adopted Amaterasu and transformed her into the Sun Goddess, ancestral to the imperial line. Some claim that the development of Amaterasu as the imperial ancestress took place around the sixth century, whereas others place it in the late seventh century when ancestor worship (*ujigami shinkō*) became well developed among the people. For a detailed discussion of interpretations by different scholars, see Matsumae (1977: 90–137) and Sakamoto et al. (1967:554).

In my view, the Sun Goddess is a deity of agricultural production and, thus, is conceptually equivalent to the other deities of production and reproduction.

7. Orikuchi (1975a:185) stresses the distinction between the *niiname/ōname* ritual and the *kanname*. While in both the *ōnamesai* and the *niiname*, the emperor offers the new crop of rice from the two fields; in the *kanname* the emperor offers new rice crops from various parts of Japan. If the two fields chosen for the *ōnamesai* are a symbolic representation of Japan as a whole, then the distinction between the two types of rituals is inconsequential, at least on a conceptual level, although it is significant from the perspective of the polity.

8. Orikuchi (1975a:195) rejects outright the sexual liaison interpretation, contrary to his own insight about the soul.

9. Some claim that there is no close correlation between the myth-histories

and the *ōnamesai* and that the myth-histories should be compared with the entirety of accession rituals rather than the *ōnamesai* alone (Hida 1988:215).

10. Some are obviously early versions and others come later. For example, the *Kojiki* and Book 1 of the *Nihonshoki* were written after the establishment of Amaterasu as the imperial ancestress.

11. Saigō (1984:78–80) stresses that Amaterasu is not "hiding" in the "cave" but that the act represents her ritual seclusion from the world in the *iwaya*, a building or structure, not a cave.

12. This is a later version of the episode in the *Kojiki* and Book 1 of the *Nihonshoki*. The English translation is in Philippi (1969:81–85).

13. In the main text (*honbun*) and sections 4 and 6 of Book 1 of the *Nihonshoki*, it is Takami Musubi rather than Amaterasu, who sends the heavenly grandson Ho-no Ninigi (Ninigi-no Mikoto), to earth, wrapped in the *madoko ohusuma* (sacred bedding) (Matsumae 1977:95–96).

14. For the *Kojiki*, see Kurano and Takeda 1958; for the *Nihonshoki*, Book 1, nos. 6 and 7 see Sakamoto et al. 1965 and 1967. *Uka-no Kami* is called *Uka-no Mitama* (*uka = uke* 'grain'; *kami* 'deity'; *mitama* 'soul of a deity').

15. After he was said to be enthroned, he was called Kamuyama Itohare Biko no Mikoto (Kurano and Takeda 1958:147).

16. The word Ō may be translated as "king," but it does not necessarily mean a male. Because rice is gendered as female it is appropriate to translate it as "queen."

17. For further discussions of the *marebito*, see Higo (1942:103–104); Matsudaira 1977; Ouwehand 1958–1959; Suzuki 1974, 1979; M. Yamaguchi 1977; T. Yoshida 1981. For the continuation of the *marebito* concept into the present see the incisive analyses of folk festivals in contemporary Japan by Higo (1942) and Matsudaira (1977).

18. Most contemporary Japanese would not personally believe that rice has a soul or that it is alive in the husk. But even today rice farmers store their rice unthreshed and thresh only small amounts as needed. Urban Japanese (women) buy relatively small amounts of rice at local stores that they can trust to supply them with rice that has been threshed only a few days before delivery. Similarly, the Japanese pay special attention to the new crop of rice; each fall at harvest time, many Japanese place special orders for the new crop of rice or shinmai (*shin* 'fresh, new'; *mai* 'rice'). Conversely, the sale of *komai* (old rice) by the government, purchased from farmers during years of overproduction and stored, has been a central issue in attacks on the government's rice policy (Hasegawa 1987). In contemporary Japan, the terms komai and shinmai are used without reference to the soul. Contemporary Japanese phrase their preference for newly threshed rice and their aversion to old rice in terms of taste rather than the soul of rice; new crop rice is tasty, whereas old rice is not palatable. Despite its thoroughly secularized form, the Japanese continue to view rice not as a lifeless object but as a special food that has life and provides a special source of energy.

19. Yanagita equates the *inadama* with the *soshin* (ancestral deity) who in turn is the Ta-no Kami (Deity of the Rice Paddy).

20. A discussion of these three symbolic principles in light of Western scholarship about the sacred and the profane is beyond the scope of this book (for further discussion of Japanese principles see Ohnuki-Tierney 1987:140–149).

21. In most cultures the moon is perceived as female, whereas the sun is usually a male figure. In Japanese mythology, however, the moon is identified with Susano-o-no Mikoto, the younger brother of the Sun Goddess.

22. Of numerous articles by Yanagita on rice, the most important for the purposes of this book are 1981a; 1982b; 1982d; and 1982c. See also Itoh 1979; 1988.

23. Mauss's position on the nature of a gift is not consistent, however, and vacillates between "pure gifts" and quasi commodity.

24. For a recent review of the divine kingship and the related concepts of priestly king and magical king see Feeley-Harnik 1985. See also Dumont 1970; de Heusch 1985; Geertz (1980:121–146); Sahlins 1985, and Tambiah 1976. Valeri (1985) uses the term *diarchic kingship*.

25. This phenomenon has been debated by scholars; Eisenstadt (n.d.) explains it in term of his scheme of Axial versus non-Axial religions; Kitagawa (1990) describes it as "eclectic," others as "multilayered," while still others see various religions as "fused" (for details see Ohnuki-Tierney [1984:145–149]).

26. In some agrarian societies, such as the Balinese and Javanese, rice is reported to "suffer the pain of severance" (van der Meer 1979:111) when it is harvested with the rice knife. Whether this act is perceived as violence is not clear. The Javanese harvest ritual enacts the marriage of a daughter of the king of gods and her husband, both transformed into rice stalks (Geertz 1960:81), but it is not connected with the kingly accession.

Chapter Five

1. For various versions of the story see Yanagita (1951:258–259).

2. For variations of this story see Yanagita's discussion on *tsuru nyōbō* (crane wife) (Yanagita 1951:382).

3. On the religious nature of economic transactions see also Komatsu and Kurimoto 1982. Although religious/symbolic interpretations of "economic transactions" represent a more recent revisionist approach, the dominant interpretation by historians, especially in the past, has been to regard the rice-tax system strictly as a politicoeconomic system that was used as a means of oppression by the landholding class (see, for example, Nagahara [1972:36–37]).

4. Not only ritual but the notion of "belief," too, was originally linked to economics. Benveniste discusses belief (*la croyance*) under the heading of "economic obligations" (Pouillon 1982:3), and many other contemporary French scholars, including Belmont (1982), Herrenschmidt (1982), and Pouillon (1982) follow this line.

5. Because rice is the source of power, the characters for spirits (*sei*) and breath/vital energy (*ki*) include a character for rice. Although these characters and their meanings have become Japanese, it is problematic to introduce characters because they, together with their meanings, came from China. Some foreign scholars misunderstand the presence of the character for rice among the four characters that the Japanese use to refer to the United States. In this particular case the character is used only for its pronunciation, not for its meaning.

6. See Barthes (1982:12–14) for his insightful but overly romantic observation of the aesthetics of Japanese food, in general, and rice, in particular.

7. Katsumata (1985) examines the egalitarianism envisioned by the common folk in different periods in history. He emphasizes that their vision of egalitarianism restricted their resentment to only the members of their own community who hoarded and became unusually rich. In other words, it did not take a more general or abstracted form directed at society at large.

8. For the concept of the stranger in various parts of the world, see Berger and Luckmann (1967:122, 156); Frankenberg 1957; Myerhoff 1980; Sahlins 1981; Schutz (1971:91–105); Shack and Skinner 1979; V. Turner (1975: especially 231–271); and van Gennep (1961:26, 27).

Chapter Six

1. Anthropologists had been and continued to be "specialists of the nonliterate and the primitive." This self-definition placed cultures like Japan, China, and India outside of their territory, unless one studied rural areas or minorities, "primitive pockets" or "cold pockets" within "civilization" or "hot society." For a critique of anthropology in this regard see Ohnuki-Tierney 1990b.

2. See chap. 7, n. 1 for a discussion of the term *society*. There is a question of when the Japanese people began to conceptualize themselves as a people. The contemporary notion of "we, the Japanese," which includes all the people on the archipelago, is a relatively new development that dates, possibly, to the Russo-Japanese War. The term *nihon* (the base where the sun rises) was originally a designation of Japan by the Chinese from their geographic perspective (Amino personal communication).

3. For details of the compilation of these myth-histories, see Sakamoto et al. (1967:6–12).

4. Tang Confucianism, which provided the model for the Japanese imperial ritual, perceived ritual as an integral part of polity (Ahern 1981; Yu-Lan [1948:214–215]), whereas in Japan the relation between ritual and politics took a complex turn after the Ancient period. In discussions of the Chinese influence on Japanese culture, especially on religion and polities, some scholars use "Confucianism" as if its character in Japan preserved the original Chinese form and content. This view is very simplistic. A far more powerful explanatory model is an anthropological understanding of the "total social phenomenon" (Mauss [1950] 1966), which maintains that most cultural institutions of any society, including the early Japanese imperial system, simultaneously embody several dimensions, such as religious, economic, and political.

5. The picture is far more complicated; one cannot simply regard the *ōname-sai* as a way to counter the Chinese-type accession ceremony as Ueyama Haruhira (quoted in Akamatsu [1989, no. 1]) suggests.

6. The term *shokunin* as the designation for craft workers and other "professionals" was first recorded in 1367 (Amino 1980:105–108; Amino 1983:186–199), which indicates the consolidation of these people as a social group by the mid–fourteenth century.

7. The residential pattern of the special status people has been controversial. Many scholars claim that they did not have permanent settlements but traveled from village to village. Ochiai (1972:66–67), however, citing Yanagita, emphatically states that many were not outsiders but were members of a community. I

suggest that special status people in the artistic/religious categories were temporary visitors to farming communities, but those whose occupations were to remove impurities were permanent members of settled communities and occupied peripheral areas.

8. Other people who were loosely included in the special status group include *mooto* (outsiders), *kojiki* (beggars), *hijiri* (saints), and the *hinin* (nonhuman). A group of people called *hinin* first appeared during the early phase of the Heian period (A.D. 794–1185) and became more visible in cities only after the mid-Heian period (Takayanagi 1981:11–13). Although the transliterated meaning of the term *hinin* is "nonhuman," during the Medieval period the term referred to individuals who voluntarily abandoned their society (Morita 1978:79–80). The *hinin* included a small number of criminals who were expelled by society and beggars who begged for economic rather than religious reasons. But many *hinin* were *hijiri* (saints) who decided to leave society (*shukke*) for religious reasons and to reject the demands and responsibilities of a secular life, such as paying taxes (Kuroda 1972; Morinaga 1967; Takayanagi 1981). As outsiders, the *hijiri*, or itinerant priests, stood for an antiestablishment element; their abandonment of society symbolically represented a critical stance against the institutionalized religion that was increasingly identified with political power (Kuroda 1972:44–45).

9. Amino (1980; 1989) stresses that during the Medieval period, nonagrarian people, including traders, artisans, artists, performing artists, and religious specialists, were directly under the jurisdiction of the emperors who gave them permission to travel across the boundaries between different regions governed by regional lords. In a controversial work, Amino (1989) argues that the Godaigo emperor (r. 1381–1339) solicited support from nonagrarian people, especially the outcastes (*hinin*), in his war against the military government whose support came from warriors and farmers. The original concept of emperors as agrarian shaman-leaders notwithstanding, emperors in this period were closely aligned with people from the nonagrarian sectors, whereas the military government was firmly based on the agrarian population.

Amino's interpretation of the multiple systems of stratification has been criticized as giving too much sociocultural significance to nonresidents. I, too, think that the structure governing residents was probably the core of Medieval society, and those who paid taxes were the central members of the society. But I also think that the structure governing nonresidents operated on a different symbolic principle—the principle of purity and impurity. Thus, I do not give equal status and power to each system but perceive each system as governed by different principles; two systems were only loosely connected and were not bound in a rigid hierarchical relationship.

10. For a scholarly controversy of the concept of caste, see Bloch ([1949] 1961) and Dumont (1970).

11. In contrast to the inflexibility with which the special status people were codified during this period, mobility was considerable across castes/classes for warriors, farmers, craftsmen, and merchants. Some individuals voluntarily moved downward in the formalized social ladder. For example, Ishida Baigan, the founder of the Shingaku school of thought, which had a profound effect on the morality of the common people during the Early Modern period, was of peas-

ant extraction but entered the merchant class before he became a full-time preacher/lecturer (Bellah 1970:134). The power holders of the Tokugawa period were warriors, wealthy farmers, and rich merchants.

12. Katsumata (1985:179–181) suggests that the ordinance was intended to protect the lives of peasants by relegating fighting to warriors and enabling peasants to devote themselves to farming. The ordinance, however, certainly facilitated the protection of the lords more than the peasants.

13. Translation by Stevens (1988).

14. They are nos. 1, 5, 8, 9, 12, 13, 14, 17, 19, 20, 22, 23, 30, 39, 44, 47, 65, 68, 70, 71, 77, 78, 79, 83, 84, 90. Picture no. 13 may illustrate seed planting by women but not necessarily rice. Morse interprets the women in print no. 90 as carrying fish in their baskets, but because no figures of fish are drawn, and the background looks like a rice field, I interpret the contents of the baskets as rice.

15. Earlier, Yanagita used the term *heimin*. Shibusawa, the founder of the well-known Achikku Miuzeamu (Attic Museum) in 1942, was the first to use the term *jōmin*. The museum was dedicated to the study of marginalized people, including the Ainu. For details see Miyata (1990:36).

16. Yanagita's interests were in women and children, whereas Orikuchi, the founder of the other Japanese school of anthropology, was concerned with the aged.

17. The late Ishida Eiichirō, a prominent anthropologist at the University of Tokyo, and others have followed this second stage of Yanagita's quest for the pure, indigenous Japanese culture in rural life.

18. I allude to the government practice today of designating exceptional artists in the traditional Japanese arts as "national treasures."

19. Tanaka Kakuei (1972–1974) came from Niigata Prefecture, and Suzuki Zenkō (1980–82) from Iwate Prefecture, although Gumma Prefecture from which Fukuda Takeo (1976–1978) and Nakasone Yashuhiro (1982–1987) came is also heavily agricultural.

20. Other common expressions include rice. For example, *yakimochi o yaku* (to be jealous) actually means to broil rice cakes. When a rice cake is placed over heat, it expands, enclosing puffed air pockets. The appearance of the broiled rice cake is perceived as analogous to the way a person's cheeks are puffed when jealous. Another expression, *mochitsuki sōba*, means a highly fluctuating stock market; it derives from the visual image of a pestle used to pound rice into rice cakes moving up and down rapidly. By the same token the term *komekami*, "rice biting," refers to the temple, which moves as one "bites" rice, that is, "food" (Yanagita 1982c:157–158).

21. For ethnographic information on the mirror-deity relationship, see Ishibashi 1914; for ethnographic details of the equivalence of water with the mirror-deity, see Nakayama 1976.

Chapter Seven

1. I avoid the term *society* here although Watsuji uses it in Japanese translation (*shakai*). I do so in view of the recent criticism of the anthropological use of *society* as an abstract notion imposed by anthropologists upon peoples who may

not have conceptualized their communities as *society*. See Ingold (1986; 1990) and Strathern (1988) for this criticism and their emphasis on social relationships and sociality. See also Wolf (1988).

2. Although this view of humans and individuals is not unique to the Japanese, as some have argued (cf. Hamaguchi 1982), many Japanese consciously conceptualize individuals as interdependent. In contrast, in some Western societies, where the concept of the individualism has been well-developed, many hold the idealized view of completely independent individuals while, in practice, their individuals, too, are interdependent.

3. This contrasts with the egalitarian emphasis in American discourse in which equal status between two speakers is the ideal. Even when a hierarchy between the two is involved, they avoid expressing the difference verbally. To a large degree similar effects are achieved nonverbally in English, however, through body language, tone of voice, and other means.

4. Although not frequently, the phrase continues to be used in contemporary Japan. For example, celebrating its tenth anniversary in 1983, Taiyō Kōbe Ginkō, a bank in Kōbe, distributed to its customers a dictionary entitled, *Wakon Kansai Jiten* (Japanese-soul, Chinese knowledge dictionary), ed. Fujidō Akiho (Tokyo: Shōbunsha).

5. See, for example, "Mt. Fuji Seen From the Izu Peninsula" by Kawase Hasui (1883–1957) in which sheaves of rice stalks are drawn with Mt. Fuji in the background. This particular modern woodblock is housed in the Museum of Fine Arts, Boston.

6. Some continued to eat meats, however, although they "converted" them into flowers. Thus, the names of flowers were given to animal meat, such as cherry blossoms for horse and peony for wild boar.

7. Some scholars view Tsukuba's work to be too deeply embedded in the *nihonjinron* (theories about the Japanese), a semi-scholarly and semi-journalistic genre of writings that try to identify who the Japanese are, often in a chauvinistic sense. I use his work, as explained in chapter 9, as an ethnographic source.

8. Published in the Record of Sangiin Gaimu Iinkai Kaigiroku, no. 5 (during the 118th session of the Diet), p. 7

9. The television report was unprecedented; a studio was set up in Tokyo where Dan Rather and other important figures were sent to report from the scene. The show was laden with symbols of "exoticism," including the image of a fan and Japanese music at the beginning of every report.

Chapter Eight

1. I thank Nell Painter at Princeton University who brought this magazine to my attention.

2. Giraffe hunting is portrayed in the film, *Hunters*. Marshall (1976:357) states that giraffes were hunted only occasionally; eland, kudu, gemsbok, wildebeest, hartebeest, springbok, warthog, and ostrich were hunted more commonly.

3. Many of the rural landscape paintings of the impressionists are devoid of peasants (Belloli 1984: especially "The Fields of France," 241–273), and in others, for example, Pissarro, only small peasant figures appear. Drawings of peas-

ants rather than rural landscapes, however, are even more numerous (Brettell and Brettell 1983).

4. They further equate the peasants with essentially "primitive peoples"—a provocative idea although I argue for a more complex association between the two.

5. Note that Japanese cuisine does not include salad.

6. For subsidies to agriculture in different countries see table 5.1 in Calder (1988:235).

Chapter Nine

1. I do not agree with his categorical statement, "It was the danger of famine that gave such urgency to agriculture and such joys to eating" (Spence 1977: 261).

2. For Jakobson (1956), Lévi-Strauss (1966:150), and Leach (1976), metaphor is characterized by similarity, whereas metonymy is characterized by contiguity, cause and effect, means and ends, and container and content. Leach separates the "cause and effect" principle to set up a third figure, signals. For details of the theoretical argument on tropes see Ohnuki-Tierney 1990c, 1991a.

3. This quotation is from James Legge's translation (1885) of F. Max Müller, ed., *The Li Ki, The Sacred Books of the East*, vols. 27, 28 (Oxford: Clarendon Press).

4. Yalman (1992:2) contrasts nation and ethnicity with only the former related to territory and state.

5. Another social group that became a minority in Japanese society is the Ainu, a hunting-gathering people whose "territory" was not anchored to space in an agrarian sense. Intra-cultural variations are considerable between the Kurile, the Sakhalin, and the Hokkaido Ainu. The Hokkaido Ainu, alone, had permanent settlements in a hunting-gathering economy. With the implementation of the Native Law in 1779, they, too, were forced to settle in "reservations" and cultivate their land and *were given rice* as their food (Takakura 1960:55–56). The history of their marginalization, however, was less directly tied to the development of "agrarian Japan."

References Cited

Ahern, Emily Martin
1981 *Chinese Ritual and Politics*. New York: Cambridge University Press.
Akamatsu Shunsuke
1989 Keni no kōzō: Tennōron no ima (The structure of authority—The current status of the debate on the emperor system). *Asahi Shinbun* no. 1 (February 6); no. 2 (February 7); no. 3 (February 8).
Akasaka Norio
1988 *Ō to tennō* (King and emperor: Comparative work on kingship). Tokyo: Chikuma Shobō.
Amino Yoshihiko
1980 *Nihon chūsei no minshūzō: Heimin to shokunin* (Portrait of the folk in medieval Japan: The common people and the "professionals"). Tokyo: Iwanami Shoten.
1983 [1978] *Muen kugai raku: Nihon chūsei no jiyū to heiwa* (*Muen, kugai,* and *raku*: Freedom and peace in medieval Japan). Tokyo: Heibonsha.
1984 Chūsei no tabibitotachi (Travelers during the Medieval period). In *Hyōhaku to teijū* (Wandering and settlement), Y. Amino et al., eds., 153–266. Tokyo: Shōgakkan.
1987 Lecture at History Workshop. Department of History, University of Chicago, October 5, 1987.
1989 [1986] *Ikei no ōken* (Atypical kingship). Tokyo: Heibonsha.
Amino Yoshihiko, Ueno Chizuko, and Miyata Noboru.
1988 *Nihon ōkenron* (Japanese kingship). Tokyo: Shunjūsha.
Anderson, Benedict
1991 *Imagined Communities*. London and New York: Verso.
Anderson, E. N.
1988 *The Food of China*. New Haven, Conn.: Yale University Press.
Aoki Kōji
1967 *Hyakushō ikki no nenjiteki kenkyū* (Chronological research on peasant uprisings). Tokyo: Shinseisha.
Aristotle
1958 *The Politics of Aristotle*. E. Barker, ed. and trans. Oxford: Oxford University Press.
Ashbrook, Tom
1988 Japan's Farmers Strike Back. *Boston Globe*, January 13, 1988.
Aston, W. G., trans.
1956 [1896] *Nihongi: Chronicles of Japan from the Earliest Times to A.D. 697*. London: George Allen and Unwin.
Augé, Marc
1982 [1979] *The Anthropological Circle: Symbol, Function, History*. Cambridge: Cambridge University Press.

Bailey, Anne M.
   1985 The Making of History: Dialectics of Temporality and Structure in Modern French Social Theory. *Critique of Anthropology* 5(1): 7–31.
Bakhtin, Mikhail
   1981 *The Dialogic Imagination*. Austin: University of Texas Press.
Barker, Randolph, and Robert W. Herdt, with Beth Rose
   1985 *The Rice Economy of Asia*. Washington, D.C.: Resources for the Future.
Barthes, Roland
   1982 [1970] *Empire of Signs*. Richard Howard, trans. New York: Hill and Wang.
Bayly, C. A.
   1986 The origins of swadeshi (home industry): Cloth and Indian Society, 1700–1930. In *The Social Life of Things: Commodities in Cultural Perspective*, A. Appadurai, ed., 285–321. Cambridge: Cambridge Unversity Press.
Bellah, Robert
   1967 The Japanese Emperor as a Mother Figure: Some Preliminary Notes. Paper presented at the Colloquium of the Center for Japanese and Korean Studies, University of California at Berkeley, October 11, 1967.
   1970 [1957] *Tokugawa Religion: The Values of Pre-Industrial Japan*. Boston: Beacon Press.
Belloli, Andrea P. A.
   1984 *A Day in the Country: Impressionism and the French Landscape*. Los Angeles, Calif.: Los Angeles County Museum of Art.
Belmont, Nicole
   1982 Superstition and Popular Religion in Western Societies. In *Between Belief and Transgression*, Michael Izard and Pierre Smith, eds., 9–23. Chicago: University of Chicago Press.
Berger, Peter L., and Thomas Luckmann
   1967 *The Social Construction of Reality*. New York: Doubleday.
Berque, Augustin
   1990 *Nihon no fūkei, seiō no keikan, soshite zōkei no jidai* (Comparative history of the Landscape in East Asia and Europe). Tokyo: Kōdansha.
Bloch, Marc
   1961 [1949] *Feudal Society*, L. A. Manyon, trans. Chicago: University of Chicago Press.
Bock, Felicia G.
   1990 The Great Feast of the Enthronement. *Monumenta Nipponica* 45(1): 27–38.
Bourdieu, Pierre
   1977 [1972] *Outline of a Theory of Practice*. Cambridge: Cambridge University Press.
   1984 [1979] *Distinction: A Social Critique of the Judgement of Taste*. Cambridge, Mass.: Harvard University Press.
   1990 *In Other Words: Essays toward a Reflexive Sociology*. Stanford, Calif.: Stanford University Press.

Braudel, Fernand

1972 [1949] *The Mediterranean and the Mediterranean World in the Age of Philip II.* Vol. 1 of 2 vols. New York: Harper and Row.

1973 [1967] *Capitalism and Material Life, 1400–1800.* London: Weidenfeld and Nicolson.

1980 [1958] *On History.* Chicago: University of Chicago Press.

Bray, Francesca

1986 *The Rice Economies: Technology and Development in Asian Societies.* Oxford: Basil Blackwell.

Brettell, Richard R., and Caroline B. Brettell

1983 *Painters and Peasants in the Nineteenth Century.* New York: Rizzoli International Publications.

Calder, Kent E.

1988 *Crisis and Compensation: Public Policy and Political Stability in Japan, 1949–1986.* Princeton, N.J.: Princeton University Press.

1989 Japanese Agricultural Policy: The Wax and Wane of Rural Bias. Paper presented at a session on "Agrarian Japan" during the Forty-first Annual Meetings of the Association for Asian Studies.

Carrithers, Michael, Steven Collins, and Steven Lukes, eds.

1985 *The Category of the Person.* Cambridge: Cambridge University Press.

Chang, K. C.

1977a Ancient China. In *Food in Chinese Culture: Anthropological and Historical Perspectives*, K. C. Chang, ed., 24–52. New Haven, Conn.: Yale University Press.

1977b Introduction. In *Food in Chinese Culture: Anthropological and Historical Perspectives*, K. C. Chang, ed., 3–21. New Haven, Conn.: Yale University Press.

Chang, K. C., ed.

1977 *Food in Chinese Culture: Anthropological and Historical Perspectives.* New Haven, Conn.: Yale University Press.

Chartier, Roger

1982 Intellectual History or Sociocultural History? The French Trajectories. In *Modern European Intellectual History: Reappraisals and New Perspectives*, D. La Capra and S. Kaplan, eds. Ithaca, N.Y.: Cornell University Press.

Clifford, James, and George E. Marcus

1986 *Writing Culture: The Poetics and Politics of Ethnography.* Berkeley: University of California Press.

Cohn, Bernard S.

1980 History and Anthropology: The State of Play. *Comparative Studies in Society and History* 12:198–221.

1981 Anthropology and History in the 1980s. *Journal of Interdisciplinary History* 12(2): 227–252.

Darlin, Damon

1988 Dissension on Rice Issue Spurs Japanese to Send "Shadow" Group to Trade Talks. *Wall Street Journal*, December 1, 1988.

Darnton, Robert
> 1985 *The Great Cat Massacre: And Other Episodes in French Cultural History.* New York: Vintage Books.

de Heusch, Luc
> 1985 *Sacrifice in Africa: A Structuralist Approach.* Bloomington: Indiana University Press.

de Man, Paul
> 1979 *Allegories of Reading.* New Haven, Conn.: Yale Univeristy Press.

Donnelly, Michael
> 1978 Political Management of Japan's Rice Economy. 2 vols. Ph.D. diss., Columbia University.

Dore, Ronald P.
> 1973 [1958] *City Life in Japan.* Berkeley: University of California Press.

> 1978 *Shinohata: A Portrait of a Japanese Village.* New York: Pantheon.

Douglas, Mary
> 1966 The Abominations of Leviticus. In *Purity and Danger*, 41–57. London: Routledge and Kegan Paul.

Dumont, Louis
> 1970 [1966] *Homo Hierarchicus.* M. Sainsbury, trans. Chicago: University of Chicago Press.

> 1986 *Essays on Individualism: Modern Ideology in Anthropological Perspective.* [Edition in French, 1983]. Chicago: University of Chicago Press.

Ebersole, Gary L.
> 1989 *Ritual Poetry and the Politics of Death in Early Japan.* Princeton, N.J.: Princeton University Press.

The Economist
> 1987 Unique, They Call It. *The Economist* (December, 1987): 32–33.

Eisenstadt, S. N.
> 1978 *Revolution and the Transformation of Societies: A Comparative Study of Civilizations.* New York: Free Press.

> n.d. The Japanese Historical Experience in Comparative Perspective. Typescript.

Ellwood, Robert S.
> 1973 *The Feast of Kingship: Accession Ceremonies in Ancient Japan.* Tokyo: Sophia University Press.

Feeley-Harnik, Gillian
> 1985 Issues in Divine Kingship. *Annual Review of Anthropology* 14:273–313.

Fernandez, James W.
> 1974 The Mission of Metaphor in Expressive Culture. *Current Anthropology* 15(2): 119–145.

> 1982 *Bwiti: An Ethnography of the Religious Imagination in Africa.* Princeton, N.J.: Princeton University Press.

> 1990 Enclosures: Boundary Maintenance and Its Representations over Time in Asturian Mountain Villages (Spain). In *Culture through Time*, E. Ohnuki-Tierney, ed., 94–127. Stanford, Calif.: Stanford University Press.

Fernandez, James W., ed.

1991 *Beyond Metaphor: The Theory of Tropes in Anthropology.* Stanford, Calif.: Stanford University Press.

Frankenberg, Ronald

1957 *Village on the Border: A Social Study of Religion, Politics and Football in a North Wales Community.* London: Cohen and West.

Frazer, James G.

1911–15 *The Golden Bough: A Study in Magic and Religion.* 12 vols. London: Macmillan.

Friedle, Ernestine

1975 *Women and Men: An Anthropologist's View.* New York: Holt, Rinehart and Winston.

Frye, Northrop

1971 [1957] *Anatomy of Criticism.* Princeton, N.J.: Princeton University Press.

Furet, Francois

1972 Quantitative History. In *Historical Studies Today*, F. Gilbert and S. R. Graubard, eds. 45–61. New York: Norton.

Geertz, Clifford

1960 *The Religion of Java.* New York: Free Press.

1980 *Negara: The Theatre State in Nineteenth-Century Bali.* Princeton, N.J.: Princeton University Press.

Genette, Gerard

1972 Metonymie chez Proust. In *Figures III*, 42–43. Paris: Editions du Seuil.

Gluck, Carol

1985 *Japan's Modern Myth: Ideology in the Late Meiji Period.* Princeton, N.J.: Princeton University Press.

Godelier, Maurice

1977 [1973] *Perspectives in Marxist Anthropology.* Cambridge: Cambridge University Press.

In press. Mirror, Mirror on the Wall . . . : The Once and Future Role of Anthropology: A Tentative Assessment. In *Assessing Cultural Anthropology*, Robert Borofsky, ed. New York: McGraw-Hill.

Goody, Jack

1982 *Cooking, Cuisine and Class: A Study in Comparative Sociology.* Cambridge: Cambridge University Press.

Gotō Shigeki

1975 *Tōkaidō gojū-san tsugi* (Fifty-three stations along the Tōkaidō). Tokyo: Shūeisha.

1976 *Kiso kaidō rokujū-kyū tsugi* (Sixty-nine stations along the Kiso road). Tokyo: Shūeisha.

Gregory, Chris A.

1982 *Gifts and Commodities.* London: Academic Press.

Gudeman, Stephen, and Alberto Rivera

1990 *Conversations in Colombia: The Domestic Economy in Life and Text.* Cambridge: Cambridge University Press.

Hamaguchi Eshun
   1982 *Kanjinshugi no shakai Nihon* (Japan: A society of contextualism [*sic*]).
   Tokyo: Keizai Shimpōsha.
Handler, Richard
   1988 *Nationalism and the Politics of Culture in Quebec*. Madison: University
   of Wisconsin Press.
Hane Mikiso
   1982 *Peasants, Rebels, and Outcastes: The Underside of Modern Japan*. New
   York: Pantheon Books.
Hanihara Kazurō
   1991 Dual Structure Model for the Population History of the Japanese. *Ni-
   chibunken Japan Review* 2:1–33.
Hardacre, Helen
   1989 *Shintō and the State*, 1868–1988. Princeton, N.J.: Princeton University
   Press.
Harootunian, Harry
   1988 *Things Seen and Unseen: Discourse and Ideology in Tokugawa Nativ-
   ism*. Chicago: University of Chicago Press.
Hasegawa Hiroshi
   1987 *Kome kokka kokusho* (The black paper on the rice nation). Tokyo:
   Asahi Shinbunsha.
Hayashiya Tatsusaburō
   1980 [1973] *Nihon geinō no sekai* (The world of performing arts in Japan).
   Tokyo: Nihon Hōsō Shuppan Kyōkai.
Herrenschmidt, Olivier
   1982 Sacrifice: Symbolic or Effective? In *Between Belief and Transgression*,
   Michael Izard and Pierre Smith, eds., 24–42. Chicago: University of Chicago
   Press.
Herzfeld, Michael
   1987 *Anthropology through the Looking-Glass*. Cambridge: Cambridge Uni-
   versity Press.
   1991 *A Place in History: Social and Monumental Time in a Cretan Town*.
   Princeton, N.J.: Princeton University Press.
Hida Yoshinobu
   1988 Sokuirei to ōnamesai no kiso chishiki (Basic knowledge of the accession
   ritual and the *ōnamesai*). In *Zusetsu tennō no sokuirei to ōnamesai*,
   H. Yamamoto, M. Satō and Staff, eds., 212–223. Tokyo: Shinjinbutsu
   Ōraisha.
Higo Kazuo
   1942 [1938] *Nihon shinwa kenkyū* (Research on Japanese myths). Tokyo:
   Kawade Shobō.
Higuchi Kiyoyuki
   1985 *Umeboshi to nihontō* (Pickled plum and Japanese sword). Tokyo:
   Shōdensha.
Hobsbawm, Eric J.
   1992 Ethnicity and Nationalism in Europe today. *Anthropology Today* 8(1):
   3–8.

Hobsbawm, Eric J. and Terence Ranger, eds.
  1986 [1983] *The Invention of Tradition.* Cambridge: Cambridge University Press.
Hocart, A. M.
  1952 *The Life-Giving Myth.* Lord Raglan, ed. London: Methuen.
  1969 [1927] *Kingship.* Oxford: Oxford University Press.
  1970 [1936] *Kings and Councilors: An Essay in the Comparative Anatomy of Human Society.* Chicago: University of Chicago Press.
Holtom, D. C.
  1972 [1928] *The Japanese Enthronement Ceremonies.* Tokyo: Monumenta Nipponica.
Hora Tomio
  1979 *Tennō fushinsei no kigen* (Origin of the apolitical nature of the emperor system). Tokyo: Azekura Shobō.
  1984 *Tennō fushinsei no dentō* (Tradition of the apolitical nature of the emperor system). Tokyo: Shinjusha.
Hubert, Henri, and Marcel Mauss
  1964 [1898] *Sacrifice: Its Nature and Function*, E. E. Evans-Prichard, trans. Chicago: University of Chicago Press. 1898 ed. in French.
Hunt, Lynn
  1986 French History in the Last Twenty Years: The Rise and Fall of the *Annales* Paradigm. *Journal of Contemporary History* 21:209–224.
Ingold, Tim
  1986 *Evolution and Social Life.* Cambridge: Cambridge University Press.
  1990 An Anthropologist Looks at Biology. *Man* 25(2): 208–229.
Inoue Hisashi
  1988 Kome no Hanashi (5)—Amerika no kome (Discussion on rice (5)—American rice). *Days Japan* 1(6): 103.
Inoue Kiyoshi
  1967 [1963] *Nihon no rekishi* (History of Japan). Vol. 1 (jō). Tokyo: Iwanami Shoten.
Inoue Mitsusada
  1984 *Nihon kodai ōken to saishi* (The kingship and ritual in Ancient Japan). Tokyo: Tōkyō Daigaku Shuppankai.
Ishibashi Fushiha
  1914 Minzokugaku no hōmen Yori mitaru kagami (Anthropological interpretations of mirrors). *Jinruigaku Zasshi* 29(6): 223–227.
Ishige Naomichi
  1983 Inasaku shakai no shokuji bunka (Dietary culture of rice cultivating societies). In *Nihon nōkō bunka no genryū.* K. Sasaki, ed., 391–414. Tokyo: Nihon Hōsō Shuppan Kyōkai.
  1985 Minshū no shokuji (Meals of the folk). In *Ie to josei* (The household and women). Tsuboi Yōbun et al., 113–180. Tokyo: Shōggakan.
  1986 Beishoku minzoku hikaku kara mita Nihonjin no shokuseikatsu (The foodway of the Japanese from the perspective of a comparative study of rice-eating peoples). In *Seikatsugaku no hōhō* (Methodological studies of the daily lives), Chūbachi Masayoshi, ed., 10–26. Tokyo: Domesu Shuppan.

Ishimori Shūzō
1984 Shi to zōtō: Mimai junōchō ni yoru shakai kankei no bunseki (Death and gifts: Analysis of human relations through the records of gifts). In Nihonjin no zōtō (Gift exchange of the Japanese), Itoh Mikiharu and Kurita Yasuyuki, eds., 269–304. Kyoto: Mineruva Shobō.

Itoh Mikiharu
1979 Ta no Kami (Deity of the rice paddy). In Kōza Nihon no kodai shinkō (Belief system in Ancient Japan), T. Matsumae, ed., 162–181. Tokyo: Gakuseisha.
1984 En to Nihon bunka (The feast and Japanese culture). Tokyo: Chūōkōronsha.
1988 Inasaku girei ni mirareru kami kannen (The concept of deity as expressed in rituals concerning rice production). Nihon Bunka Kenkyū Hōkoku (March): 73–79.

Jakobson, Roman
1956 On Aphasia. In Fundamentals of Language, R. Jakobson and M. Halle, 76–82. The Hague: Mouton.

JETRO (Japan External Trade Organization)
1989 White Paper on International Trade: Japan 1989. Tokyo: Japan External Trade Organization.

Kaberry, Phyllis M.
1939 Aboriginal Woman, Sacred and Profane. London: Routledge and Kegan Paul.

Kano Yoshikazu
1987 Rice Wars? Journal of Japanese Trade and Industry 6(2): 40–42.

Kantorowicz, Ernst H.
1957 [1981] The King's Two Bodies: A Study of Medieval Political Theology. Princeton, N.J.: Princeton University Press.

Kapferer, Bruce
1988 Legends of People, Myths of State: Violence, Intolerance, and Political Culture in Sri Lanka and Australia. Washington: Smithsonian Institution Press.

Katsumata Shizuo
1985 [1982] Ikki (Protests). Tokyo: Iwanami Shoten.

Kawasoe Taketane
1980 [1978] Kojiki no sekai (The world of Kojiki). Tokyo: Kyōikusha.

Kelly, William W.
1989 The Price of Prosperity and the Benefits of Dependency: Rice Reserves and Reserve Regions in Contemporary Japan. Paper presented at the session on "Agrarian Japan" during the Forty-first Annual Meetings of the Association for Asian Studies.
1991 The Taut and the Empathic: Antinomies of Japanese Personhood. Paper read at the Institute for Culture and Communication, the East-West Center for a conference on Self and the Social Order: China, India, and Japan. August 5–9, 1991.

Kitagawa, Joseph M.
1990 Some Reflections on Japanese Religion and Its Relationship to the Imperial System. Japanese Journal of Religious Studies 17(2–3): 129–178.

Kitō Hiroshi
  1983a Edo jidai no beishoku (Rice diet during the Edo period). *Rekishi Kōron* 89:43–49.
  1983b *Nihon Nisennen no Jinkōshi* (Japanese demographic history for two thousand years). Tokyo: PHP Kenkyūjo.
Kobayashi Issa
  1929 *Issa haiku zenshū* (Collected *haiku* poems of Issa). Tokyo: Shunjūsha.
Koharu Kyūichirō
  n.d. *Kachi kachi yama, tsuru no ongaeshi* ("Mountain on fire" and "The crane returning her gratitude"). Tokyo: Hikari no Kuni Shōwa Shuppan.
Kokuritsu Rekishi Minzoku Hakubutsukan, ed.
  1987 [1985] *Nihon no rekishi to bunka* (Japanese history and culture). Tokyo: Daiichi Hōki Shuppan.
Komatsu Kazuhiko
  1983 *Kamigami no seishinshi* (Spiritual history of deities). Tokyo: Dentō to Gendaisha.
Komatsu Kazuhiko, and Kurimoto Shinichirō
  1982 *Keizai no tanjō* (Birth of the economy). Tokyo: Kōsakusha.
Kondo, Dorinne
  1990 *Crafting Selves: Power, Gender, and Discourses of Identity in a Japanese Workplace.* Chicago: University of Chicago Press.
Kōshitsu Bunka Kenkyūkai, ed.
  1988 Ōnamesai: Yuki sukiden no shogi (*Ōnamesai*: Various rituals for the *yuki* and *suki* fields). In *Zusetsu tennō no sokuirei to Ōnamesai*, H. Yamamoto, M. Satō and Staff, eds., 88–95. Tokyo: Shinjinbutsu Ōraisha.
Koyama Shūzō
  1983 *Hida Gofudoki* ni miru Edo jidai no shoku seikatsu (Diet during the Edo period as recorded in *Hida Gofudoki*). *Rekishi Kōron* 89:35–42.
Koyama Shūzō, Sugiyama Toshio, Akimichi Tomoya, Fujino Yoshiko, and Sugita Shigeharu
  1981 "*Hida Gofudoki*" ni yoru shokuryō shigen no keiryōteki kenkyū (Quantitative research on food resources as recorded in *Hida Gofudoki*). *Kokuritsu Minzokugaku Hakubutsukan Kenkyū Hōkoku* 96(3): 363–596.
Koyanagi Teruichi
  1972 *Tabemono to Nihon bunka* (Food and Japanese culture). Tokyo: Hyōgensha.
Kurabayashi Shōji
  1988 Ōnamesai no henkaku (Changes in the *ōnamesai*). In *Zusetsu tennō no sokuirei to ōnamesai*. H. Yamamoto, M. Satō and Staff, eds., 36–37. Tokyo: Shinjinbutsu Ōraisha.
Kurano Kenji, and Takeda Yūkichi, eds.
  1958 *Kojiki Norito* (*Kojiki* and *Norito*). Tokyo: Iwanami Shoten.
Kuroda Toshio
  1972 Chūsei no mibunsei to hisen kannen (Social Stratification during the Early Medieval period and the concept of baseness). *Buraku Mondai Kenkyū* 33:23–57.
Kurushima Hiroshi
  1986 Kinsei no seneki to hyakushō (Military duty and peasants during the

Early Modern period). In *Nihon no shakaishi* (Social history of Japan). 8 vols. N. Asao, Y. Amino, K. Yamaguchi, and T. Yoshida, eds., 4:273–317. Tokyo: Iwanami Shoten.

Lakoff, George, and Mark Johnson
1980 *Metaphors We Live By.* Chicago: University of Chicago Press.

Leach, Edmund
1965 [1954] *Political Systems of Highland Burma.* Boston: Beacon Press.
1968 [1964] Anthropological aspects of language: Animal categories and verbal abuse. In *New Directions in the Study of Language*, E. Lenneberg, ed., 23–63. Cambridge, Mass.: Massachusetts Institute of Technology Press.
1976 *Culture and Communication.* Cambridge: Cambridge University Press.
1982 *Social Anthropology.* Glasgow: Fontana Paperbacks.

Lee, Richard
1968 What Hunters Do for a Living, or, How To Make Out on Scarce Resources. In *Man the Hunter*, Richard B. Lee and Irven DeVore, eds., 30–48. Chicago: Aldine/Atherton

Le Goff, Jacques
1972 Is Politics Still the Backbone of History? In *Historical Studies Today.* F. Gilbard and S. R. Graubard, eds., 337–355. New York: Norton.

Lévi-Strauss, Claude
1963 [1962] *Totemism.* Trans. by R. Needham. Boston: Beacon Press.
1966 [1962] *The Savage Mind.* George Weidenfeld and Nicolson Ltd. trans. Chicago: University of Chicago Press.
1967 [1958] *Structural Anthropology.* New York: Doubleday.
1969a [1949] *The Elementary Structure of Kinship.* London: Eyre and Spottiswoode.
1969b [1964] *The Raw and the Cooked.* Vol. 1 in *Introduction to a Science of Mythology.* John and Doreen Weightman trans. New York: Harper Torchbooks.
1983 [1976] *Structural Anthropology.* Vol. 2 of 2 vols. Chicago: University of Chicago Press.

Lowenthal, David
1985 *The Past Is a Foreign Country.* New York: Cambridge University Press.

Macé, François
1985 Genmei Tajō tennō no sōgi ga imisuru maisō gireishijō no danzetsuten (A break in the history of the funeral rituals as indicated by the funeral for the Empress Genmei). *Shūkyō Kenkyū* 266:55–77.

Marshall, Lorna
1976 Sharing, Talking and Giving: Relief of Social Tensions among the !Kung. In *Kalahari Hunter-Gatherers: Studies of the !Kung San and Their Neighbors*, Richard B. Lee and Irven DeVore, eds., 349–371. Cambridge: Harvard University Press.

Martin, Samuel
1964 Speech Levels in Japan and Korea. In *Language in Culture and Society*, Dell Hymes, ed., 407–415. New York: Harper and Row.

Matsudaira Narimitsu
1977 *Matsuri—Honshitsu to shosō: Kodaijin no uchū* (Festivals—Their es-

sence and multiple dimensions: The universe of the Ancient Japanese). Tokyo: Asahi Shinbunsha.

Matsumae Takeshi

1977 *Nihon no kamigami* (Japanese deities). Tokyo: Chūōkōronsha.

1988 *Inari myōjin* (Inari deity). Tokyo: Chikuma Shobō.

Matsuyama Toshio

1990 Sanson no seisan katsudō to sonraku seikatsu no shosō: Hida Kohachi-gagō o chūshin ni (Productive activities of mountain villages and village life: Primarily in Kohachigagō, in Hida District). In *Nihon sonrakushi kōza* (Lectures on the history of Japanese villages), Nihon sonrakushi kōza Henshū Iinkai, ed., 7: 65–89. Tokyo: Yūzankaku.

Mauss, Marcel

1966 [1950] *The Gift: Forms and Functions of Exchange in Archaic Societies.* London: Cohen and West.

1985 [1938] A Category of the Human Mind: The Notion of Person; The Notion of Self. In *The Category of the Person*, M. Carrithers, S. Collins, and S. Lukes, eds., 1–25. Cambridge: Cambridge University Press.

Mayer, Adrian C.

1991 Recent Succession Ceremonies of the Emperor of Japan. *Japan Review* 2:35–61.

Mennell, Stephen

1985 *All Manners of Food: Eating and Taste in England and France from the Middle Ages to the Present.* Oxford: Basil Blackwell.

Miller, Roy A.

1967 *The Japanese Language.* Chicago: University of Chicago Press.

Mintz, Sidney W.

1985 *Sweetness and Power: The Place of Sugar in Modern History.* New York: Penguin Books.

Miura Shūgyō

1988 Tairei seido no enkaku (Outline of the imperial ritual). In *Zusetsu tennō no sokuirei to ōnamesai* (Illustrated outline of the imperial accession ritual and ōnamesai). H. Yamamoto, M. Satō, and Staff, eds., 142–146. Tokyo: Shinjinbutsu Ōraisha.

Miyamoto Tsuneichi

1981 Nihonjin no shushoku (The staple food of the Japanese.) In *Shoku no bunka shinpojūmu '81: Higashi Ajiya no shoku no bunka* (Symposium on the culture of food: Dietary culture of East Asia). Tokyo: Heibonsha.

Miyata Noboru

1975 [1970] *Miroku shinkō no kenkyū* (Research on the belief in Maitreya). Rev. ed. Tokyo: Miraisha.

1987 *Shūmatsukan no minzokugaku* (Folklore of the end of the world). Tokyo: Kōbundō.

1988 *Rēkon no Minzokugaku* (Folklore of the soul). Tokyo: Nihon Editā Sukūru Shuppan.

1989 Nihon ōken no minzokuteki kiso (Ethnographic basis of the Japanese kingship. *Shikyō* 18:25–30.

Miyata Noboru (*cont.*)
    1990 *Minzokugaku* (Folklore study). Tokyo: Hōsō Daigaku Kyōiku Shin-
        kōkai.
Moon, Okpyo
    1989 *From Paddy Field to Ski Slope: The Revitalization of Tradition in Japa-
        nese Village Life.* Manchester, England: Manchester University Press.
Moore, Sally Falk
    1986 *Social Facts and Fabrications: "Customary" Law on Kilimanjaro,
        1880–1980.* Lewis Henry Morgan Lecture Series. Cambridge: Cambridge
        University Press.
Morinaga Taneo
    1967 [1963] *Rūnin to hinin: Zoku Nagasaki bugyō no kiroku* (The exiled and
        the *hinin* outcastes: The records of the commissioner of Nagasaki Bugyō,
        Cont.). Tokyo: Iwanami Shoten.
Morisue Yoshiaki
    1953 *Nihonshi no kenkyū* (Research on Japanese history). Tokyo: Ōbunsha.
Morita Yoshinori
    1978 *Kawara makimono* (The scrolls of the "River Banks"). Tokyo: Hōsei
        Daigaku Shuppankyoku.
Morse, Peter
    1989 *Hokusai: One Hundred Poets.* New York: George Braziller.
Murakami Shigeyoshi
    1977 *Tennō no saishi* (Imperial rituals). Tokyo: Iwanami Shoten.
    1986 *Tennō to Nihon bunka* (The emperor and Japanese culture). Tokyo:
        Kōdansha.
Muraki Tsuyoshi
    n.d. *Shitakiri suzume* (Sparrow with her tongue cut). Osaka: Kōyō Shuppan.
Myerhoff, Barbara
    1980 [1978] *Number Our Days.* New York: Simon and Schuster.
Nagahara Keiji
    1972 [1970] *Nihon keizaishi* (Economic history of Japan). Tokyo: Yūhikaku.
Nagaoka, Jeffrey
    1987 Losing Appetite for the Rice Diet. *PHP Intersect* (December 1987): 33–
        36.
Nakayama Tarō
    1976 Mizukagami Tenjin (Mizukagami Tenjin). *Nihon Minzokugaku* 1:181–
        188. Tokyo: Yamato Shobō.
Natsume Sōseki
    1984 [1965] Kōfu (The miners). In *Sōseki zenshū* (Complete works of Sōseki).
        Vol. 3 of 34 vols. Tokyo: Iwanami Shoten. Originally published as a daily
        newspaper column beginning January 1, 1907.
Newby, Howard
    1979 *Green and Pleasant Land?* London: Hutchinson
Nihiname Kenkyūkai, ed.
    1955 *Nihiname no kenkyū* (Research on the *nihiname*). Tokyo: Yoshikawa
        Kōbunkan.

Ninomiya Shigeaki
1933 An Inquiry Concerning the Origin, Development, and Present Situation of the *eta* in Relation to the History of Social Classes in Japan. *Transactions of the Asiatic Society of Japan* 10:47–154.
Nōda Tayoko
1943 *Mura no josei* (Women of the village). Tokyo: Mikuni Shobō.
Noguchi Michihiko
1978 Chūsei no shomin seikatsu to hisabetsumin no dōkō (The life of the Common People and Movements of the Discriminated People during the Medieval period). In *Buraku Mondai Gaisetsu* (Introduction to *Buraku* problems), Buraku Mondai Kenkyūjo, ed., 86–99. Osaka: Kaihō Shuppansha.
Nōrin Suisanshō Keizaikyoku Tōkei Jōhōbu (Statistics and Information Department, Ministry of Agriculture, Forestry, and Fisheries), ed.
1990 *Dai 65-ji Nōrin Suisanshō Tōkeihyō (Shōwa 63—Heisei Gannen)* (The sixty-fifth statistical yearbook of the Ministry of Agriculture, Forestry, and Fisheries, Japan, 1988–1989). Tokyo: Nōrin Tōkei Kyōkai.
Ōbayashi, Tarō
1973 *Inasaku no shinwa* (Rice cultivation myths). Tokyo: Kōbundō.
Ōbayashi, Tarō et al.
1983 *Sanmin to ama* (Mountain people and sea people). Tokyo: Shōgakkan.
Ochiai, Shigenobu
1972 *Mikaihō Buraku no kigen* (Origin of *Buraku*). Kōbe: Kōbe Gakujutsu Shuppan.
Oda Yūzō
1986 Kodai Chūsei no Suiko (Interest during the Ancient and Medieval periods). In *Nihon no shakaishi* (Social history of Japan). 8 vols. N. Asao, Y. Amino, K. Yamaguchi, and T. Yoshida, eds., 4:93–116. Tokyo: Iwanami Shoten.
Ohnuki-Tierney, Emiko
1974 *The Ainu of the Northwest Coast of Southern Sakhalin*. New York: Holt, Rinehart and Winston. Reprint, 1984. Prospect Heights, Ill.: Waveland Press.
1976 Regional Variation in Ainu Culture. *American Ethnologist* 3(2): 297–329.
1981 *Illness and Healing among the Sakhalin Ainu—A Symbolic Interpretation*. Cambridge: Cambridge University Press.
1984 *Illness and Culture in Contemporary Japan: An Anthropological View*. Cambridge: Cambridge University Press.
1987 *The Monkey as Mirror: Symbolic Transformations in Japanese History and Ritual*. Princeton, N.J.: Princeton University Press.
1990a The Ambivalent Self of the Contemporary Japanese. *Cultural Anthropology* 5:196–215.
1990b Introduction: The Historicization of Anthropology. In *Culture through Time*. E. Ohnuki-Tierney, ed., 1–25. Stanford: Stanford University Press.

Ohnuki-Tierney, Emiko (*cont.*)
1990c Monkey as Metaphor?: Transformations of A Polytropic Symbol in Japanese Culture. *Man* 25:399–416.
1991a Embedding and Transforming Polytrope: The Monkey as Self in Japanese Culture. In *Beyond Metaphor: The Theory of Tropes in Anthropology*, James W. Fernandez, ed., 159–189. Stanford, Calif.: Stanford University Press.
1991b The Emperor of Japan as Deity (*Kami*): An Anthropology of the Imperial System in Historical Perspective. *Ethnology* 30 (3): 199–215.
In press The Power of Absence: Zero Signifiers and Their Transgressions. Typescript. Forthcoming in *L'Homme*.

Okada Seishi
1970 *Kodai ōken no saishi to shinwa* (The ritual and myth of the ancient emperor system). Tokyo: Hanawa Shōbō.

Ōmae Kenichi
1986 *Shin Fukokuron* (A new theory on the wealth of nations). Tokyo: Kōdansha.

Orikuchi Shinobu
1965a [1924] *Marebito* (Stranger). In *Orikuchi Shinobu zenshū* (Collected works of Orikuchi Shinobu), 1:78–82. 32 vols. Tokyo: Chūōkōronsha.
1965b [1925] *Marebito [sic.]* no otozure (Visits by *Marebito*). In *Orikuchi Shinobu zenshū* (Collected works of Orikuchi Shinobu), 2:33–35. 32 vols. Tokyo: Chūōkōronsha.
1975a [1928] Ōnamesai no hongi (The meaning of the *ōnamesai*). In *Orikuchi Shinobu zenshū* (Collected works of Orikuchi Shinobu), 3:174–240. 32 vols. Tokyo: Chūōkōronsha.
1975b [1928] Shindō ni Arawareta Minzoku Ronri (Ethnographic interpretation of Shintoism). In *Orikuchi Shinobu zenshū* (Collected works of Orikuchi Shinobu), 3:145–173. 32 vols. Tokyo: Chūōkōronsha.
1976a [1947] Ijin to bungaku (The stranger and literature). In *Orikuchi Shinobu zenshū* (Collected works of Orikuchi Shinobu), 7:303–317. 32 vols. Tokyo: Chūōkōronsha.
1976b [1933] Kakinomoto Hitomaro (Kakinomoto Hitomaro). *Orikuchi Shinobu zenshū* (Collected works of Orikuchi Shinobu), 9:461–493. Tokyo: Chūōkōronsha.
1983 [1947] Matsuri no hanashi. *Orikuchi Shinobu zenshū* (Collected works of Orikuchi Shinobu), 15:271–280. 32 vols. Tokyo: Chūōkōronsha.

Ortner, Sherry
1989 *High Religion: A Cultural and Political History of Sherpa Buddhism.* Princeton, N.J.: Princeton University Press.

Ōshima Kiyoshi
1984 *Shokuryō to nōgyō o kangaeru* (Thoughts on food and agriculture). Tokyo: Iwanami Shoten.

Ōta, Yoshinobu
n.d. The Ryūkyū as the Other: Discourse and Politics of Representation in Japanese Folklore Studies. Typescript.

Otomasu Shigetaka
  1978 Yayoi nōgyō no seisanryoku to rōdōryoku (Productivity and labor power of Yayoi agriculture). *Kōkogaku Kenkyū* 25(2): 17–28.
Ōtsuka Hatsushige, and Mori Kōji, eds.
  1985 *Toro iseki to yayoi bunka: Ima toinaosu wajin no shakai* (The Toro site and Yayoi culture: Reexamination of the wajin society). Tokyo: Shōgakkan.
Ouwehand, Cornelius
  1958–59 Some notes on the God Susano-o. *Monumenta Nipponica* 14(3–4): 138–161 (384–407).
Parry, Jonathan
  1985 Death and Digestion: The Symbolism of Food and Eating in North Indian Mortuary Rites. *Man* 20:612–630.
Parry, Jonathan, and Maurice Bloch
  1989 *Money and the Morality of Exchange.* Cambridge: Cambridge University Press.
Pharr, Susan J.
  1990 *Losing Face: Status Politics in Japan.* Berkeley: University of California Press.
Philippi, Donald L., trans.
  1969. *Kojiki.* Princeton, N.J.: Princeton University Press; Tokyo: University of Tokyo Press.
Pollack, David
  1986 *The Fracture of Meaning: Japan's Synthesis of China from the Eighth through the Eighteenth Centuries.* Princeton, N.J.: Princeton University Press.
Pouillon, Jean
  1982 Remarks on the Verb "To Believe." In *Between Belief and Transgression,* Michael Izard and Pierre Smith, eds., 1–8. Chicago: University of Chicago Press.
Ray, Benjamin C.
  1991 *Myth, Ritual, and Kingship in Buganda.* Oxford: Oxford University Press.
Redfield, Robert
  1953 [1959] *The Primitive World and Its Transformations.* Ithaca, N.Y.: Cornell University Press.
Reich, Michael R., Yasuo Endō, and C. Peter Timmer
  1986 Agriculture: The Political Economy of Structural Change. In *America versus Japan,* Thomas K. McCraw, ed., 151–192, 417–420nn. Boston: Harvard Business School Press.
Reischauer, Edwin O., and Albert M. Craig
  1978 *Japan: Tradition and Transformation.* Boston: Houghton Mifflin.
Richards, Audrey I.
  1961 [1939] *Land, Labour and Diet in Northern Rhodesia.* Oxford: Oxford University Press.
Ricoeur, Paul
  1980 *The Contribution of French Historiography to the Theory of History.* Oxford: Clarendon Press.

Robert, Paul
   1962 *Dictionnaire alphabétique et analogique de la langue Française.* Paris: Société du Nouveau Littré.
Rosaldo, Michelle Zimbalist
   1974 Women, Culture and Society: A Theoretical Overview. In *Women, Culture and Society*, M. Z. Rosaldo and L. Lamphere, eds., 17–42. Stanford, Calif.: Stanford University Press.
Rosovsky, Henry
   1966 Japan's Transition to Modern Economic Growth 1868–1885. In *Industrialization in Two Systems: Essays in Honor of Alexander Gerschenkron*, H. Rosovsky, ed., 91–139. New York: John Wiley and Sons.
Sahara Makoto
   1990 *Komezukuri to Nihonjin* (Rice cultivation and the Japanese). Tokyo: Mainichi Shinbunsha.
Sahlins, Marshall
   1981 *Historical Metaphors and Mythical Realities: Structure in the Early History of the Sandwich Islands Kingdom.* Ann Arbor: University of Michigan Press.
   1985 *Islands of History.* Chicago: University of Chicago Press.
   1988 Cosmologies of Capitalism: The Trans-Pacific Sector of "The World System." *Proceedings of the British Academy* 74:1–51.
Saigō Nobutsuna
   1984 [1967] *Kojiki no sekai* (The world of the *Kojiki*). Tokyo: Iwanami Shoten.
Sakamoto Tarō, Ienaga Saburō, Inoue Mitsusada, and Ōno Susumu, eds.
   1965 *Nihonshoki* (Ge). *Nihonshoki*, vol. 2 of 2 vols. Tokyo: Iwanami Shoten.
   1967 *Nihonshoki* (Jō). *Nihonshoki*, vol. 1 of 2 vols. Tokyo: Iwanamai Shoten.
Sakurai Katsunoshin
   1988 Ōnamesai to Kannamesai (*Ōnamesai* and *Kannamesai*). In *Zusetsu tennō no sokuirei to ōnamesai*, H. Yamamoto, M. Satō and Staff, eds., 32–34. Tokyo: Shinjinbutsu Ōraisha.
Sakurai Tokutarō
   1981 Kesshū no genten: Minzokugaku kara tsuikyū shita shochiiki kyōdōtai kōsei no paradaimu (The source of solidarity: Folklorists' search for a paradigm for the structure of corporate groups). In *Shisō no bōken* (Explorations into thought Structure), K. Tsurumi and S. Ichii, eds., 187–234. Tokyo: Chikuma Shobō.
Sansom, George
   1943 [1931] *Japan: A Short Cultural History.* New York: Appleton-Century-Crofts.
   1961 *A History of Japan 1334–1615.* Stanford, Calif.: Stanford University Press.
Santamaria, Ulysses, and Anne M. Bailey
   1981 A Note on Braudel's Structure as Duration. *History and Theory* 21:78–83.

Sasaki Kōmei
   1983 *Inasaku izen* (Before rice cultivation). Tokyo: Nihon Hōsō Shuppan Kyōkai.
   1985 Ine to Nihonjin: Inasaku bunka to hi-inasaku bunka no aida (The Rice plant and the Japanese: Between rice culture and nonrice culture). In *Toro iseki to Yayoi bunka—Ima toinaosu wajin no shakai* (The Toro site and Yayoi culture—The question of the society of the Ancient Japanese), Ōtsuka Hatsushige and Mori Kōichi, eds., 36–62. Tokyo: Shōgakkan.
   1986 *Jōmon bunka to Nihonjin* (The Jōmon culture and the Japanese). Tokyo: Shōgakkan.
Scheiner, Irwin
   1973 The Mindful Peasant: Sketches for a Study of Rebellion. *Journal of Asian Studies* 32(4): 579–591.
Schutz, Alfred
   1971 *Studies in Social Theory.* Vol. 2 in *Collected Papers.* The Hague: Martinus Nijhoff.
Shack, William A., and E. P. Skinner, eds.
   1979 *Strangers in African Societies.* Berkeley: University of California Press.
Shibamoto, Janet.
   1987 Japanese Sociolinguistics. *Annual Review of Anthropology* 16:261–278.
Shimogaito Hiroshi
   1986 *Okome to bunka* (Rice and culture). Osaka: Zen-Ōsaka Shōhisha Dantai Renrakukai.
   1988 *Zoku okome to bunka* (Rice and culture, Continued) Osaka: Zen-Ōsaka Shōhisha Dantai Renrakukai.
Shimonaka Yasaburō
   1941a [1936] Shindō daijiten (Comprehensive dictionary of Shintoism). Vol. 2. Tokyo: Heibonsha.
   1941b [1937] Shindō daijiten (Comprehensive dictionary of Shintoism). Vol. 3. Tokyo: Heibonsha.
Shirota Kichiroku
   1987 *Akagome Denshō: Tsushima Tsutsumura no minzoku* (The oral tradition on red rice: Folklore found in Tsutsu Village, Tsushima). Fukuoka City: Ashi Shobō.
   1989 Akagome no Higi (Secret ritual for red rice). *Nikkan Āgama*, no. 103:072–080.
Shweder, Richard A., and Joan G. Miller
   1985 The Social Construction of the Person: How Is It Possible? In *The Social Construction of the Person*, K. J. Gergen and K. E. Davis, eds. 41–69. New York: Springer-Verlag.
Shweder, Richard, and Maria A. Sullivan
   1990 The Semiotic Subject of Cultural Psychology. In *Handbook of Personality: Theory and Research*, L. A. Pervin, ed., 399–418. New York: Guilford.
Simmel, Georg
   1950 [1907] *The Sociology of Georg Simmel.* Glencoe: Free Press.

Smith, Charles
  1987 The Price of Rice. *Far Eastern Economic Review* 136(29): 22–23.
Smith, W. Robertson
  1972 [1889] *The Religion of the Semites.* New York: Schocken Books.
Smith, Thomas C.
  1959 *The Agrarian Origins of Modern Japan.* Stanford, Calif.: Stanford University Press.
  1988 *Native Sources of Japanese Industrialization.* Berkeley: University of California Press.
Soda Osamu
  1989 *Kome o kangaeru* (Thinking about rice). Tokyo: Iwanami Shoten.
Spence, Jonathan
  1977 Ch'ing. In *Food in Chinese Culture: Anthropological and Historical Perspectives*, K. C. Chang, ed., 259–294. New Haven, Conn.: Yale University Press.
Stevens, John
  1988 Rice-Paddy Culture. *PHP Intersect* (November 1988): 43.
Strathern, Marilyn
  1988 *The Gender of the Gift.* Berkeley: University of California Press.
Sugiyama Kōichi
  1988 Higashi Ajiya no nōkōshin-kan (A comparative study of agricultural deities in East Asian peasant communities). *Nihon Bunka Kenkyūjo Kenkyū Hōkoku* 24:71–100.
Suzuki Mitsuo
  1974 *Marebito no kōzō* (The structure of *Marebito*). Tokyo: Sanichi Shobō.
  1979 Marebito (Strangers). In *Kōza Nihon no minzoku* (Folk cultures of Japan). Vol. 7, *Shinkō* (Belief systems). T. Sakurai, ed., 211–239. Tokyo: Yūseidō Shuppan.
Takagi Shunsuke
  1983 [1979] *Eeja naika* (It's All Right). Tokyo: Kyōikusha.
Takakura Shininchirō
  1960 The Ainu of Northern Japan: A Study in Conquest and Acculturation, J. A. Harrison, trans. *Transactions of the American Philosophical Society* (n.s.), vol. 50, pt. 4. Philadelphia: American Philosophical Society.
Takayanagi Kinpō
  1981 *Edo jidai hinin no seikatsu* (The life of the *hinin* outcastes during the Edo period). Tokyo: Yūzankaku Shuppan.
Takeuchi Satoshi
  1988 Hardline stand against rice imports softens. *Japan Economic Journal*, October 15, 1988, 3.
Taki Kōji
  1990 [1988] *Tennō no shōzō* (Portraits of the emperor). Tokyo: Iwanami Shoten.
Tambiah, S. J.
  1969 Animals Are Good to Think and Good to Prohibit. *Ethnology* 8(4): 423–459.

1976 *World Conqueror and World Renouncer: A Study of Buddhism and Polity in Thailand against a Historical Background.* New York: Cambridge University Press.

Tanaka, Stefan
In press. *Japan's Orient: Rendering Pasts into History.* Los Angeles: University of California Press.

Tanaka Takashi
1988 "Niiname" kara "Ōname" e (From the *Niiname* to the *Ōname*). In *Zusetsu tennō no sokuirei to ōnamesai*, H. Yamamoto, M. Satō, and Staff, eds., 28–30. Tokyo: Shinjinbutsu Ōraisha.

Tanizaki Junichirō
1959 [1933] In-ei Reisan (In praise of shadows). Tokyo: Chūōkōronsha. In *Tanizaki Junichirō zenshū* (Collected works of Tanizaki Junichirō). 30 vols. 22:2–41.

Thompson, E. P.
1971 The Moral Economy of the English Crowd in the Eighteenth Century. *Past and Present* 50:76–136.

Thorson, Larry
1989 Rice to Roses: Life of Japanese Farmers Changing. *Asahi Evening News*, June 13, p. 6.

Tracey, David
1988 Slugging It Out over Gas and Rice. *PHP Intersect* (October 1988): 15–16.

Trevor-Roper, Hugh
1983 The Invention of Tradition: The Highland Tradition of Scotland. In *The Invention of Tradition*, E. Hobsbawm and T. Ranger, eds., 15–41. Cambridge: Cambridge University Press.

Tsuboi Hirofumi
1984 [1982] *Ine o eranda Nihonjin* (The Japanese who chose the rice plant). Tokyo: Miraisha.

Tsukuba Tsuneharu
1986 [1969] *Beishoku, nikushoku no bunmei* (Civilizations of rice consumption and meat consumption). Tokyo: Nihon Hōsō Shuppankai.

Tsunoda, Ryūsaku, and L. Carrington Goodrich
1968 *Japan in the Chinese Dynastic Histories.* Kyoto: Perkins Oriental Books.

Tsūshō Sangyōshō (Ministry of Trade and Industry), ed.
1989 *Tsūshō Hakusho* (White paper on international trade and industry). Tokyo: Ōkurashō Insatsukyoku.

Tuan, Yi-Fu
1986 *The Good Life.* Madison: University of Wisconsin Press.

1989 *Morality and Imagination: Paradoxes of Progress.* Madison: University of Wisconsin Press.

Turner, Christie, Jr.
1976 Dental Evidence on the Origins of the Ainu and Japanese. *Science* 193:911–913.

1991 Report on the 1990 Kyoto Symposium: Japanese as Members of the Asian and Pacific Populations. *Nichibunken Newsletter* 8:2–4.

Turner, Victor
   1967 *The Forest of Symbols: Aspects of Ndembu Ritual.* Ithaca, N.Y.: Cornell
        University Press.
   1975 [1974] *Dramas, Fields, and Metaphors: Symbolic Action in Human So-
        ciety.* Ithaca, N.Y.: Cornell University Press.
Ueda Kazuo
   1978 Buraku no bunpu to jinkō (Distribution of *buraku* settlements and pop-
        ulation). In *Buraku mondai gaisetsu* (Introduction to *buraku* problems).
        Buraku Kaihō Kenkyūsho, ed., 3–10. Osaka: Kaihō Shuppansha.
Ueda Kenji
   1988 Ōnamesai seiritsu no haikei (The background of the establishment of
        the *ōnamesai*). In *Zusetsu tennō no sokuirei to ōnamesai*, H. Yamamoto,
        M. Satō, and Staff, eds., 31–32. Tokyo: Shinjinbutsu Ōraisha.
Valeri, Valerio
   1985 *Kingship and Sacrifice: Ritual and Soceity in Ancient Hawaii.* Chicago:
        University of Chicago.
van der Meer, N. C. van Setten
   1979 *Sawah Cultivation in Ancient Java: Aspects of Development During the
        Indo-Javanese Period, 5th to 15th Century.* Canberra: Australian National
        University Press.
van Gennep, Arnold
   1961 [1909] *The Rites of Passage.* Chicago: University of Chicago Press.
Vansina, Jan
   1978 *The Children of Woot: A History of the Kuba Peoples.* Madison: Uni-
        versity of Wisconsin Press.
   1985 *Oral Tradition as History.* Madison: University of Wisconsin Press.
Vlastos, Stephen
   1986 *Peasant Protests and Uprisings in Tokugawa Japan.* Berkeley: Univer-
        sity of California Press.
Waida, Manabu
   1975 Sacred Kingship in Early Japan: A Historical Introduction. *History of
        Religions* 15(1): 319–342.
Walthall, Anne
   1986 *Social Protest and Popular Culture in Eighteenth-Century Japan.*
        Tucson: University of Arizona Press.
Walthall, Anne, ed. and trans.
   1991 *Peasant Uprisings in Japan: A Critical Anthology of Peasant Histories.*
        Chicago: University of Chicago Press.
Watanabe Tadayo
   1987 Ine to kome o meguru Ajiyateki shiya (Asian perspectives on rice). In
        Ajiya inasaku bunka no tenkai (Developments of rice culture in Asia),
        T. Watanabe, ed., 5–32. Tokyo: Shōgakkan.
   1989 Nihonjin to inasaku bunka (The Japanese and rice culture). *Nikkan
        Āgama*, no. 103:081–091.
Watson, James L., and Evelyn S. Rawski, eds.
   1988 *Death Ritual in Late Imperial and Modern China.* Berkeley: University
        of California Press.

Watsuji Tetsurō
1959 *Rinrigaku* (Ethics). Vol. 1 of 20 vols. Watsuji Tetsurō zenshū (Collected works of Watsuji Tetsurō). Tokyo: Iwanami Shoten.
Williams, Brackette F.
1989 A Class Act: Anthropology and the Race to Nation across Ethnic Terrain. *Annual Review of Anthropology* 18:401–444.
Williams, Peter
1992 Uruguai raundo kōshō seikō to shippai no kiro (The crossroad of the negotiation of the Uruguay round). *Gaikō Fōramu* 46(July): 53–58.
Williams, Raymond
1973 *The Country and the City.* New York: Oxford University Press.
Wolf, Eric
1988 Inventing Society. *American Ethnologist* 15:752–761.
Yalman, Nur
1989 The Dimensions of Cultural Pluralism. A keynote address to the symposium on *Internationalization and Cultural Conflict*, the Department of Anthropology, University of Osaka, July 1989.
1992 The Perfection of Man: The Question of Supra-Nationalism in Islam. A keynote address to the symposium on *Nationalism*, the Department of Anthropology, University of Osaka, March 1992. In *Shisō* 823 (January 1993): 34–49.
Yamaguchi, Iwao
1987 Maintaining Japan's Self-Sufficiency in Rice. *Journal of Trade and Industry* 6(2): 40–42.
Yamaguchi, Masao
1977 Kingship, Theatricality, and Marginal Reality in Japan. In *Text and Context: The Social Anthropology of Tradition*, R. K. Jain, ed., 151–179. Philadelphia: Institute for the Study of Human Issues.
Yamamoto Hikaru, Satō Minoru, and Staff, eds.
1988 *Zusetsu tennō no sokuirei to ōnamesai* (Illustrated account of the imperial accession and the *ōnamesai*). Tokyo: Shinjinbutsu Ōraisha.
Yamamura, Kōzō
1988 From Coins to Rice: Hypotheses on the *Kandaka* and *Kokudaka* Systems. *Journal of Japanese Studies* 14(2): 341–368.
Yamaori Tetsuo
1978 *Tennō no shūkyōteki keni towa nanika* (The identity of the religious authority of the emperor). Tokyo: Sanichi Shobō.
1990a Kakureta tennōrei keishō no dorama: Daijōsai no bunka hikaku (Hidden drama of the imperial succession: Comparative cultural analysis of Daijōsai). *Gekkan Asahi* (February 1990): 80–85.
1990b *Shi no minzokugaku* (Folklore of death). Tokyo: Iwanami Shoten.
Yanagita Kunio
1981a [1953] Ine no sanya (Parturient hut for rice). In *Yanagita Kunio-shū* (Collected works of Yanagita Kunio), 36 vols. 1:178–209. Tokyo: Tsukuma Shobō.
1981b [1917] Yamabitokō (Thoughts on the mountain people). In *Yanagita*

Kunio-shū (Collected works of Yanagita Kunio), 36 vols. 4:172–186. Tokyo: Tsukuma Shobō.

Yanagita Kunio

1982a [1949] Fuji to Tsukuba (Mt. Fuji and Mt. Tsukuba). *Yanagita Kunio-shū* (Collected works of Yanagita Kunio), 36 vols. 31:129–139. Tokyo: Tsukuma Shobō.

1982b [1940] Kome no chikara (Power of rice). *Yanagita Kunio-shū* (Collected works of Yanagita Kunio), 36 vols. 14:240–258. Tokyo: Tsukuma Shobō.

1982c Kome no shima kō (Thoughts on the islands of rice). *Yanagita Kunio-shū* (Collected works of Yanagita Kunio), 36 vols. 31:157–158. Tokyo: Tsukuma Shobō.

1982d Kura inadama kō (Thoughts on the soul of rice). *Yanagita Kunio-shū* (Collected works of Yanagita Kunio), 36 vols. 31:159–166. Tokyo: Tsukuma Shobō.

1982e [1931] Shokumotsu no kojin jiyū (Personal freedom on food). *Yanagita Kunio-shū* (Collected works of Yanagita Kunio), 36 vols. 24:160–186. Tokyo: Tsukuma Shobō.

Yanagita Kunio, ed.

1951 *Minzokugaku jiten* (Ethnographic dictionary). Tokyo: Tōkyōdō.

Yayama, Tarō

1987 Rebellion in a Model Farm Community. *Japan Echo* 14:62–67.

Yokoi Kiyoshi

1982 [1975] *Chūsei minshū no seikatsu bunka* (The life of the folk during the Medieval period). Tokyo: Tōkyō Daigaku Shuppankai.

Yokota Kenichi

1988 Ōnamesai seiritsu jidai hosetsu (Additional explanation for the age of the establishment of the *ōnamesai*). In *Zusetsu tennō no sokuirei to ōnamesai*, H. Yamamoto, M. Satō, and Staff, eds., 27–29. Tokyo: Shinjinbutsu Ōraisha.

Yoshida Shūji

1992 Shimpojūmu idengaku ga shimeshita saibai ine no kigen (The origin of the rice plant as identified through genetic analysis). *Minpaku* 16(6): 18–19.

Yoshida, Teigo

1981 The Stranger as God: The Place of the Outsider in Japanese Folk Religion. *Ethnology* 20(2): 87–99.

Yoshimura Takehiko

1986 Shihō to kōnō (Service and tributes). In *Nihon no shakaishi* (Social history of Japan), 8 vols. N. Asao, Y. Amino, K. Yamaguchi, and T. Yoshida, eds. 4:13–54. Tokyo: Iwanami Shoten.

Yoshino Hiroko

1986 *Daijōsai: Tennō sokuishiki no kōzō* (The *Daijōsai*: The structure of the imperial accession ritual). Tokyo: Kōbundō.

Yu-Lan, Fung

1948 *A Short History of Chinese Philosophy.* New York: MacMillan.

Zimmermann, Francis

1987 [1982] *The Jungle and the Aroma of Meats.* Berkeley: University of California Press.

Index

abdomen, 51, 65

Abel, 119

actors (social), 80, 116, 128–30, 137n.4. *See also* agents

aesthetics: of objects made from rice plants, 14, 78; of rice, 75–77, 79. *See also* woodblock prints

affluence, and rice consumption, 40–41, 42

agents, 6–7, 99, 137n.4. *See also* actors

agrarian deities. *See* deity(ies)

agrarian ideology, 87–98, 102, 104, 105–6, 122–23; and daily life of Japanese, 81, 88–90, 95–97; and minorities, 131–34. *See also* agrarian Japan; countryside; rice: domestic vs. foreign; "Village Japan"; rice agriculture: ideology of

agrarian Japan, representations of, 81–83, 87, 92–93. *See also* agrarian ideology

agrarian rituals. *See* harvest rituals; ritual(s)

agricultural cycle: and deities, 36; and rituals, 55–56. *See also* seasons

agricultural protectionism, in cross-cultural perspective, 10–11, 125–26. *See also* Japanese government; rice farmers: double subsidization of

agricultural reproduction. *See* human reproduction

agricultural subsidies. *See* rice farmers

agricultural trade. *See* trade issues

agriculture: length of time Japan's economy depended primarily on, 81; and permanent settlement, 30; regional variations in, 35; representations of Japanese, 10, 81–83, 120, 122–23; rice symbolism more important than, 132; slash and burn, 34, 35; and state formation, 139n.1; as transformation of nature, 120–22, 125. *See also* hunting-gathering; "nonrice cultivation culture"; rice agriculture; wet-rice agriculture

Ainu, 5, 31, 69, 114, 116, 119, 139n.1; as marginalized others, 146n.15, 148n.5

akagome (red rice), 14, 72

akita komachi (rice variety), 15

Amaterasu Ōmikami (Sun Goddess and imperial ancestress), 47–53, 54, 83, 141n.6. *See also* imperial system

Ame-no iwaya. See "Heavenly cave" episode

Ame-no Uzume no Mikoto (shaman-deity), 50–51

Americans, 103. *See also* United States; Western countries

Amino Yoshihiko, 34, 35, 36, 67, 71, 85, 102, 145n.9

ancestor worship, 95–96, 141n.6. *See also* Amaterasu Omikami

Ancient period, 32; Japanese self in, 83–85; monetary transactions in, 67; political power of emperors in, 59; rice symbolism in, 44–53, 94

animals: in European representations of nature, 124–25; foreigners likened to, by nativist Japanese, 104; humans distinguished from, 103; in Japanese representations of nature, 123; as strangers in folktales, 63, 64, 65, 77. *See also* meat; sacrifice

Annales school, 6, 137n.3

anthropology: historicized, 6–7, 82–83; as specialists in nonliterate and primitive peoples, 144n.1; structuralism in, 137n.4; "Village Japan" in, 82

aramitama. See aratama

aratama (violent power), 53, 54, 55, 101

artists: as others, 84, 85, 92, 145nn. 7, 8, and 9. *See also* aesthetics

Asia: rice in, 12–13. *See also* Names of Asian countries

"Asian," 138n.6

Australia, 115, 132

awa (Italian millet), 34, 35, 37, 40, 50, 139n.4

azuki (red beans), 14, 35

Bakhtin, Mikhail, 99

Bali, 143n.26

barley, 16

Barthes, Roland, 6, 143n.6

Baruya (of New Guinea), 69

beans, 14, 35, 139n.4

bear meat, and Ainu, 79, 114, 116

Bellah, Robert, 62, 87

Bemba, 117, 118

178 INDEX

money (*cont.*)
69. *See also* currency; monetary transactions; rice: as pure money; rice tax;
wealth
Monmu (Emperor), 44–45
Moore, Sally Falk, 129, 134, 137n.4
Motoori Norinaga, 75, 77, 87
mountains, 64, 89, 92, 106
Mt. Fuji, 89, 105
mugi (wheat), 4, 139n.4; aesthetics of, 79;
contrasted with rice, 13; Japanese government's control over, 16; as staple
food, 12, 34, 37
musu, 56
musubi, 49
Musubi no Kami, 141n.6
myth-histories: and agrarian folk rituals,
45, 50–51; and imperial system, 58; and
ōnamesai, 50–51, 141n.9; religious basis
of, 67; rice deities in, 51–53; rice symbolism in, 44, 66, 102, 132, 133; themes of,
52–53, 55, 57, 132; writing of, 45,
142n.10. See also *Kojiki*; *Nihonshoki*

naichimai. See rice: domestic vs. foreign
Nakasone Yashuhiro, 146n.19
naorai, 48, 58. *See also* commensality: between emperor and deity
Napoleon, 59
nationalism, 99; in contemporary Japan,
113, 131–32; cross-cultural perspectives
on, 132–33; of Nativist scholars, 75, 77,
140n.2; use of rice for, 93, 98, 134. *See
also* Nativist scholars
National Museum of Ethnology (Kokuritsu
Minzokugaku Hakubutsukan), 12, 33
Nativist scholars, 75, 97; and agrarian
Japan, 87–88, 105, 121; and domestic vs.
foreign rice issue, 104, 122–23; nationalism of, 74–77, 140n.2. *See also* agrarian
ideology; agrarian Japan
Natsume Sōseki, 104–5
"natural," definition of, 81
natural foods. *See* health food movement
"naturalization," 6, 98, 133–34. *See also*
marginalization; marginalized others;
"natural"
nature, transformation of, 120–22, 125,
133. *See also* agricultural cycle; countryside; past; rice paddies; seasons
new rice crop (*shinmai*): attention to, in
contemporary Japan, 142n.18; blessings

on, 45; loan repayments with, 67, 72; offerings of, 47, 48, 50, 57, 67, 140n.2,
141n.7, 142n.18. See also *kannamesai*;
onamesai
New Year rituals: gifts for, 72; rice offerings during, 96; without rice, 36, 37,
42
"New Year without rice cake," 36
nigimitama. See *nigitama*
nigirimeshi (molded rice), 41
nigitama (peaceful power), 53–57, 74, 101
Nihon (Japan), origins of term, 102, 144n.2
Nihonshoki (myth-history), 44, 46–47, 50–
51, 54, 83. *See also* myth-histories
niinamesai, 46–47, 140n.3, 141n.7. *See
also* harvest rituals
ningen (humans), 100. *See also* personhood
Ninigi-no Mikoto (grandson), 51, 52, 55
nōmin (farmers), 92. *See also* peasant(s)
nonagrarian populations, 82–83, 98,
145n.8. *See also* marginalized others;
nonsettled population; urbanites
"nonrice cultivation culture," 33, 34–36;
importance of, in Japan, 81, 82; marginalization of farmers in, 98
nonsettled population (*hiteizūmin*): in
Japan, 10, 39, 82, 133–34. *See also*
marginalized others; minorities; residents
vs. nonresidents
nutrition: of white rice, 15, 106, 138n.3.
See also food(s): energy value of

Occidentalism, 135. *See also* Western
countries
occupations: devaluation of nonagrarian,
87, 90–91; diversity of, in Japan, 82; importance of rice symbolism to people in
nonagrarian, 97–98; stratification by, 84,
85–86. *See also* "caste" system; "nonrice
cultivation culture"; rice farmers; *samurai*; *shokunin*
Ōjin emperor, 44
"old rice" (*komai*), 55, 142n.18
Ōmae Kenichi, 23–24
ōnamesai (harvest/imperial accession ritual), 45–51, 61, 62, 83–84, 94, 118,
140nn. 3 and 5, 141nn. 7 and 9, 144n.5.
See also imperial system
"Oriental": term of, 103, 138n.6
Orientalism, 135
Orikuchi Shinobu, 46, 49–50, 53, 58–59,
140n.2, 141nn. 5, 6, 7, and 8, 146n.16